NEIGHBORHOOD RECOVERY

Reinvestment Policy for the New Hometown

JOHN
KROMER

RUTGERS UNIVERSITY PRESS
New Brunswick, New Jersey, and London

Library of Congress Cataloging-in-Publication Data

Kromer, John, 1948–
     Neighborhood recovery : reinvestment policy for the new hometown /
John Kromer.
          p. cm.
     Includes bibliographical references and index.
     ISBN 0-8135-2716-3 cloth : alk. paper). — ISBN 0-8135-2717-1
(pbk. : alk. paper)
     1. Urban renewal—United States. 2. Urban policy—United States.
3. Community development. Urban—United States. 4. Neighborhood—
United States. 5. Urban economics. I. Title.
HT175.K76 1999
307.3'416'0973—dc21   99-28161
                                                                          CIP

British Cataloging-in-Publication data for this book is available from the British
Library

Manufactured in the United States of America

Contents

Acknowledgments

Neighborhood Recovery is a collection of experiences and insights I accumulated while active as a Philadelphia city government administrator, urban neighborhood resident, and community organization member. During those years of activity, many people inspired and encouraged me and helped broaden my understanding of the issues discussed in this book.

Kathleen and Andrew gave me their love, understanding, and patience. The creative ideas and sensible advice of my friend Joanne Barnes Jackson were invaluable to me and influenced the content of this book in many ways. Mayor Edward G. Rendell, whose leadership during the past decade laid the foundation for Philadephia's best neighborhood reinvestment policy and programs, took a big risk in appointing a relatively inexperienced outsider to a key city leadership position, and his support and encouragement were constant and unfailing. The staff of the Office of Housing and Community Development (OHCD) provided daily examples of personal commitment, creative endeavor, boldness, and courage. Because of them, my experience at OHCD was continually exciting and rewarding. Many staff at the Redevelopment Authority of the City of Philadelphia, the Philadelphia Housing Development Corporation, and the Philadelphia Housing Authority devoted extraordinary amounts of time and energy to the collaborative activities I initiated or supported, and their program delivery expertise produced outstanding results described. Hundreds of other people, most of them associated with nonprofit or neighborhood-based organizations, were responsible for the success stories described in this book. Many of these implementers of neighborhood reinvestment policy brought me fresh insights, good advice, and friendship.

Witold Rybczynski, who holds the Martin and Margy Meyerson Chair in Urbanism at the University of Pennsylvania, helped me make contact with Rutgers University Press. Marlie Wasserman, Director of the Press, guided my thinking about the organization of this book, helped me recover from a couple of false starts, and provided a wealth of constructive comments and suggestions. In her review of the manuscript, Victoria Wilson-Schwartz made dozens of useful suggestions that led to substantial improvements in every chapter. During the July 1998 Program for Senior Executives in State and Local Government at the Harvard University Kennedy School of Government, I had a good opportunity to think through the structure of the book and begin writing. My participation in the program was supported by a Fannie Mae Foundation Fellowship.

Most of the photographs that appear in this book are the work of Jane Whitehouse, and I am grateful for her help, as well as for the permission granted by the City of Philadelphia to reproduce these photos here. The photograph of the computer screen display in chapter 2 was made possible by the University of Pennsylvania Cartographic Modeling Laboratory. The photograph of the Northwest Philadelphia homes in chapter 4 was provided by John Gibbons. The title of chapter 10 is taken from "Explain It to Me" by Liz Phair, from *Exile in Guyville* (Matador Records, Inc.). I appreciate the generosity of Scott McGhee Artists in granting permission for the use of these lyrics.

I am very appreciative of help given me in many forms by other people, too numerous to list individually here, who share an interest in the improvement and future well-being of urban residential communities.

Acronyms

ACC	Annual Contributions Contract
APM	Asociacion de Puertorriqueños en Marcha (Association of Puerto Ricans on the March)
ASHI	American Society of Home Inspectors
CBC	Campus Boulevard Corporation
CDBG	Community Development Block Grant
CDC	Community Development Corporation
CETA	Comprehensive Employment and Training Act
CISP	Communities in Schools of Philadelphia
CNU	Congress for the New Urbanism
CSP	Comprehensive Service Program
CUED	Council for Urban Economic Development
DCED	Department of Community and Economic Development
GGHDC	Greater Germantown Housing Development Corporation
GPF	Greater Philadelphia First
HUD	U.S. Department of Housing and Urban Development
LCA	Ludlow Community Association
LISC	Local Initiatives Support Corporation
MAVDC	Mount Airy Village Development Corporation
NAHRO	National Association of Housing and Redevelopment Officials
NIMBY	"Not in my back yard"
NKCDC	New Kensington Community Development Corporation
OARC	Ogontz Avenue Revitalization Corporation

OCRA	Omnibus Consolidated Recissions and Appropriations Act
ODAAT	One Day at a Time
OHCD	Office of Housing and Community Development
PEC	People's Emergency Center
PECCDC	People's Emergency Center Community Development Corporation
PHA	Philadelphia Housing Authority
PhAME	Philadelphia Area Accelerated Manufacturing Education, Inc.
PHFA	Pennsylvania Housing Finance Agency
PIC	Private Industry Council
PICA	Pennsylvania Intergovernmental Cooperation Authority
RDA	Redevelopment Authority
RFP	Request for Proposals
SOSNA	South of South Neighborhood Association
TDC	total development cost
TRAC	Tenants' Rental Assistance Corporation
UCH	Universal Community Homes
WCRP	Women's Community Revitalization Project
YCO	Yorktown Community Organization

Neighborhood Recovery

INTRODUCTION

Some of the most creative and innovative neighborhood reinvestment strategies ever to be attempted in any American city were tried out in Philadelphia during the administration of Mayor Edward G. Rendell, in which I served as director of housing. Over an eight-year period, I had an unprecedented opportunity to design and manage local-government policy that helped bring to life a variety of development and service activities—from new housing construction ventures to after-school internships for high-school students—producing tangible results in neighborhoods across the city. With the mayor's backing, I spent more than a billion dollars (not counting overhead costs) to mobilize programs and services as a response to one overriding priority: to help distressed neighborhoods recover from a generation of economic loss and reposition themselves for survival and success in today's economy. I wasn't a housing czar, a politician, or a confidant of powerful elected officials; but, thanks to a political alliance forged between Mayor Rendell and Philadelphia's City Council, I received consistent political and legislative support for every one of my policy goals and funding priorities. This combination of control over policy, access to lots of public money, and sustained political support made it possible for me to attempt and accomplish more than any of my predecessors in

Philadelphia and most of my counterparts in other older American cities. Many people had written about, debated, and proposed solutions to serious problems confronting urban neighborhoods. Due to an extraordinary combination of circumstances, I was given a better opportunity than most of these people to deal with one of the biggest problems—economic disinvestment—in the most direct way imaginable.

This book explains how I made use of this extraordinary opportunity. The ten chapters which follow describe my efforts to influence fundamental changes in the economies of neighborhoods struggling with a protracted postindustrial history of economic disinvestment: an unprecedented loss of businesses, jobs, and people, and the associated physical deterioration of formerly attractive residential communities. Neither autobiography, insider tell-all, nor urban history, this book is part war story, part how-to manual, part advocacy for more effective public policy. Philadelphia's experience in pursuing neighborhood reinvestment goals is not necessarily the best or the only model for other cities confronting similar problems. A number of city governments have surpassed Philadelphia's record of performance in addressing some of these goals. Other city governments have adopted reinvestment approaches that are fundamentally different from Philadelphia's, because their neighborhood economies differ from Philadelphia's in significant ways. Rather than presenting an ideal model of neighborhood reinvestment policy, my purpose in writing this book is to promote better understanding of a subject rarely addressed in literature about cities and public policy: an explanation of the key challenges and opportunities that need to be recognized and managed effectively in order for urban neighborhoods to recover and thrive. My experience in Philadelphia and the specific cases described throughout this book are readily comparable to similar, often identical, challenges and opportunities that can decisively influence the future of neighborhoods in many other American cities.

To deal with the problem of disinvestment in a meaningful way, cities have to improve the physical condition of their neighborhoods and help community residents get ready to compete for good jobs in today's economy. These tasks are economic issues; they are different from, but just as important as, social issues such as crime, public schools, drug abuse, and child welfare that are the focus of much of the current dialogue about cities and their neighborhoods. Even the ideal urban social policy, a policy that addresses these critical social issues and produces phenomenal benefits for cities, will not automatically rebuild devastated neighborhoods— just as a great housing-construction program will not, by itself, also produce safe streets and an outstanding public school system. While closely related to other urban concerns, neighborhood reinvestment is a distinct issue that has to be addressed through a public policy focused specifically on the problem of economic disinvestment, a problem with its own special nature and characteristics. Because of this distinction between neighborhood reinvestment and social issues, policy and programming managed by police, fire, drug-prevention, and child-welfare departments and service agencies are not addressed in this book.

My primary focus in the chapters that follow is housing, because most urban neighborhoods are overwhelmingly residential in character. The first chapter describes some of the strategic issues that have to be considered in organizing a sensible reinvestment policy. Subsequent chapters address the topics of neighborhood strategic planning, housing finance, homeownership, the role of community-based organizations, public housing, work readiness and job training for neighborhood residents, housing for homeless people and others with specialized housing and service needs, and the importance of advocacy in influencing and advancing neighborhood reinvestment policy. The final chapter describes how cities can evaluate and improve existing reinvestment policy to achieve the best possible results in the future. Each chapter is accompanied by an anecdote illustrating some of my firsthand experience with the topic under discussion.

Some of the principles described in these chapters are relevant to strategies for commercial and industrial development in urban neighborhoods. However, I do not address development opportunities associated with these uses in depth, because housing markets are different from the market for neighborhood retail services or the market potential of neighborhood-based development sites to attract industries that participate in the mainstream economy. The strong interest generated by Michael E. Porter's 1995 *Harvard*

Business Review essay[1] has shown that much is to be gained by more discussion and debate about the nonresidential reinvestment issues that I do not directly pursue in this book.

Good neighborhood reinvestment policy is guided by three underlying principles, emphasized in different ways from chapter to chapter.

☐ Resources are limited, but opportunities are great. There is not enough public money on hand to quickly and decisively address the worst conditions of disinvestment in urban neighborhoods. At the same time, there are more opportunities now than ever before for supporters of neighborhood reinvestment to make better use of the substantial funding and other resources that are available. New and improved forms of innovation and collaboration to take advantage of current opportunities are essential to a successful reinvestment effort.

☐ The right organizational approach is neither "top-down" nor "bottom-up." The critical task of leading and guiding an effective neighborhood reinvestment strategy cannot be exclusively government directed and controlled nor exclusively community directed and controlled. Instead, city and neighborhood leaders have to support an effective organizational combination: government agency management of a rational public policy, and neighborhood-based management of community initiative—the pursuit of the dreams and ambitions of neighborhood residents. Each city must seek out and define in its own way the organizational joining of local government policy and community initiative that produces the best results.

☐ Everyone is entitled to participate. No special academic credentials, technical training, or life experience is needed in order for an interested person to participate in and influence neighborhood reinvestment policy. Everyone has an understanding of the core values on which a successful reinvestment approach is based: the values of a secure, comfortable home, attractive physical surroundings, and an engaging, interesting social environment. Anyone who lives or works in the metropolitan region has expert knowledge of these core values, accompanied by a history of relevant experience. For this reason, any interested person has the standing and credentials to participate in the creation and execution of neighborhood reinvestment policy.

This book is intended to inform, support, and encourage people who recognize these principles, who care about urban neighborhoods, and who want to make constructive commitments of their time, energies, and resources to the future economic well-being of these special places.

1

A STRATEGIC PROBLEM

One winter morning, a few years before his election and several more years before Al Gore dubbed him "America's Mayor," I stood in line behind Ed Rendell at the A-Plus Mini Market at Ridge and Midvale. He bought a newspaper and a soda and engaged the cashier in friendly conversation. At the time, he was a local celebrity in decline, facing an uncertain future. Ed Rendell had been the city's most popular district attorney in years, then a two-time loser in successive campaigns for governor in 1986 and mayor in 1987. What was he going to do now?

I thought about introducing myself, but what could I say that would be of any interest? In two past elections, I had been the volunteer campaign manager for State Representative Robert O'Donnell—not a very hard task, given O'Donnell's long incumbency and strong political base. I had been struggling to complete my first real estate development venture, a small retail center in West Philadelphia—too insignificant to be of interest to anyone outside the immediate neighborhood. My full-time job as an associate at a little development consulting firm downtown was not worth mentioning. I wasn't bringing the firm any profitable work, and I was lucky to still be on the payroll. What was there to talk about? If Rendell was a has-been, my situation was even worse. To paraphrase that line from *Tootsie*, you couldn't really be considered a has-been if you were never particularly important in the first place.

A few years later I volunteered to work on housing issues for Ed Rendell's 1991 mayoral campaign. I had once been employed as a project manager at the city's Office of Housing and Community Development (OHCD), during four years that straddled the mayoral terms of Frank Rizzo and William Green, a best-of-times/worst-of-times period. The experience had been fascinating, rewarding, discouraging, bitterly disappointing. I learned how public investment could influence positive change in a deteriorated neighborhood. I implemented a simple rehabilitation financing program for vacant houses, combining a city subsidy with a Title I loan. I learned how dissension and poor leadership could undermine good public policy. I helped design a construction program that trained unemployed young adults in the building trades, at no additional expense to the city budget—then saw the program rejected by OHCD's Contract Review Committee without explanation.

Housing and neighborhoods stayed on my mind during the 1980s. Ed Rendell had been a progressive district attorney and, I reasoned in 1991, he might be responsive to some of my insights on progressive housing policy. The Rendell '91 campaign welcomed me as a volunteer housing-issues coordinator. When I came on board early in the campaign year, no one was covering housing and neighborhoods in a big way—not surprisingly, because these issues aren't the ones that make or break a mayoral campaign. Instead, the recurring hot topics are taxes, crime, the police, the schools, jobs, the economy. A candidate has to demonstrate some interest in housing and neighborhoods, make some intelligent statements about these issues during the course of the campaign, then move back to the big topics that draw the interest of the most voters.

I drafted the campaign's housing platform, *The Rendell Housing Strategy: A New Opportunity for Philadelphia Neighborhoods,* and fielded inquiries and proposals from individuals and groups representing various housing and neighborhood constituencies. The experience was refreshing and fun. I met the candidate only once, at a housing-roundtable event in July that afforded no real opportunity for one-on-one discussion.

A lot of people I knew weren't that enthusiastic about Ed Rendell.

They viewed him as a sleazy politician, a loser, a has-been. They thought he would favor downtown development at the expense of neighborhood interests. They thought he would dispense community development money to private developers who supported his campaign. None of these people would have tagged him a future "America's Mayor."

I pressed ahead. In addition to managing housing issues, I helped coordinate the Northwest Philadelphia campaign organization, joining forces with a network of committeepeople and ward leaders who supported Ed Rendell. Rendell won the primary. In July, Rendell's Republican opponent, Frank Rizzo, dropped dead. Some of the city's most knowledgeable political observers say that Rizzo would have won decisively in November, but after his death the Republicans weren't able to regroup in time. Rendell's general-election landslide must have included a greater-than-usual number of voters who felt deprived of any real alternative.

At the election-night victory party, Rendell stood on a low stage, surrounded by television cameras and hundreds of cheering campaign workers. With him on the platform were some of the private developers and real estate lawyers that my friends and acquaintances suspected would be favored with community development money in a Rendell Administration. Among those surrounding the mayor-elect, I didn't recognize any representatives of affordable housing or neighborhood constituencies.

Two months later, on the weekend before the mayor-elect's inauguration, I was asked to manage OHCD on an interim basis—possibly for a few days—while a housing director was recruited. I hadn't spoken with Ed Rendell since that July meeting, much less discussed our views on housing policy. Housing was still not a hot topic. The city was on the brink of bankruptcy. Everyone in the mayor-elect's transition team seemed to understand the importance of housing and neighborhood issues, but the primary tasks at hand were meeting the municipal payroll, determining the true magnitude of the deficit, and organizing a financing plan before the city crashed and had to be put on life-support.

Late one night a week or so after the inauguration, I finished the day's work and sat alone in the housing director's office, staring at the ceiling-high window, a darkened screen overlooking Market Street.

On the other side of the street was a vacant lot the size of a city block. Within the past few days, the mayor had ordered cuts in housing agency administrative budgets and had decided to bring in a panel of experts to develop a housing reorganization plan. The funding cuts could mean layoffs of good staff people. I knew all about that; my previous tenure at OHCD had ended with a layoff notice. The reorganization, to be designed by a group of out-of-towners, could mean big disruption, with limited gains for the city and its neighborhoods.

I didn't feel betrayed by or disillusioned with the mayor; on the contrary, I felt flattered to be given the opportunity to manage OHCD on a temporary basis. I didn't want to be appointed housing director. What I might have wanted was irrelevant in any case, since no one considered me sufficiently qualified to be a serious candidate for the job.

What bothered me was the realization that nothing had come of my attempts to influence Philadelphia's housing and neighborhood policy. Despite the energy and initiative I brought to the campaign and the postelection transition period, I had somehow missed the opportunity to make an impact on the new administration—if there really ever had been an opportunity.

You know that feeling you get when you go outside in the morning and find your car window smashed, with bits of sparkling glass strewn across the seats and on the pavement—that feeling of washed-out emptiness, beyond the anger and bitterness? That's how I felt that night, staring out at the screen of darkness.

Blighted urban neighborhoods, particularly the older communities left behind in the wreckage of the American industrial age, are today's biggest threat to the economic well-being of the cities and metropolitan regions where they are located. The only way to overcome this threat is by solving a fundamental strategic problem: how do you bring stability and economic success to the places hardest hit by a half-century or more of disinvestment? Within a few decades, many inner-city communities have changed from geographic centers of wealth to clusters of economic failure and loss. In any metropolitan region, urban neighborhoods are the places where the worst physical deterioration, the greatest social need, and the least potential for economic improvement can be found. The urban communities which are the focus of this problem share three characteristics.

□ *Age*. Nearly all urban neighborhoods currently suffering from economic disinvestment—an unprecedented, decades-long loss of businesses, jobs, and people—grew up and established their identities during the century prior to 1950, when the nation's industrial economy was flourishing.

□ *Level of Physical Deterioration*. The vacant properties, deteriorated occupied housing, obsolete factory buildings, and failing commercial corridors located in urban neighborhoods are serious deficiencies which, for the most part, will not be corrected through private market activity, because investment in these places is too expensive or risky.

□ *Level of Service Need*. A larger proportion of the population of these neighborhoods has a greater need for government-funded human services—subsidized day care for children, job-readiness training for out-of-school adolescents, literacy and job-training services for adults, continuing care and case management for older people—than residents of other areas of the city and region.

These conditions can be found in a variety of urban communities, from factory-town neighborhoods built up around now-obsolete manufacturing plants to working-class, rowhouse blocks experiencing population loss and housing vacancy, from Victorian-era "streetcar suburbs" struggling to reduce the departure of middle-class families to the older suburban-city neighborhoods now experiencing economic and social problems previously associated with the central city alone. If urban neighborhoods decline and fail during the early decades of the twenty-first century, the economies of the cities and metropolitan regions surrounding them will suffer badly. Alternatively, if these neighborhoods are able to achieve stability and economic success during the coming decades, the economic potential and competitive standing of their cities and metropolitan regions will improve substantially.

During the early twentieth century, many urban neighborhoods succeeded as great job centers for the people who lived in and around them. To succeed during the first decades of the twenty-first century, most urban neighborhoods will have to reestablish themselves as great places to live, learn, play, shop, and socialize—

primarily for people who work somewhere else, in and around the city and region. The most desired neighborhoods of the twenty-first century will succeed not as industrial centers but as new home-towns, as places that best represent traditional values of belonging, sharing, and collaborative spirit for new generations of residents. In the most idealized terms, a hometown is a place where young people, older people, and families enjoy living, and can afford to live, with or near one another. The physical plan of the commu-nity, a network of mostly residential blocks with higher housing density than is found in suburban tracts, makes it easy for residents to get acquainted with their neighbors, communicate with one an-other, and organize themselves to respond to an opportunity or a problem. Retail stores and services are located within walking dis-tance or can be reached easily by public transportation. People cel-ebrate the sense of community that binds the neighborhood together, the recognition that some residents share with one an-other a common race, ethnicity, age, or economic status. At the same time, people recognize and appreciate the diversity of the neighborhood, the capacity of the community to accommodate a variety of individuals and families, who are able to live together comfortably and enjoy one another's company.

Can urban neighborhoods, particularly today's ruined, post-industrial ghost towns, really become new hometowns? To those who have experienced the worst qualities of these neighborhoods—the windswept vacant lots, the graffiti-scarred factory buildings, the armed boys selling drugs, the sound of gunfire at night—the idea seems ludicrous. And for some neighborhoods, it is. Some formerly vital urban communities will disintegrate and disappear from the map of the twenty-first-century city. Others will retain long-term slum status, as places where destitute individuals and families live in overcrowded and substandard conditions. Without fundamen-tal change in America's public housing system, public housing cam-puses will retain their status as communities of desperation. Not one of these residential environments is going to be regarded by anyone as a new hometown candidate.

On the other hand, certain urban neighborhoods, many located in or near downtown areas, already possess most of the defining characteristics of a new hometown. Philadelphia's celebrated Rittenhouse Square, the neighborhood surrounding a city-block-sized park located a short distance west and south of City Hall, is home for middle- and upper-income working professionals, retired empty-nesters who want to live near the attractions of the central city, and students from the University of Pennsylvania and other nearby academic institutions. The working people live in expensive con-dominiums above the treetops overlooking the park, in big historic brownstones or brick-fronts one or two blocks south of the square, or in more recently developed townhouses two or more blocks fur-ther south and west. The empty-nesters live in high-priced condo-miniums or apartment buildings around or near the square. Most of the students live a few blocks further away, in older apartment buildings and large row homes converted to multifamily use. Res-taurants, delis, grocery stores, and convenience stores are scattered throughout the community. A well-maintained branch of the public library faces the square. Lawyers, doctors, and dentists maintain their practices at street level in converted older residential build-ings or above-ground in nearby office buildings. One of the city's top elementary schools, Albert M. Greenfield, is located near the western edge of the community. Two extraordinary food centers, the historic Reading Terminal farmers' market and the much more recently arrived Fresh Fields supermarket, are located within a short bus ride or a medium-length walk. Many Philadelphia attractions—the downtown office center, cultural institutions, stores, public and private schools—are within walking distance or readily accessible through public transportation or a relatively inexpensive taxi ride.

But Rittenhouse Square and other downtown neighborhoods aren't really part of the big strategic problem confronting cities and metropolitan regions. These higher-income communities don't pos-sess all three characteristics—age, level of physical deterioration, and level of service need—of urban neighborhoods struggling to recover from economic disinvestment. The Rittenhouse Square area defined itself as a residential community prior to the industrial era and successfully redefined itself for postindustrial success during the de-cades after 1950. For the most part, physically deteriorated proper-ties in the area are acquired and upgraded through private-market activity. The service needs of this community's population are at a much lower level than those of community residents in other areas of the city and region.

Better-off communities such as Rittenhouse Square are not worry-free. Public safety, the maintenance of streets and public spaces, and an array of "quality-of-life" concerns—from aggressive panhandling to nuisance bars—are serious issues. But none of these issues involves the key strategic problem evident in a much greater number of urban neighborhoods: recovery from economic disinvestment.

Between the wrecked, outlying ex-communities nearing extinction and the high-end, mostly downtown-oriented communities like Rittenhouse Square are dozens of urban neighborhoods experiencing varying degrees of instability and deterioration. All of these neighborhoods possess the three characteristics which define the strategic problem, and all of them are also alike in one significant respect: they are all going to require public intervention, usually in the form of a sustained commitment of government resources over a period of years, if they are ever going to reach their maximum potential to become new hometowns, communities of choice for new generations of residents.

Because they are so isolated from the mainstream metropolitan economy, lack major neighborhood-based employers, and possess the weakest real estate markets in the region, an upturn in the business cycle or real estate market will not bring corresponding economic benefit to these neighborhoods. Even extraordinarily successful downtown development, with filled-to-capacity convention centers, stadiums, hotels, themed visitor attractions, and a revived retail core, while generating good jobs for many neighborhood residents, will not bring substantive improvements to distressed urban neighborhoods. In fact, a fast-growing urban economy can have the opposite effect, substantially worsening conditions for residents of city neighborhoods. As Colorado Springs underwent rapid growth during the 1980s and 1990s, with rising population, housing construction, business development, and many new entry-level jobs, the city's homeless population also grew.[1] In Atlantic City, after twenty years of casino-related development, about 78 percent of casino-related jobs were held by out-of-towners,[2] while one out of four Atlantic City residents lived below the poverty level.[3] These negative by-products of economic success are the consequence of two unexpected and undesired changes that occur when a local economy takes off: the price of rental and sales housing shoots up, quickly making existing housing unaffordable to the city's lowest-income residents; and many of the new jobs generated by the growing economy are taken by people who live outside the city or who move in from somewhere else, crowding out less-qualified, long-unemployed neighborhood residents.

The realization that the private market does not connect positively with distressed urban neighborhoods, and may even place some residents of these neighborhoods at a severe disadvantage during a boom period, causes people with real estate development or business administration expertise—people such as downtown development agency managers, private real estate developers, and business school graduates—to steer clear of such neighborhoods as places to work or transact business. As a result, the pursuit of stabilizing and revitalizing these neighborhoods is left, more often than not, to people with backgrounds in community organizing, social work, or public administration—but with few or no real estate or business skills. Ironically, the people who know most about how to achieve what urban neighborhoods desperately need—economic stability and a return to participation in the local and regional economy—are not engaged professionally in improving these neighborhoods. Conversely, many of the people who are devoting their professional lives to tackling the region's number-one economic development problem, the problem of upgrading the economy of urban neighborhoods, have little or no training and professional experience in real estate or business.

My own background illustrates this situation. Following completion of a liberal-arts college education and four years of employment with nonprofit community organizations, I began my initial period of work at OHCD as a project manager for a series of neighborhood improvement programs targeted for two large areas of the city. Although I pursued opportunities to use city funding creatively to leverage other resources and generate greater benefit for the targeted areas, I rarely encountered private-sector developers or businesspeople who were interested in or capable of co-venturing with the city. I encountered this problem in another form after my layoff from OHCD, when I devoted two years to an aggressive job search in which I tried to market my public-sector skills and experience to private-sector employers, through dozens of interviews with midlevel and senior managers of banks, mortgage banking companies, investment banking concerns, and real estate development firms. Although most of the targets of my job-search strategy acknowledged my basic communications skills and managerial abilities, none of them regarded my government-program, neighborhood-focused professional background as a particularly relevant or useful qualification for employment in their fields. As a result, I ended up spending most of the decade prior to my return to city government working on consulting projects involving government-subsidy programs and came back to government with little private-sector experience.

Since the private economy won't decisively influence the fundamental problem of economic disinvestment, the shaping of a public intervention, a neighborhood reinvestment policy, is fundamentally important. During the eight-year period in which I served as OHCD director, I had the benefit of an extraordinary combination of resources and strategic advantages to support my neighborhood reinvestment approach for Philadelphia: annual budgets of more than $100 million during each year of my tenure; Mayor Rendell's consistent political support; and continuing endorsement, concurrence, or acquiescence from City Council, other city agencies, most nonprofit and private developers, and most housing advocates.

It wasn't easy, though. As public-policy designers and implementers, we at OHCD had to behave in an open, forthright, evenhanded, and consistent manner. Some of our fellow stakeholders (to use that irritating term of 1990s rhetoric) did not recognize a corresponding obligation to observe comparable standards of conduct. Various elected officials, disappointed when development ventures they supported did not receive OHCD funding awards, publicly denounced us as unfair, dishonest, insensitive, uncollaborative, cynical, and out of touch with deserving consumers. A nationally respected political fund-raiser told Mayor Rendell that my refusal to alter policy in order to accommodate a housing-finance proposal he supported reflected a "bureaucratic determination" to exclude program initiatives other than my own ("John won't last long in the next administration," the mayor joked at a meeting with city staff the following week). Some municipal union members who were unhappy with our Redevelopment Authority's progressive new management approach conducted a vituperative campaign of personal attacks against agency leadership, bringing to one regulatory authority charges of corruption and conflicts of interest, submitting to human-relations commissions complaints of racial and sexual discrimination, and requesting that the Sons of Italy investigate a policy of "ethnic cleansing" being practiced against Italian-American employees. All these allegations were found to be groundless. Some housing agency staff appointed to positions of authority embarrassed us and undermined the integrity of our programs. I dismissed a deputy director, well regarded by the mayor, after receiving a report that, in violation of the city's conflict-of-interest policy, he had executed a consulting contract with one of the nonprofit agencies we funded. I caused the dismissal of another deputy director when I was informed that he had authorized dozens of hours of unearned overtime compensation for a pal, an office-support worker who, I was told, had once used a city-owned cellular phone to make a long-distance call from San Juan on one of the holidays recorded as a work day in his time records. Vanloads of angry housing advocates tried to stage a sleepover on my front lawn one weekend (they goofed; my family and I were away in Colorado, and the police broke up the demonstration). Career government-agency professionals responsible for monitoring our programs nickeled and dimed us over regulatory minutiae year in and year out. As we tried to author and enforce a rational public policy, we constantly encountered conflicts, misunderstandings, and annoyances of every variety.

But the potential opportunities and associated benefits were extraordinary. A billion-dollar budget, available during an extended period of relative political stability—not the most funding and not the best environment, but a much better combination of the two than had been available to any community development director in the history of the city's programs. Under these circumstances, what reinvestment policy would be most effective? And what were we going to do?

Prior to entering city government leadership and during the early months of my tenure at OHCD, I imagined that public policy was formulated in a "war room" located somewhere in City Hall, probably a high-ceilinged, curtained place where, behind closed doors, the mayor and a group of important people—city department heads, City Council leaders, possibly a few private-sector executives—sat in armchairs around a table and deliberated on the big issues. As the first months of the Rendell Administration went by, it became increasingly clear that the war room did not exist and that nearly all of the policy issues that I had imagined being discussed and resolved by this select group of power brokers were my decisions to make. In the first years of the administration, Mayor Rendell and I met several times a month and discussed many issues—from the capabilities of Philadelphia's community development corporations to the level of funding to be devoted to homeless housing programs—but we never worked out the details of the annual OHCD budget and the city's overall neighborhood reinvestment policy together. Instead, I organized the budget and plan for the upcoming program year and, after reviewing this material and discussing potential opportunities and problems likely to emerge during the year, the mayor supported all of the priorities I had proposed, along with nearly everything else in the plan.

It wasn't that Mayor Rendell didn't care about neighborhoods and didn't pay any attention to our reinvestment programs. On the contrary, he was acutely aware of the seriousness of the problems affecting Philadelphia communities, and he devoted a lot of time to securing more funding for neighborhoods and supporting neighborhood development ventures that he felt would make a difference. However, following an initial period of getting acquainted with me and my leadership style, the mayor delegated most policymaking responsibility to me, just as other big-city mayors, even those who identify themselves with neighborhood policy issues, delegate substantial responsibility to the people they select as the leaders of their neighborhood programs. A good mayor has to use all available time attracting businesses and jobs to the city, improving the public school system, promoting public safety, and marketing the city in a variety of ways. These first-priority activities are far more important to neighborhoods than a strong mayoral role in managing neighborhood reinvestment policy on a day-to-day basis, because, when effective, they strengthen the local economy and generate new jobs for neighborhood residents. Mayoral delegation of neighborhood reinvestment policymaking responsibility is essential in any city.

What should our policy look like? History had already demonstrated the soundness of one fundamental principle: if public intervention is handled properly, neighborhood reinvestment will succeed, and both the neighborhood and the city at large will benefit. Two examples from Philadelphia's past illustrate how a well-designed and -managed neighborhood reinvestment policy can work.

The Society Hill neighborhood, one of the first residential settlements in seventeenth-century Philadelphia, was generally acknowledged to be one of the worst slums in Philadelphia during the years immediately following World War II. Although the community had a traditional urban street pattern, many historic houses, and an advantageous location at the eastern edge of the downtown area, Society Hill was overwhelmed by a chaotic mix of land uses: poorly maintained rooming houses, other deteriorated and vacant residential property, a massive, overcrowded food distribution center on Dock Street, and dilapidated commercial buildings scattered throughout the community.

During the postwar years, as the federal government began to make a substantial commitment to upgrading the nearby Independence Hall area, a reinvestment plan for Society Hill was drafted and authorized. A survey of the neighborhood's historic assets was completed. The Redevelopment Authority (known as the RDA) had the area certified as "blighted" and obtained City Council authorization to undertake property acquisition through eminent domain. The food distribution center was relocated to South Philadelphia. Following a design competition that resulted in the selection of a proposal by I. M. Pei, the site where the center had been located was developed as Society Hill Towers, a group of three thirty-story apartment buildings with extraordinary views of the nearby Delaware River and the downtown area. The community surrounding the towers retained its traditional low-rise character. With land acquisition and development funding support made available through the RDA during the 1950s and 1960s, more than six hundred historic houses were restored, based on standards established by the

Historic Society Hill houses, with Society Hill Towers in background

Philadelphia Historical Commission. Vacant lots were developed for residential use, most as modern, single-family townhouses compatible in scale and density with existing residences. Narrow streets were closed and recreated as brick-paved, landscaped pedestrian walkways, extending into or through city blocks being redefined as primarily residential in character. Some interior-block spaces were developed as small parks or play areas for young children. Many trees were planted throughout the community. Cement sidewalks were replaced with brick, and Franklin-lantern lighting was installed on every block.

As a result of two decades of public investment and publicly supported development, Society Hill was transformed into an attractive residential community offering desirable housing for a middle-class market, as well as great access to the downtown business district, to clusters of neighborhood-oriented food stores and retail services, and to the city's entertainment attractions and night life.

Subsequently, in the 1970s and afterward, Society Hill established itself as a gentrified, mostly upper-income, mostly residential community, as one of the region's neighborhoods of preference. Property values, and associated property tax revenues, increased at a much higher rate than in most other city neighborhoods. Most sales and rental housing in Society Hill is now priced at or near the top of the market. There are no vacant properties and no destructively adverse land uses, although quality-of-life concerns similar to those experienced in the Rittenhouse Square area are significant and are taken seriously.

Robert Butera, executive director of the Pennsylvania Convention Center Authority, formerly a Montgomery County legislator who had lived most of his life in the suburbs, described the attractions and benefits of Society Hill residency,

> When suburbanites ask me why I moved to the city, I offer a one-sentence reply: "We can walk everywhere!" In the suburbs, walking *anywhere* is inconceivable. . . .
>
> My neighborhood consists of people who have lived in all parts of the Philadelphia region, of the U.S. and, indeed, in all parts of the world. It's this wide variety of people and the interaction among them that distinguishes the city from the suburbs, and I mean that in the best sense. To me, life's daily routine is more fascinating in the city: a casual walk to the local bakery might result in three or four conversations with people who have vastly different backgrounds and interests but a commonality of neighborhood.[4]

Society Hill is not the best example of how public intervention can help older urban neighborhoods make a comeback, because—although it did possess the three defining characteristics of neighborhoods in need of reinvestment—it has, like Rittenhouse Square, advantageous qualities that most distressed neighborhoods don't have and can't get. Society Hill's downtown location, historic houses, and proximity to Independence Hall and other attractions are extraordinary advantages. Given these advantages, it is certain that the area would have been substantially upgraded during the 1950s and 1960s through private-market activity, without any government intervention or the expenditure of a single public dollar. However, the total improvement of this community and the level of resulting economic benefit to the neighborhood and the city would never have been achieved without public intervention and associated government funding. A sustained delivery of public resources was needed to produce what is now one of the nation's most attractive and desirable residential communities.

The history of the Yorktown community illustrates another form of successful public intervention.[5] Yorktown, located about ten blocks north of Philadelphia's downtown, is bounded by the Temple University campus, a rail line, and two major four-lane streets: Broad Street, the city's primary north-south route, and Girard Avenue, a well-traveled commercial corridor.

Post–World War II disinvestment had made the area a landscape of vacant buildings and lots, substandard rental housing with inadequate utilities, and deteriorated, nonresidential land uses. Unlike Society Hill, Yorktown had no adjacency to the downtown area or other locational advantages that eventually would have attracted private-market interest.

However, the area was not entirely devoid of strategic advantages. The nearby presence of the Temple main campus provided a stable, well-maintained center of investment which could serve as a geographic anchor for adjacent development and as a protective buffer.[6] Temple was also a major employer of many North Philadelphia residents, some of whom might want to live in an improved neighborhood within walking distance of campus. Access to downtown by public transit and car was excellent. And many African-American citizens already valued North Philadelphia for its affordable, economically diverse neighborhoods, community-oriented churches, and attractive neighborhood facilities and social institutions.

Leaders of Philadelphia's African-American community played a decisive role in securing a commitment to public intervention in

Yorktown townhouses

the area. The Reverend Dr. William H. Gray, Jr., pastor of the nearby
Bright Hope Baptist Church, told the *Evening Bulletin*, "This is the
first time and place in the United States that Negroes have been
named as developers for urban renewal."[7]

As in Society Hill, the Redevelopment Authority played a key
role in the public intervention. Unlike Society Hill, development
in this area, designated as the Southwest Temple Urban Renewal
Area, consisted exclusively of new sales housing construction completed by a single developer. By 1958, the RDA had acquired and
cleared a 163-acre development tract. A plan for the construction
of more than six hundred new single-family houses was established,
and the entire site was conveyed to a private developer, Norman
Denny. The Yorktown plan implemented by Denny brought to the
inner city some of the design features of suburban residential
development, including front yards, driveways, garages, and streets
ending in cul-de-sacs.

The Yorktown Community Organization (YCO), founded in 1961 to "foster conduct and living habits which are conducive to a wholesome neighborhood,"[8] promoted the development of the new community and organized incoming residents. Protective Covenants published by YCO established standards of property maintenance (example: "Lawns shall be mowed and weeds removed at least once a week between May 1 and November 1 of each year").

The completion of Yorktown in the 1960s created a new, suburban-style residential neighborhood at a key city location and provided an attractive alternative to traditional forms of urban residency. By the 1990s, the Yorktown community still included a substantial number of residents who had been the first buyers of the newly constructed homes thirty years earlier and had remained since then. Although Yorktown housing now has the dated appearance of the 1960s-era suburban communities on which it was modeled, most of the houses and yards are attractive and well maintained. Street-oriented activity is ongoing: kids playing in yards or on sidewalks, grown-ups tending gardens or washing cars, pedestrians walking to places in or near the community. Yorktown property values increased by 116.5 percent during the 1970s, the first full decade after the completion of development, and 1980s and 1990s median values in Yorktown were significantly higher than those in other Philadelphia neighborhoods with comparable market orientation. Yorktown has become recognized as a key North Philadelphia asset and as a community of preference for African-American homeowners.

Yorktown residents responding to a 1995 survey described some of the benefits of living in this community.

"Proud homeowners; good transportation; only a few minutes from Center City."

"Good public services; double protection with Temple and City police. Convenient to Temple University."

"Location . . . homeowners who take care of their property."[9]

That's how public intervention brought successful reinvestment to Society Hill and Yorktown and generated significant economic benefit to these neighborhoods and to the city as a whole. Because the population at large has become so well acquainted with the failure of government programs in urban neighborhoods—often through negative media coverage such as news stories about the abandonment and demolition of derelict public housing sites—it is important to recognize that an effective neighborhood reinvestment policy can produce outstanding results.

So why don't we just extend these past successes and produce dozens of Society Hills and Yorktowns throughout cities such as Philadelphia? The policy would be simple: establish a neighborhood plan, clear away the old or adverse elements of the physical environment, restore or upgrade existing neighborhood assets through construction on vacant lots and the installation of site improvements such as parks, street trees, and sidewalk lighting. The result: new neighborhoods and a revitalized city.

This simplified policy approach wouldn't work in most urban neighborhoods today, because both the funding base for public intervention and the nature of public engagement in neighborhood reinvestment have changed radically since the 1950s and 1960s. During the first two decades after World War II, a lot of federal money was available to support the total improvement of target areas designated for urban renewal. Property restoration and site improvements in Society Hill, designated as the Washington Square East Urban Renewal Area, were funded with generous federal awards to the city. In Yorktown, an award of about $5.5 million (about $28 million in 1990s dollars), made available through Title I of the National Housing Act, supported two-thirds of the cost of acquiring the massive housing development site.[10] Millions of dollars of matching state funds were also made available for these renewal activities. During this postwar period, most city governments didn't yet realize that they were headed for fiscal trouble, and substantial local-government funding was also committed for neighborhood renewal projects. Philadelphia's Capital Program supported targeted neighborhood development in Society Hill, Yorktown, and elsewhere, through municipal borrowing to finance new streets, curbs, sidewalks, and utilities.

Starting in the 1970s, federal funding to cities began a long, protracted decline. Local governments, by this time experiencing significant tax losses as residents and businesses left the city, decided not to make up the shortfall with local funding and, in fact, cut back on their own commitments to large-scale neighborhood development. Philadelphia's Washington Square West, a mostly residential neighborhood adjacent to Society Hill, gained an unhappy appreciation of this post–Great Society policy shift. Following an initial period, prior to 1970, of planning for a Society Hill–style reinvestment approach, the neighborhood had been designated an urban renewal area and the Redevelopment Authority had acquired property, demolished older buildings, and relocated many residents and businesses. By the mid-1970s, the Authority owned about one-fifth of the neighborhood, an inventory consisting of most of the area's vacant buildings and lots. By this time, however, federal urban renewal programs had been superseded by the block-granting of federal aid to cities initiated in the Nixon era. As a result, Washington Square West, unlike Society Hill, had no federal money, and no associated city funds, specifically earmarked for housing restoration or for amenities such as brick paving, small parks, or street lighting. During the next two decades, most publicly owned land in Washington Square West eventually got developed, but progress was slow, and the community never achieved the total improvement of its more fortunate neighbor.

What would it take to finance a replication of Yorktown today? The federal Title I funding commitment to Yorktown, expressed in 1990s dollars, is roughly equivalent to Philadelphia's entire housing production budget for a single year of the 1990s decade. Using federal money available to Philadelphia in the 1990s to create another Yorktown would have meant denying funding for vacant house rehabilitation and new housing construction everywhere else in the city—a politically infeasible approach, as well as bad policy. Even if such a set-aside were possible, a commitment of Philadelphia Capital Program funds for associated 1960s-style infrastructure development could not have happened in the 1990s. Philadelphia didn't have the municipal borrowing capacity to debt-finance another Yorktown during this decade. In addition, large-scale local spending for such an initiative would never have been authorized by the Pennsylvania Intergovernmental Cooperation Authority (PICA), the state panel established early in the decade to monitor Philadelphia's fiscal practices, following a state intervention to help the city avoid bankruptcy.

The relative scarcity of funding requires that public money be used with care in order to make neighborhood reinvestment as effective as it can be in today's difficult environment, where neither the private market nor the public sector alone can produce an economic turnaround and bring a quick end to disinvestment. As indicated above, most neighborhoods outside the immediate orbit of the downtown area don't possess locational advantages similar to those of Rittenhouse Square, advantages that will attract new investment without significant public intervention. Not more than a few neighborhoods—perhaps only three or four in a decade—will be fortunate enough to become the top political priorities of local government and receive bigger, more sustained commitments of available public funding than all the other neighborhoods. Many of the remaining communities (in fact, the vast majority of urban neighborhoods) will be struggling for available public resources to support a goal of reinvestment that will take a decade—or decades— to achieve.

Given the critical shortage of resources, shouldn't local leaders advocate for more state and federal funding to help older urban neighborhoods? And, if sufficient funding can't be obtained to produce strong short- or mid-term results in most neighborhoods, why even bother trying to pursue a systematic reinvestment policy?

Government leaders and neighborhood advocates have learned that appeals for more public money to support urban neighborhoods usually have little or no effect in today's political environment. In 1989, OHCD director Edward A. Schwartz staged a two-week walk from Philadelphia to the state capital in Harrisburg to advocate for more state funding for affordable housing in Philadelphia. Nearly a decade later, Cheri Honkala of the Kensington Welfare Rights Union staged a similar event, marching from Philadelphia to Harrisburg to demand more resources for the homeless. The result of both these initiatives: modest media coverage, sympathetic responses from other neighborhood advocates, and a politely delivered negative response from state government officials. Mayor Rendell hoped that if city governments balanced their budgets, improved the delivery of municipal services, and managed available resources more responsibly, then federal and state officials might be persuaded to make a greater funding commitment to cities. Instead, despite progressive changes in local municipal government policy and practice across the country that restored financial stability, measurably improved services, and reduced crime in many cities during the 1990s, federal and state support for Philadelphia and many other older cities shrank rather than increased during this decade.

Neighborhood advocates should certainly continue to press for more nonlocal funding when there is a realistic prospect of getting it, because more money is needed to help older urban neighborhoods recover from disinvestment. Even the most progressive municipal management reforms and cost-cutting initiatives are not going to generate sufficient savings to finance the level of public investment that neighborhoods require. But at the moment, major new federal or state funding for urban neighborhood reinvestment seems to be an unlikely prospect.

The other reason why we can't replicate Society Hill and Yorktown everywhere is because neighborhood reinvestment today necessitates a much higher level of government and neighborhood collaboration than was required or desired in the 1950s and 1960s. During the urban renewal era, the biggest community-related issue, from the perspective of most of the local government administrators responsible for implementing Society Hill and Yorktown reinvestment activity, was getting rid of the people who occupied dwelling units and businesses that didn't measure up to redevelopment plan standards. The area that became Yorktown was completely emptied of people prior to the start of the new housing construction activities. Society Hill residents in local rooming houses and apartments were moved out of the neighborhood, as were nonconforming businesses such as junkyards, auto repair shops, and small manufacturing concerns. In today's environment, government can no longer just weed out existing residents and businesses in the postwar style. The relocation and displacement of urban community members to make way for expressway construction, institutional expansion by hospitals and universities, downtown business-district development, and residential gentrification projects in the 1950s and 1960s met with such a negative public response that some cities stopped using eminent-domain acquisition altogether, while others made sure that relocation activity associated with any city-supported development was minimized.

In addition, as the result of post-1960 federal legislation establishing new standards of compensation for government-related displacement, relocation is now too expensive and time-consuming to undertake on such a large scale. In the 1990s, the provision of federally mandated relocation benefits cost about twenty-five thousand dollars per displaced household. Funding for this expense is not available through a federal set-aside; unless extra state or local dollars are made available for this purpose, the money has to come from the same limited annual HUD funding used to support all citywide community development activities. Business relocation is even more costly. The fact that an existing business is characterized as a blighting influence does not reduce a city government's obligation to make full compensation for business loss, moving expenses, and machinery and equipment replacement. The total cost of moving out a down-at-the-heels tavern or a run-down auto repair shop can be phenomenal.

Even if relocation were more politically palatable and even if the expense of displacing people and businesses could be paid by someone else, there is very little public or political tolerance today for government action to depopulate and make over any urban community, no matter how deteriorated. Community members are not willing to have their surroundings declared economically unviable and are not ready to move out in order to set the stage for the future development of another Society Hill or Yorktown. Many of the residents and businesses that have made a commitment to remain in a particular community despite decades of steady disintegration are not going to get out now for the sake of supporting a government reinvestment program that will benefit someone else. (Giving community members a guarantee that they can move back after completion of development is risky from a legal point of view and would be unworkable from a management point of view if attempted on a large scale.) Elected officials representing voters in even the most fallen-down neighborhoods are not going to put themselves in the position of advocating depopulation for the sake of some greater public good which may not be achieved during their terms of office.

Because most community members are not going to be leaving the neighborhoods where they live now for the sake of advancing a depopulation and rebuilding policy, local government and neighborhood interests have to collaborate in order to make neighborhood reinvestment effective in today's economic and political environment. This collaboration can be time-consuming and complicated. Some community members need housing, services, and jobs, and a reinvestment plan for their neighborhood has to address these needs. Many community members would like to see public resources used to improve the neighborhood, and some of them would be willing to work with local organizations and public agencies to make improvement happen. A number of these prospective community participants in the reinvestment process would, under the right circumstances, contribute a lot of their intelligence, energy, and time to support an improvement plan that made sense to them. Other community members are themselves a primary source of some of the neighborhood's biggest problems and may prove difficult or impossible to deal with. Some community members want to participate in managing and leading a reinvestment plan for the neighborhood. Some of their ideas will be creative, workable, and relevant; others will be unrealistic, unworkable, and potentially disastrous. Future planning for neighborhood reinvestment has to encompass all these opportunities and problems and has to engage community members in a meaningful way over the long term.

Reinvestment works when government-community collaboration is successful, when the right balance is struck between public policy and neighborhood initiative. This balance is essential. A Marshall-Plan approach to older urban neighborhoods, in which a mega-agency headed by a development czar with a big budget and unquestioned authority totally remakes the urban landscape won't happen and can't work in the post–urban renewal era. Neither can the opposite, a community-empowerment approach, in which government programs are taken over and managed by enlightened residents who possess innate community-building skills and sensitivity surpassing the capabilities of public-agency bureaucrats; most neighborhood residents don't have and can't readily acquire the capability to manage government programs.

The insufficiency of public funding and the complexity of government-community collaboration do not justify giving up on inner-city neighborhoods and concluding that no significant improvement can be achieved there. Though current resources are inadequate, a city such as Philadelphia, with access to more than $100 million annually in neighborhood reinvestment funding, cannot claim with any credibility that nothing of value can be done without a lot more money. To the contrary, despite funding reductions and the largely negative history of urban neighborhoods during the final decades of the twentieth century, the post–urban renewal period has produced many valuable, though smaller-scale demonstrations of the fundamental lesson of Society Hill and Yorktown: if a public intervention is managed properly, the resulting neighborhood reinvestment will succeed and last. Many affordable-housing development ventures of the 1970s are today as attractive, clean, and well maintained as some of the newest private housing development in the region. The best-organized neighborhood economic development ventures of the 1980s, from small stores to supermarkets, are still operating successfully now. Many of the kids who were trained in the best job-readiness programs and many of the formerly homeless people who passed through the best transitional housing systems of the 1990s are working and living independently today. Post-1970 community development initiatives, though less dramatic and more dispersed than the large-scale, total-improvement projects of the past, prove that neighborhood reinvestment can work. Of course, many post-1970 neighborhood initiatives have failed, too. The whole urban neighborhood environment, when examined closely, is a landscape strewn with models of past success and failure. Neighborhood supporters have to learn what works and devote their energies and ambitions to pursuing the most promising opportunities for future success. The following chapters describe the best ways to design, launch, and sustain a successful neighborhood reinvestment policy, supported by long-term collaboration between government and neighborhood interests.

2

ADVANCING
THE PLAN

Our little group paused in a canyon of vacancy and abandonment. The midwinter sky was gray-marbled white. Our hands and feet were starting to get really cold. The disjointed rowhouse block was a perfect example of urban community commingled with urban ruin. On the corner, an empty, fire-damaged storefront, then six abandoned houses, then a cluster of owner-occupied houses—some well maintained, others needing repair—then a run-down garage, a weed-filled lot, and a smaller group of occupied houses in poorer condition.

What sense could be made of this landscape? Should the city acquire all the vacant houses and fix them up? If that happened, would anyone come to buy them? Should the corner storefront be rehabilitated to renew its past use as ground-floor retail with upstairs apartments? If so, who would come in and operate a successful store there? Or should the corner building just be demolished? In fact, why not acquire and demolish the whole block? You could relocate the remaining households to a better block or a better neighborhood. But the well-kept condition of some of the occupied houses showed that the families living there had committed years to maintaining a half-decent environment on the street they had chosen as their home. Were we going to try to force them out?

In the face of all these uncertainties, who was going to make decisions about the future of this block? Should government launch an ambitious improvement program here—or just stay away and let the inevitable downgrading continue?

These vacant houses and lots were like rocks at the bottom of a deep canyon. The rocks are numerous, varied in shape, size, and color. You can touch them, examine them, kick them. To an outsider who hasn't studied them and has no deeper knowledge of them, they're just a lot of . . . rocks. But someone who has spent time learning about rocks views them differently, with a knowledge of their age and history, of the changes they have undergone with the passage of time, of the reasons why they are here and the conditions that will affect their future.

We wanted to deal with the vacant properties in a similar way, not simply as outside observers, but as people with a base of knowledge and understanding. One or two of the graduate students were starting to shiver, but they weren't going to begin complaining in front of the OHCD staff. Using a couple of felt-tip markers, Nia colored in the vacant properties on a photocopy of an old insurance map that showed property lines and addresses more clearly than the newer city base maps; each vacant house got marked in red, each vacant lot in green. With a digital camera, Sherene took individual shots of every vacant house and lot on the block. As part of the set-up for every shot, Michelle and Karl positioned a portable metal signboard in front of each property, arranging magnetic numbers to display the city-designated street code and the street address. Hope penciled in a one-page survey form, entering responses to standard yes/no questions: Is the house fire-damaged? Does it have front-wall cracks? Are the openings sealed? Is the vacant lot fenced, filled with trash, paved, posted for sale? We knew that the whole process was ridiculously labor-intensive and could be made much simpler with improved technology, such as digital cameras with built-in caption-writing capability. Unfortunately, the market demand for sophisticated vacant-property survey equipment was apparently nonexistent. In the meantime, we had enough students and interested community members to meet the high labor requirements of the project.

We left the block and headed for a warm place. Later that day the survey information and the digital images were entered into a data base and merged with city government data files identifying, for each property, the name and address of the owner of record, the amount and length of tax delinquency, the status of the property on the city demolition list, and other information that in years past could have been obtained only through multiple visits and phone calls to a half-dozen government offices. Now all the available information about a particular property could be displayed on a single screen or printed out on a single page. Data sorting could generate a list of the most tax-delinquent properties in the neighborhood, identify the biggest va-cant property owners in the neighborhood, and reveal the addresses of all the vacant properties owned by public agencies. With this re-source, questions about blocks such as the one we had just surveyed could more readily be addressed on a neighborhood basis, rather than through ad hoc, property-by-property decision making.

For their semester project back at the University of Pennsylva-nia, the graduate students computer-mapped existing conditions of vacancy in the neighborhood, then created a series of reinvestment strategy options, some mutually exclusive, some overlapping. One map illustrated the results of an aggressive relocation/demolition strategy, another an aggressive preservation/rehabilitation strategy, another a strategy of building from strength by fixing up blocks surrounding the sites of completed development. Penn's Cartographic Modeling Laboratory staff integrated the data into an elaborate software sys-tem that could display each map in its original form, then as a de-tailed aerial photograph, then as a three-dimensional model that could be tilted, rotated, and examined at street level or from two hundred feet above the rooftops.

Other people besides our survey team of OHCD staff, community organization members, and Penn students were dealing with vacant property in creative ways, based on their own neighborhood planning perspectives, ambitions, and interests.

Universal Community Homes, a community development corpo-ration active in a portion of the neighborhood just surveyed by the students, had already computer-mapped a target area to illustrate the development strategy UCH supported: use all available resources to develop nearly every vacant property west of Broad Street, out to Sixteenth Street. UCH's map showed how this goal could be accom-plished through a combination of government-subsidized and market-rate housing development over a five-year period. The organization had

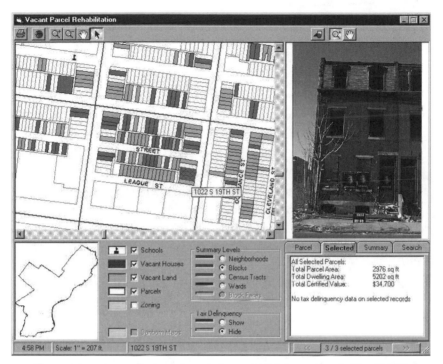

Computer screen display of vacant property information in the OHCD database

already completed construction, started construction, or obtained financing for the first phases of housing and retail development specified in the plan: new apartments, houses for sale, and a new corner store.

Out in New Kensington, a pint-sized partnership called Greensgrow Farms had obtained a three-quarter acre factory site as the location for its hydroponic urban-agriculture venture: a specialty lettuce farm which sold its harvest to high-priced downtown restaurants. The land was crisscrossed with PVC piping supporting tilted rows of gleaming white, plastic-coated metal drainage chutes. Spaced evenly along each chute was a series of little greenish-brown cubes sprouting green, red, and white lettuce leaves. Narrow streams of water flowed down the chutes soaking the grow-cubes, then fell two feet into a collection tank, then cycled back up to the top of the chutes again. Standing in the center of the lot with eyes closed, listening to dozens of columns of water falling on either side, you could imagine yourself at the Italian Water Garden display at the Longwood Gardens horticultural center.

In Eastern North Philadelphia, a tireless community development corporation director and a persistent Redevelopment Authority project manager methodically acquired more than a hundred small- and medium-sized vacant parcels to assemble an entire city block as the site for Borinquen Plaza, a new retail center to be developed by the Asociacion de Puertorriqueños en Marcha (Association of Puerto Ricans on the March, known as APM). With a small supply of working capital in hand, Rose Gray had tracked down vacant property owners and negotiated a series of cash purchases before the city made a commitment to participating in the development of the block. Later, Kirk Goodrich steered a complicated eminent-domain taking of properties owned by long-deceased residents or long-departed businesses. Streets and alleys were closed and struck from the official map of the city. A new block was being formed, and a big community asset was being created.

In neighborhoods across the city, neighborhood plans were guiding and determining the future of other vacant properties and establishing new definition and character for older communities.

A neighborhood strategic plan can fill a volume of five hundred pages or fit on a matchbook cover. Neighborhood strategic plans can differ from one another in format, scope, perspective, and emphasis. The focus of a strategic plan can be a multineighborhood cluster with fluid boundaries, a precisely delineated target area, a street corridor, or a single building. Neighborhood strategic plans can distinguish themselves from one another in many ways, but all of them share one defining quality: they all contain an argument, explicit or implicit, that urban neighborhood problems are solvable. When this argument is presented effectively, the strategic plan serves an important purpose: the plan begins to counter the perception that neighborhood deterioration is unstoppable and that neighborhood problems are so big and complicated that no one can handle them.

Strategic planning is not needed in neighborhoods where vacant buildings are being fixed up and reoccupied, where businesses are opening and expanding, and where government-owned property is well maintained or is scheduled for capital improvements funded within the current program year. Instead, neighborhood strategic planning should take place in those communities where disinvestment is so widespread and long-standing that no course of action other than a public intervention will work.

Before strategic planning begins, these neighborhoods have to be understood not just as blighted areas in need of fix-up but as communities where three extraordinary social and economic transformations of our time are having their greatest impact. These interrelated transformations, which began prior to the mid–twentieth century and will not run their course until sometime in the twenty-first, can be summarized as follows.

☐ *Work.* An economy with a dominant manufacturing sector supported by city-based production sites and a large, relatively unskilled workforce is being transformed into an economy in which service activities predominate, production sites are dispersed globally, and the reduced manufacturing sector is supported by fewer workers with more skills. The result: older urban neighborhoods experience a massive loss of job sites, and many residents of these neighborhoods find themselves unqualified for work in today's economy.

☐ *Place.* A metropolitan geographic pattern in which a populous central city is surrounded by lower-density suburbs, agricultural zones, and undeveloped areas is being transformed into a pattern in which central-city population is dwarfed by suburban and exurban population and in which central cities and older suburban cities contain the region's highest proportion of people living in poverty and in greatest need of support services. The result: many older urban neighborhoods experience substantial population loss, and formerly middle-income, working-class, or mixed-income communities gain a substantial proportion of people with incomes below poverty level.

☐ *Race.* A society in which nonwhites were excluded from nearly all managerial and executive leadership positions is being transformed into a society in which more nonwhites are moving into middle- and executive-level positions in government, business, and institutional entities and in which, within some of the most populous regions of the United States, nonwhites will eventually occupy many such leadership positions. However, in order to achieve the best possible integration of nonwhites into middle- and top-level leadership positions, many more racial and ethnic minority group members have to be educated and trained for successful careers in the metropolitan workforce than ever before. The result: older urban neighborhoods, currently the home of many, if not most, of the region's nonwhites, have to be recognized as the places where the most work needs to be done to help people move out of poverty into the middle class, in order to increase minority participation in the management and leadership of society and reduce the threat of future racial and economic polarization.

In the public discussion, academic discourse, political debate, and citizen advocacy of recent decades, dialogues about these three transformations have been loaded with value judgments, scapegoating, and blaming: big corporations sold out the American worker by moving overseas; American consumers betrayed American companies by purchasing foreign-made goods produced by cheap labor; "white flight" caused the decay of urban communities; incoming black migration caused the decay of urban communities; Federal Housing Administration redlining policies and federal highway subsidies caused the enrichment of the suburbs and the decline of the cities; affirmative action policies brought a generation of leaders to positions of authority they did not earn or deserve; white racism sustained a system which continued to block most nonwhites from positions of authority.

Some of these charges and contentions contain some truth, but none of them are relevant to the task of strategic planning for reinvestment in older urban neighborhoods. All three transformations were decisively influenced by fundamental changes in regional, national, and international social and economic structure rather than by any single policy or group of people. Changes in technology, transportation, communications systems, and finance made the growth of the service economy and the decline of manufacturing inevitable, bringing associated consequences for activities as varied as business location decisions and consumer buying trends. The twentieth-century migration from cities to suburbs, as unstoppable as the nineteenth-century westward migration, was an inevitable reaffirmation of the uniquely American passion to possess a substantial, secure, free-standing homestead[1] and was fueled by a phenomenal increase in post–World War II median income (an increase of 96.6 percent between 1950 and 1973).[2] U.S. demographics guaranteed that the participation of nonwhites in leadership positions would grow and will continue growing, as a larger nonwhite population votes more of its members into public office and exerts greater influence on business decisions and institutional policies.

A primary task of neighborhood strategic planning and, more broadly, of American leadership in the twenty-first century, is the effective management of these three transformations to produce the greatest benefit for society. Activities related to the transformations of place and, to a lesser extent, work, are the primary focus of most neighborhood strategic plans. In light of the fundamental changes in place and work that are now well under way, most older urban neighborhoods have to be developed and marketed as attractive residential communities; not as job centers, but as great places to live, mostly for people who work elsewhere in the city or region. Nonresidential land uses that do not support this new presentation of the neighborhood have to be removed or adapted. In most communities that previously had significant industrial orientation, the housing density of any new development should be lowered to achieve consistency with the reduced size of the city. Demolished factory sites and former rowhouse blocks that had nineteenth-century densities of twenty-five dwelling units or more per acre should be redesigned to support densities as low as ten to twelve units per acre and create blocks with fewer people, bigger houses, and more yard space. The neighborhood should be planned as a residential environment that can attract and keep people who have the means to live elsewhere if they so choose, as well as people with limited housing choice.

The scope and magnitude of these three transformations make planning for older urban neighborhoods particularly difficult. Urban neighborhood disinvestment linked to these transformations is an unprecedented problem with no clear or predictable resolution. Prior to the 1950s, the economic history of many urban neighborhoods was consistently positive; nearly every decade witnessed a growth in business development, jobs, and population. The reversal of this trend first became apparent after 1950. Now, a half-century later, many urban neighborhoods continue to lose businesses, jobs, and people, and no one knows when or whether the decline will bottom out and a new upward trend begin.

Disinvestment-related problems are, moreover, formidable in their scope and complexity. Consider, for example, the problem of vacant property. A 1995 OHCD policy paper estimated that Philadelphia neighborhoods contained a total of twenty-seven thousand vacant houses, two-thirds of which would cost substantially more than $100,000 each to rehabilitate. The total cost of fixing up all of the city's vacant houses was estimated to be $2.7 billion, an amount approximately thirty-five times the size of OHCD's annual "housing production" budget at the time.[3] Given this disparity between needs and resources, how could Philadelphia ever hope to be able to address its vacant house problem? And, to make the issue more complicated, why should the city devote any resources at all to fixing up houses, in light of the preceding half-century of population loss? With five hundred thousand fewer people in 1995 than in 1950, Philadelphia didn't have a housing shortage; to the contrary, the city now had far more houses than it needed to accommodate its reduced population. Why add to the oversupply by using public funding to promote the repair and reoccupancy of even a single vacant house?

In addition, some of the most critical problems of older urban neighborhoods can only be addressed through a combination of capital investment and service support requiring an unprecedented degree of coordination and cooperation between different government agencies with little or no prior history of collaboration. For example, a development agency can rehabilitate a vacant house for a homeless person to live in—but developing housing is only a partial response to the problem of homelessness. A house can't treat drug addiction, provide child care, or supply a chronically unemployed person with marketable skills. Without effectively delivered supportive services and case management, the problems which led to that person's homelessness will not be addressed, and the newly rehabilitated house will be neglected and eventually abandoned. The house-rehabilitation activities and the service-support activities are, in many cases, funded from different state and federal programs (with their own associated funding cycles and funding-award criteria) and often involve at least two different sets of staff, employed by agencies unlikely to have any formal structural connection or past experience in working together.

For an elected official, a public agency manager, a nonprofit organization director, a community organizer, or a neighborhood resident, the recognition that urban neighborhood problems are unprecedented, formidable in scale and complexity, and impossible to address without calling on a multiplicity of disparate resources can be a source of almost overwhelming frustration and discouragement. In the absence of a reliable guide to future action, these people are likely to respond to urban neighborhood problems with proposals that are off-target, unrealistic, or unworkable: cities should find a way to get more state and federal money; city leaders should find more money in the city budget; a housing czar should be appointed; a government or public/private task force with a "holistic" orientation should make policy; the private sector should be brought in to take charge of the situation in a businesslike fashion; more attention should be devoted to public safety, public schools, and programs for children and youth before any substantive neighborhood reinvestment planning even begins; urban neighborhoods should be declared disaster areas; urban areas should be systematically depopulated through large-scale relocation.

The neighborhood strategic plan is a constructive alternative to these impractical responses to the issues confronting older urban neighborhoods. The neighborhood plan describes a series of activities to be implemented, a sequence of improvements that, as they are completed, solve a neighborhood problem, provide certain direct benefits to the neighborhood, and, more implicitly, demonstrate capable management of one or more of the transformations described above. A newly constructed block of government-subsidized houses built on a former factory site improves a blighted location and creates new affordable housing. A well-designed block of houses, constructed at lower density, with generous bedroom sizes and amenities such as porches and large side or rear yards, provides the same direct benefits but also produces a residential environment that can compete more effectively with other residential-community options in the metropolitan economy of the twenty-first century.

A good neighborhood plan breaks down a disinvestment-related problem into manageable elements. For example, if the neighborhood is suffering from a proliferation of vacant, abandoned properties, the neighborhood plan can include an index of the addresses of the vacant properties, a classification of the neighborhood's vacant property inventory based on significant characteristics (e.g., structural condition, amount of tax delinquency), a proposed treatment plan for the properties, a description of how the proposed treatment will be supported through available funding programs (e.g., government subsidies, private rehabilitation loans), and—because sufficient funding is not likely to be available to deal with all the vacancy in the neighborhood during the course of a single year—an implementation schedule that establishes an order of priority for the use of these resources over a period of years.

Neighborhood strategic planning does not guarantee quick solutions to long-standing problems, but a good neighborhood strategic plan can show how to organize resources to address these problems rationally and systematically. Resolving the problem of vacant property involves more than just the desire to fix up all the vacant houses in a particular neighborhood. Instead, through the neighborhood plan, different activities, such as those summarized below, can be specified to address current and potential vacancy.

☐ *Prevent* future vacancy by promoting the local real estate market, assisting first-time homebuyers with housing counseling and down payment or settlement grants, to reduce the possibility that houses for sale will remain vacant for extended periods and eventually be abandoned.

☐ *Preserve* existing owner-occupied housing through creating or expanding city-funded repair programs with capability to repair or replace major systems on an "on call," year-round basis.

☐ *Plan* for the neighborhood's future by making strategic decisions about where to demolish and where to rehabilitate vacant housing, how to improve vacant lots, and how to use city and state development funding to address community priorities for vacant-property development.

☐ *Repair* recently vacated houses in reasonably good condition, using rehabilitation loan financing supplemented by modest city subsidies (Philadelphia's moderate-rehabilitation financing program provides a subsidy of up to twenty-five thousand dollars per house).

☐ *Mothball* other vacant houses in good condition through low-cost "encapsulation," to protect these structures against further damage and save them for future rehabilitation.

☐ *Plant* grass and vegetables on vacant lots, with technical assistance provided through the state Department of Agriculture extension service or the local horticultural society.

☐ *Leverage* development financing for affordable rental housing ventures through the federal Low-Income Housing Tax Credit program, which

can provide equity investment to support more than two-thirds of total development cost.

☐ *Collaborate* with city agencies and the local public housing authority
to establish consensus on plans for the improvement or disposition
of publicly owned property in the community.

☐ *Spread out* new housing development, in recognition of the declining
population of older cities, to build houses on larger lots with generous yard space.

☐ *Demolish* vacant houses too expensive to rehabilitate, and plan for
new development on the resulting vacant lots.

Associating these activities with individual vacant properties located
in a strategic plan area can produce a specific, community-supported
treatment for every vacant property in the neighborhood.

In addition to vacant property, there are two other problem
categories that are best addressed through a strategic planning approach: neighborhood commercial corridors and publicly owned
property. Some neighborhoods in reasonably good condition need
to organize strategies for blocks of storefront properties that once,
during the century prior to 1950, attracted many shoppers and generated many jobs for community residents. The larger neighborhood commercial corridors, some located in older "factory town"
districts, others in newer "streetcar suburb" communities, once supported a level of consumer demand, and an associated total retail
square footage, rivaling that of the entire downtown area of a
medium-sized city. However, late twentieth-century population loss
produced a radical, irreplaceable drop in consumer base. The emer-
gence of accessible, attractive retail malls in nearby suburbs (and a
limited number of highway-oriented urban locations) caused a devastating drop in retail market share for commercial corridors in urban neighborhoods. Following decades of decline brought on by
these circumstances, most older neighborhood retail corridors have
to be reorganized as smaller, more concentrated business centers.
The neighborhood plan should show where and how retail consolidation will occur on these corridors and should specify new re-
uses for formerly retail real estate not to be included in the reduced
commercial area.

Neighborhoods that have a publicly or institutionally owned
property or group of properties that are of significant size and are

vacant or deteriorated should consider organizing a neighborhood plan focused on these problem sites. Particular consideration should be given to poorly maintained, deteriorated, and/or vacant parks, playgrounds, public housing sites, hospitals, schools, and former municipal buildings, such as vacant libraries or fire stations.

The literature of planning and the social sciences contains extensive definition and description of tasks associated with plans for neighborhood renewal, including activities such as analyzing demographic data, documenting existing conditions, conducting market demand studies, evaluating alternative policy/program approaches, and illustrating everything with maps, graphs, charts, tables, and sometimes cartoons and posters. All of these activities and their related products can be important elements of a great neighborhood strategic plan, but none of them is indispensable. The authors of the plan need to determine which of these tasks and documentation products are essential to implementation—to a series of completed improvements proposed in the plan—and decide whether and how these essential elements should be incorporated into the plan, in some form that can be copied, circulated, published, and displayed. All these elements should support the defining argument of the strategic plan: that reinvestment activities proposed in the plan address a neighborhood problem in a decisive way.

The scarcity of capital investment resources and the potential for changes in both public policy and in government and private financing programs, as well as in government and community leadership, mean that the neighborhood plan has to be dynamic and adaptable over a period of years. The neighborhood plan document, in whatever form it may be published, is a marketing and presentation tool that, in some respects, will start to become outdated almost from the moment it is published, as uncertainties get resolved during the course of implementation. For example, the number of properties scheduled to be included in the first phase of housing production may have to be reduced because of delays in the public acquisition/disposition process. Negotiations aimed at establishing a joint-venture relationship with a private developer may fail, so that development activities planned for immediate implementation by the joint venture are instead scheduled for implementation by a local community development corporation over a longer period. Unexpected neighborhood opposition to proposed rental development on a particular vacant lot may lead to a rethinking and postponement of development plans. Because changes of this kind are an inevitable part of the implementation of neighborhood reinvestment activities guided by a strategic plan, the plan document itself decreases in importance as implementation proceeds. For neighborhoods in need of reinvestment, the organization and presentation of the plan document is important, but consistency in implementation is critical. Notwithstanding the revisions and adaptations that may have to be made during the years following publication of the plan document, implementation activities must consistently uphold the core goals and priorities set forth in the plan.

Success in implementation is dependent on four factors: community support, developer/producer capacity, funding availability, and overall feasibility. Depending on the neighborhood and the goals being pursued, the relative impact of each of these factors can vary greatly, as is illustrated by the neighborhood strategies undertaken by the three organizations introduced at the beginning of this chapter.

Universal Community Homes' ambition was to develop, or influence the development, of, all vacant property within UCH's target area and, through this activity, to create a mostly residential, mixed-income neighborhood that would regain in the twenty-first century its pre-1950 status as a neighborhood of preference for many citizens. Loss of jobs and population had caused the decline of the neighborhood; implementation of a rational reinvestment plan could regenerate the neighborhood as an attractive residential community within walking distance of the city's business center. Some of the blocks in the improved community would resemble some of the low-rise blocks of the nearby Rittenhouse Square area and would enjoy some of the same locational advantages, but these blocks would contain a much broader income mix and much greater racial diversity than Rittenhouse Square. All UCH sales and rental housing development and other vacant property improvement activities were guided by this overriding goal of redefining UCH's target area as an attractive place to live.

UCH did not experience significant difficulty in securing community support for its strategic plan, in part because the organization's founder, Kenneth Gamble, a lifelong community resident, was well known and respected in the neighborhood target area. Mr. Gamble, a co-founder of Philadelphia International Records (originator of the "Sound of Philadelphia" in 1960s and 1970s popular music) and a developer of small rental properties in the area, provided initial financial support for the new organization and recruited neighborhood residents to serve on UCH's board of directors. Although some friction developed between UCH and South of South Neighborhood Association (SOSNA), an OHCD-funded community organization representing an area that included UCH's target zone, no one disputed the value of developing vacant property in the UCH target area for primarily residential reuse.

As a new organization with no prior development track record, UCH addressed the issue of developer capacity in a systematic way. After the basic legal structure of the organization had been established, two full-time staff were hired. Both individuals recruited for the staff positions had strong experience and qualifications in business administration, rather than the community planning or neighborhood organizing backgrounds more typically associated with community organization work. Since community support for the strategic plan was already in place, community planning/organizing qualifications did not have as much value to UCH as the business management skills needed to operate a successful development organization.

UCH staff made a priority of organizing an initial development project through a joint venture with an experienced private developer, Pennrose Properties. This first development project, Universal Court, involved new construction and rehabilitation of forty units of rental housing at a strategically important neighborhood intersection then occupied by a combination of vacant row buildings and vacant land. The relatively small scale of Universal Court and Pennrose's strong housing development track record and excellent access to investment capital made it relatively easy for the joint venture partnership to demonstrate the overall feasibility of the project and to compete successfully for OHCD funding.

Participation in the Universal Court venture provided UCH

Universal Court, street frontage

with enough knowledge and experience to develop subsequent housing ventures on its own, without a private-sector partner. This knowledge and experience, supplemented with some guidance from consultants, helped UCH address the key issues associated with the organization's next venture: securing funding and determining overall feasibility. UCH's experience also laid the foundation for ownership of a key neighborhood asset, the inventory of rental property to be developed and maintained by UCH during successive years of strategic plan implementation, by this minority-governed organization.

A very different strategic planning perspective influenced New Kensington Community Development Corporation (NKCDC), an established community development group representing a mostly white working-class neighborhood located a few miles northeast of the city's downtown, to invite Greensgrow Farms to locate its hydroponic lettuce farm on a vacant factory site within NKCDC's neighborhood service area. The leadership of NKCDC, an organization with nearly a decade's experience in organizing and planning

Universal Court, interior courtyard, prior to start of grand opening
ceremony

for development, providing housing counseling services, and rehabilitating vacant houses, decided to organize a grass-roots planning
project called "New Kensington 2000." The project included a series of community meetings to discuss neighborhood needs, followed by the creation of a plan for addressing these needs during
subsequent years. NKCDC's neighborhood planning approach, in
contrast to UCH's, involved inviting a great many people to consider a broad range of neighborhood improvement options for a
very large target area. Community meetings held over a period of
months to discuss neighborhood problems attracted hundreds of
residents interested in expressing their views and anxious to see
positive change in the community. These big discussions produced
some surprises, one of them particularly noteworthy: many residents ranked housing rehabilitation—a primary focus for NKCDC
in recent years—as lower in priority than the improvement of un-
sightly vacant lots scattered throughout the community, the result
of three decades' worth of demolition of deteriorated rowhouses

and obsolete factory buildings. For NKCDC, the process of securing community support for its strategy produced a new assignment
and a change of direction.

Following the publication of its strategic plan document, *New
Kensington 2000*, NKCDC began strengthening its relationship with
Philadelphia Green, a nonprofit program of the Pennsylvania Horticultural Society which helps community groups organize neighborhood beautification projects and open-space improvements,
such as the creation of vegetable gardens and small parks or play
areas on vacant or underused land. Following completion of a survey to identify all vacant land in the neighborhood, NKCDC com-
piled a list of dozens of small vacant lots (the sites of demolished
rowhouses with twelve- to twenty-foot-wide street frontages) that
adjacent property owners wanted to acquire and develop as side
yards or parking spaces. Larger vacant lots that had been designated
for future housing development were scheduled for landscaping to
improve their appearance over the short term. In light of NKCDC's
previous community development experience and planning/orga-
nizing capability, the organization could take on its new role of
vacant land planner and manager without specialized training, the
hiring of new staff, or a capacity-building experience comparable
to the joint venture UCH needed as a stepping-stone in order to
increase its housing production capability.

As with UCH's experience in housing development, funding
and feasibility issues related to NKCDC's open-space approach were
addressed simultaneously. OHCD and the Philadelphia-based William Penn Foundation awarded funding to support NKCDC and
Philadelphia Green work on New Kensington open space issues over
a two-year period. Additional OHCD funding was committed for
eminent-domain acquisition of eighty vacant lots, to support a test
of the feasibility of transferring lots to some of the adjacent owners who had expressed interest in developing side yards or parking
areas. A portion of the foundation grant paid for a tractor, used by
NKCDC to grade and clean up more than three hundred parcels of
vacant land in locations around the community. Because NKCDC's
approach was an initiative without precedent, there were no standards for assessing overall feasibility. Did it really make sense for
NKCDC to buy a tractor? Would the cleaned-up parcels stay clean,

or would they again fill up with weeds and litter? Could the garden center that NKCDC developed on a corner lot with the help of workers from the federal AmeriCorps program generate enough income from plant and garden-supply sales to sustain itself as a small-business venture? Because OHCD and the foundation viewed the NKCDC open-space initiative as a creative new approach to addressing the vacant property problem in Philadelphia, the two funders were willing to support most of the initial costs of this initiative without confirmation of its feasibility and to bear most of the associated risk of failure. For OHCD, the greatest risk was that, following completion of the eminent-domain acquisition of the eighty small lots (at a cost to the city of about five thousand dollars each), adjacent property owners would not follow through on their expressed interest in taking over and improving the lots. As it turned out, the opposite problem was encountered: some of the adjacent property owners were so eager to move ahead with improving the vacant lots they were scheduled to receive that grass planting and driveway paving began before the acquisition process had been completed and legal title transferred.

In light of the elevation of vacant land as a neighborhood strategic plan priority, NKCDC was immediately receptive to Greensgrow's expression of interest in operating a lettuce farm on a vacant lot in the community. Greensgrow had initially been considering a location in another neighborhood, but an unfriendly response from a local community organization influenced the partnership to look elsewhere. OHCD paid for acquisition of the land, and Greensgrow financed the installation of the hydroponic system. Greensgrow hired a neighborhood kid to help with the harvest, and residents of the houses surrounding the little farm were pleased with the improvement of the long-vacant site. In the event that Greensgrow's venture proved unprofitable or relocated to another site, NKCDC could program the land for some other open-space use or for housing, the use originally planned for this property.

In undertaking its neighborhood strategy, the Asociacion de Puertorriqueños en Marcha (Association of Puerto Ricans on the March) had two advantages that neither UCH nor NKCDC possessed: a long organizational history as a community-based human services provider and a neighborhood environment with enough concentrations of abandoned property to make possible the assemblage of medium- and large-sized sites for new construction. Over a period of years beginning in the 1970s, APM had opened three mental health clinics, three "community living arrangement" residences for mentally ill people, and a shelter for children. APM had also administered a drug and alcohol abuse prevention program, an AIDS awareness and education program, and a children and family services program. The organization had experience in managing and delivering an array of human services, and most people in the neighborhood regarded APM as a responsible and reliable member of the community. APM's service area, twelve square blocks of Eastern North Philadelphia located north and east of Temple University, was a community in need of wholesale redefinition. The remnants of the old neighborhood economy—the ruined factories, the deserted rowhouses, the empty storefronts—were falling to pieces. Nearly every block had vacant lots and vacant houses. On more than a few blocks, the vacant buildings outnumbered the remaining occupied houses. None of the factory buildings was suitable for development and reuse; all of them had to be demolished, one by one. Germantown Avenue, a major thoroughfare which bisected the neighborhood diagonally on its way from the downtown area to Northwest Philadelphia and the suburbs, had lost its vitality decades ago. Most of the remaining retail and industrial activity on the avenue, formerly crowded with busy stores and working factories, was limited to a single block extending north from Diamond Street.

In 1989, APM created a housing development affiliate; a few years later, the organization hired Rose Gray as development director. Gray had grown up in the mostly white, middle-class Oxford Circle area and had no past ties to the community, but she knew all about real estate development. Gray had spent a career in the construction business but had become increasingly bored with private-sector work. The prospect of managing a production-oriented strategic plan for APM excited her. Because of the level of confidence that APM had built up through years of community service, it was not hard to organize a community dialogue to discuss neighborhood improvement activities. After a year of meetings and planning, APM decided to focus on developing property in the

Germantown Avenue corridor as a top priority. APM's board spent a day in Ocean City going over the final version of a ten-year reinvestment strategy. Gray decided to make a commitment to spend the next decade implementing the strategy. Through the planning process and the hiring of Gray, APM had addressed from the outset the issues of community support and developer capacity.

APM's plan document was only 37 pages long, as compared to the 356–page *New Kensington 2000*. The whole intent and projected results of the APM approach were effectively captured on a single page: a color-photocopied map defining a series of Germantown Avenue development sites.

APM subsequently entered into a highly productive period of development activity, during which the organization completed one real estate venture every nine to twelve months: the creation, through new construction and the rehabilitation of vacant buildings, of sales and rental housing, including housing for mentally ill people or people with AIDS—the kind of housing that most community development corporations were afraid to handle. After the completion of more than 150 units of new housing, enough new buying power had been created (in a neighborhood that had experienced population loss and declining median income for decades) to justify the development of new retail services. With local-government support, APM permanently closed a block-long stretch of Germantown Avenue to assemble a site for the Borinquen Plaza shopping center.

Funding and feasibility issues were much more difficult for APM to address than for UCH and NKCDC. APM's ambitious development schedule required the organization to compete more frequently for large city subsidies that had to be combined with Low Income Housing Tax Credit investment equity and "soft" second mortgage financing from the Pennsylvania Housing Finance Agency. APM-sponsored special-needs ventures necessitated extensive planning for service delivery and case management and the securing of separate funding awards and service contracts for these activities. None of the APM development ventures could have been implemented without both the multilayered development financing and the fully funded service package.

For each of the three organizations, the strategic plan, designed

Jardines de Borinquen, an APM rental venture

to address the problem of vacancy through a distinctive approach based on available resources, guided subsequent implementation activities. Choices made during the course of strategic planning led to a sequencing of improvement activities and a designation of priorities that excluded other alternatives. UCH's decision to focus on the build-out of its designated target area meant that all development funding available to UCH would be directed to this area; housing production activities in nearby areas would have to be implemented by someone else or not implemented at all, at least not in the short term. NKCDC's expanded focus on vacant lots meant that less staff time would be devoted to housing rehabilitation and that fewer houses would be produced by the organization. APM's focus on the Germantown Avenue corridor as a development zone had the effect of drawing resources away from already occupied residential blocks that could have used APM's help in addressing serious problems of vacancy and deterioration.

As these examples illustrate, the creators and implementers of neighborhood strategic plans have to be consistent but flexible,

ambitious in striving for big results but conservative in assessing
the availability of financing resources. Neighborhood strategies
must be incremental, multiyear, adaptable. A strong presentation
of published words, numbers, and graphics in the plan document
is needed to guide supporters of the plan to success in implementation; but success in implementation is also strongly influenced
by the ability of plan supporters to recognize and act on the need
for adaptation and midcourse changes, some of which may vary
significantly from the published plan document.

This dynamic is what makes neighborhood strategic plans so
uniquely suitable as guides to reinvestment in older urban neighborhoods. The redevelopment plans that governed development
activity in old urban renewal areas, such as Society Hill and Yorktown, aren't workable in most urban neighborhoods today, because
of the absence of government funding for large-scale acquisition
and construction projects involving the development or improvement of hundreds of dwelling units. Even a limited redevelopment-
plan approach, in which all the vacant and deteriorated properties
in a targeted area are publicly acquired, then conveyed, when the
opportunity arises, to well-financed private developers (as happened
in Washington Square West, Society Hill's less fortunate neighbor)
is not workable in most neighborhoods. City governments are unlikely to be willing to commit much funding to a long-term "land-
banking" approach, in which local government must take
responsibility for maintaining a vacant property inventory while
waiting for interested and qualified developers to appear.

Although community participation leading to the creation of
a neighborhood strategic plan can resemble a "charette" (in architecture, an extended brainstorming session, in which students work
out the solution to a planning or design challenge under pressure
of a deadline), the success of a neighborhood strategic plan depends
not only on a commitment to support the agreed-upon solution
but also on a willingness to make significant changes in the implementation process, without reconvening the charette participants,
when such changes are needed to achieve the desired results.

The distinctive characteristics of the neighborhood strategies
described in the preceding paragraphs provide part of the explanation for why relatively few examples of the "new urbanism" ap-

proach to planning and design have been undertaken in older urban neighborhoods. The new urbanism is a blend of three elements: a critique of the car-dependent, low-density, overbuilt metropolitan and highway-corridor regions that grew up fast during the past three decades; a set of principles for reengineering existing suburbs and creating more livable new communities; and a marketing strategy for private developers mindful of the need to create residential environments that are superior to the isolated, boring products typical of late-twentieth-century construction. In the words of one of its supporters, the new urbanism "represents a rediscovery of planning and architectural traditions. . . . [New urbanist] approaches . . . revive principles about building communities that have been virtually ignored for half a century. Public spaces like streets, squares and parks should be a setting for the conduct of daily life; a neighborhood should accommodate diverse types of people and activities; it should be possible to get to work, accomplish everyday tasks (like buying fresh food or taking a child to day care) and travel to surrounding communities without using a car."[4] To date, the new urbanism has demonstrated its best results in environments where a "clean slate" is available for development— a cleared expanse of many acres ready for new construction—and in real estate markets where middle- and upper-income buyers predominate. Older urban neighborhoods offer a strikingly different landscape. Instead of a clean slate, these neighborhoods offer a hodgepodge of vacant houses and lots, obsolete industrial structures, and other nonresidential uses, such as commercial garages and warehouses.

But the most important underlying issue separating the new urbanism from strategic planning and associated implementation activities in older urban neighborhoods is the issue of control. In suburban and new-town development ventures, the key participant is the developer, who controls the resources needed to implement a scheme, subject to resolution of regulatory issues with local authorities. Even the two U.S. Department of Housing and Urban Development (HUD) funding programs strongly influenced by the Congress for the New Urbanism (CNU), HOPE VI (for transforming obsolete public housing projects into attractive mixed-income communities) and the Homeownership Zone program (for developing large-scale sales housing ventures linked to neighborhood retail, service, and public transit resources) involve a relatively high degree of control by the developer and local authorities. In these HUD programs, all development funding and most of the local approvals needed in order to implement the total plan are in place prior to construction start. In contrast, the reinvestment activity taking place in most older urban neighborhoods involves multiple key participants—developers, community organizations, government agencies, professional services providers, and funding sources—all with limited control over the neighborhood strategy and the resources needed to implement it. Older urban neighborhoods are a changing economic and political landscape. During implementation of a multiyear reinvestment strategy, community priorities may shift, political administrations may change, and public funding resources may be denied, cut, or delayed, fundamentally altering the timing and results of the strategy. This limitation on control presents a real challenge for people interested in bringing about positive change in older urban communities.

Although the new urbanism does not offer a strategic approach that works as well for older urban neighborhoods as it does for suburban "new towns," the founders of the Congress for the New Urbanism never claimed that the principles for which they advocated were a cure-all for the combination of problems confronting urban neighborhoods. CNU leaders have emphasized the linkage between policy, design, and management issues and have made it clear that good design, the focus of the new urbanism, cannot solve social problems or resolve policy and management issues.[5] These distinctions help explain why the new urbanism has not been useful to many older urban neighborhoods from a strategic point of view. In suburban and exurban areas, the design of a three-hundred-acre tract controlled by a single developer with access to financing can decisively influence the nature and results of development. In older urban neighborhoods, while design is still critically important, policy and management issues, the core of neighborhood strategic planning, predominate.

Under some circumstances, a neighborhood may not be ready to launch an ambitious strategic planning initiative leading to publication of a neighborhood plan, despite the best efforts of neighborhood activists to move the community in that direction. In neighborhoods where supporters of reinvestment are ambitious and focused, the absence of a completed neighborhood plan does not necessarily mean that no worthwhile reinvestment activity can take place. Mount Airy Village Development Corporation (MAVDC), a relatively young organization with no past experience in completing publicly funded development ventures, obtained an OHCD grant to organize a plan for the twenty-block segment of Germantown Avenue that extended through the Mount Airy neighborhood in Northwest Philadelphia. A highly regarded retail consultant, E. L. Crow, was engaged by MAVDC and, following series of meetings to bring the consultant together with representatives of MAVDC and other community interests, Crow produced a report outlining a recommended reinvestment approach. Rather than laying the foundation for a strong neighborhood plan, the consultant's report and the process leading to its completion generated a protracted controversy in the neighborhood. The issues of contention, some well founded, others alleged but not proven, were many: that the consultant's assessment of the target area was seriously flawed; that the consultant's recommendations were wrong; that the general community had never been sufficiently informed about or involved in the planning process; that the recommended approach unfairly proposed more favorable treatment for selected blocks in one portion of the corridor (where businesses owned by several MAVDC representatives happened to be located). Regardless of the extent to which the criticisms of MAVDC, the consultant, or the process were justified or not, one thing was certain: the neighborhood plan was not going to be completed in the near future.

Despite these setbacks, Mount Airy leaders interested in advancing Germantown Avenue reinvestment accomplished a lot in the months following the breakdown of the neighborhood planning process. MAVDC competed successfully for an OHCD contract to provide housing counseling services for first-time homebuyers; with funding support provided through the contract, an office was opened on the avenue, and MAVDC quickly established a reputation as one of the most capable of the city's neighborhood-based counseling providers. The owners of the Sedgwick Theater, a big, vacant, old-fashioned movie house, obtained a small prede-velopment grant from OHCD and the Local Initiatives Support Corporation (LISC) to explore the feasibility of developing the front-lobby portion of the building as a cultural center, with an art gallery, a performance space, and a reception/dining area for catered events. The study was completed and the plan put into effect, and this new use of the lobby turned a profit in its first year of operation. A coalition of local groups expanded an annual arts festival held each spring and attracted thousands of residents and visitors to the avenue for the multi-day event. Despite the lack of a unified plan for Germantown Avenue, community initiative was producing important results.

A well-organized plan that is reflective of community interests and sentiments can have a powerful influence in shaping perceptions of the community both within and outside the neighborhood. A coalition of six Latino groups known as Ceiba (the name of a Central American rain forest tree noteworthy for its long, outwardly radiating branches) mobilized organizational resources to complete a big, well-documented plan that included mapping, evaluating, and specifying reinvestment goals and reinvestment activities for an enormous area where the core of the city's Latino population lived and worked. To walk through all the neighborhoods included in the plan, you would need to organize a day-long hike. The completed Ceiba neighborhood strategy delivered a strong message to the community and the world at large: we are organized, working together, committed to the improvement of our neighborhoods, and we are here to stay. Although some of the Ceiba member organizations proved better able to implement than others (with the least capable groups unable to move to a reliable implementation schedule), a substantial amount of improvement activity that occurred during the remainder of the decade was linked to the neighborhood plan and could be understood in terms of the plan. Just as important, the spirit of the plan, the message of unified, determined endeavor, had been successfully articulated and absorbed in the neighborhood and downtown.

The Frankford Plan provides another good example of how a neighborhood strategic plan can be an effective vehicle for presenting a theme of positive change and unified effort to an audience within and outside the community. Frankford, located in lower northeast Philadelphia a dozen blocks above New Kensington, is a mix of houses and factories; whites and people of color; community development corporations and human services agencies; intact, densely settled rowhouses and big Victorian twins on large lots. In 1991, a coalition of religious congregations known as Frankford Group Ministries launched a broad, multifaceted neighborhood planning initiative that ultimately brought together sixty-six co-sponsoring organizations, from the Frankford Lions Club to Mater Dolorosa School. The product of this planning initiative, the 234–page Frankford Plan document, covered a variety of issues, from transportation and parking to safety and clean streets. The completion of the planning process and the publication of the plan in 1993 was widely publicized and gained recognition as a big event in the history of the community. In the years after publication, many activities, from housing development ventures to holiday parades, were organized and promoted as elements of the Frankford Plan. The Frankford Plan was repeatedly cited by community representatives as supporting documentation in presentations to the mayor, City Council, the Zoning Board, the City Planning Commission, foundations, corporations, banks, and other prospective supporters of community goals. Within the Frankford community, as everywhere else on earth, there existed serious animosities and rivalries among individuals and groups; some were so long-standing that they might never be resolved. But these problems never came up when the Frankford Plan was mentioned. Everyone respected and supported the Frankford Plan. It was one big, positive expression of neighborhood commonality and unity.

A Frankford Plan banquet was held in the spring of every year, and the event filled up Romano's Caterers at Adams Avenue and Wingohocking Street. At the banquet you would hear the accomplishments of the past year celebrated, and plans for the coming months announced. You would see elected officials shake hands and make speeches, and you would applaud as awards were presented. Despite the formality of the setting, the cloth napkins, the suits and ties, the atmosphere was relaxed and congenial. When the speeches ended, waves of conversation, music, and laughter engulfed the hall. Everyone was aware that much improvement was still going to be needed in Frankford during the coming year and the years that followed. But the event confirmed what everyone already knew: the plan was working. The room glowed with excited anticipation of future opportunity and success.

3

TROPHIES AND
LANDMARKS

Noel Eisenstat, the RDA's executive director, was an obsessed over-achiever who was as effectively wired, plugged-in, and networked as a medium-sized telephone company. His capacity to retain and inter-relate personal, programmatic, and political data was extraordinary. Mention the name of a person you'd met recently on an out-of-town trip—an associate professor at the University of Chicago, for example—and Noel would matter-of-factly say something like, "Oh, yeah, she went to graduate school with my wife's cousin's husband." Noel's internal data reserves were complemented by a remarkable depth of knowl-edge and analytical skill. At a moment's notice, he could deliver an off-the-cuff history of, say, the complicated Southwark Plaza public hous-ing development plan, in a narrative and expository style as captivat-ing as one of Bobby McFerrin's masterful a capella performances.

Noel's appearance—overweight, near-sighted, and balding—belied an agility, speed, and toughness that took his adversaries by surprise. He enjoyed and excelled at high-risk debate tactics. In a heated dis-cussion with a roomful of people, he could switch his role in the dia-logue as quickly and effortlessly as a channel-surfing TV viewer pressing buttons on a remote—from bully to mediator to advocate to educa-tor, and back again. He would barge into a tepid conference-room presentation—"That's bullshit! That's utter bullshit!"—effectively disrupting the meeting and generating a wave of annoyance and hostility. Moments later, he would interject new information or a unique perspective on the issue under discussion so persuasively that the anger dissipated and the room was drawn to his point of view.

The Redevelopment Authority was supposed to serve as the city's housing finance agency and vacant-property broker, responsible for managing the key neighborhood-reinvestment commodities of money and land. Most people rated the agency as below-average to poor before Noel took over. Noel was out to change the Authority's decades-long history of weakness and inadequacy. He scrutinized, laid his hands on, and worked over every one of the two dozen individual steps in the eminent domain process for acquiring blighted property, a process that hadn't functioned effectively since the 1960s. He reassigned or got rid of incompetent public agency staff when he could, and worked around those he couldn't move or dismiss. He changed work rules and infuriated the municipal employees' union; labor grievances sprouted and blossomed like early-spring tulips on JFK Plaza. Returning from vacation with an incipient beard, Noel told Mayor Rendell's chief of staff that he wouldn't shave until a recalcitrant commissioner returned his phone calls; phone communication resumed soon afterwards, and the beard disappeared. By the time Noel was done, the eminent domain process was delivering more than a thousand blighted properties a year to Philadelphia's reinvestment program.

Managing money for development financing was even more difficult than managing real estate transactions, because the prospect of access to lots of public dollars served as high-octane fuel for the ambition, competitive energy, and greed of developers and would-be developers around the city. Noel and I agreed on an approach that worked for both of us: OHCD, as the policymaking agency, would establish overall goals and priorities and publish development proposal underwriting criteria; the RDA, as the financing agency, would evaluate development proposals, negotiate with developers, and award public money based on the OHCD policy and criteria. Our staffs respected this division of responsibility and stayed out of each other's way. We taught developers and city officials to respect this approach too. When a councilperson convened a meeting at City Hall with a neighborhood group and a private developer to promote a multimillion dollar development venture, I would say, "The idea looks great, but you'll have to get a proposal past Noel." In the midst of a heated discussion set off by a developer's anger at project financing modifications required by RDA staff before his proposal could be considered for city subsidy, Noel would execute an exaggerated shrug and say, "I'm just a functionary; we're just here to implement OHCD's policy." On the few occasions when the discussion turned ugly, Noel would stand up, declare, "We're not getting anywhere; this meeting is over," and walk out.

Our approach wasn't buck passing, and it was different from a good-cop/bad-cop routine. My outward demeanor was friendly and conciliatory, but people found Noel easier to engage in substantive discussion of project-implementation issues. Noel could be argumentative and overly critical, but he was also a consistent, reliable, accessible source of information and good advice for anyone willing to pay attention. When all was said and done, Noel was delivering land and money in much larger quantities than ever before to development ventures that addressed city priorities and standards and that made sense.

Rental housing was a special challenge, because rental housing development ventures needed to obtain both city and state financing, the latter in the form of Low Income Housing Tax Credit investment equity, awarded in competitive funding rounds managed by the Harrisburg-based Pennsylvania Housing Finance Agency (PHFA). To leverage as much tax credit financing for Philadelphia as possible, Noel engaged in a gentle but persistent courtship of PHFA. Noel's staff mastered PHFA underwriting standards and applied them consistently to proposals they were scrutinizing. Noel loaded up a van with his senior managers and drove them to Harrisburg to spend a full day talking over Philadelphia financing proposals with their PHFA counterparts. Philadelphia-Harrisburg communications opened up; RDA and PHFA staff compared their perspectives on pending Philadelphia development financing decisions via phone, fax, e-mail and lots of face-to-face consultations. One time, to close out the review and coordination of financing approvals for a series of high-stakes development ventures, Noel and an RDA deputy director drove to meet PHFA officials at a rendezvous midway between Philadelphia and Harrisburg, a roadside restaurant called—this is true—"Mom's." Outstanding issues were resolved over a high-fat, high-starch luncheon, and Philadelphia got the PHFA financing we all wanted.

Noel booked the mayor's box at Veterans Stadium for an evening and invited PHFA officers and managers to a Phillies game. The event was a big success. RDA and PHFA staff ate cheesesteaks, drank beer from oversized plastic cups, talked over pending financing decisions, and kept an eye on the baseball game. Mayor Rendell walked in during the fourth inning and worked his way through the upbeat crowd of PHFA and RDA celebrants. The handshakes, backslapping, and laughter conveyed a heartfelt message: you guys are really important to us, and we appreciate your help. The Philly Phanatic barged in and exchanged high-fives with senior PHFA staff. Something extraordinary was happening: city and state government agencies, traditionally out of touch or at odds with each other, were celebrating a Philadelphia victory—the RDA's success in securing tax credit financing for worthwhile Philadelphia development ventures. In that year Noel and his staff had won more than half of Pennsylvania's entire tax credit allocation: $8.9 million, out of $17.7 million available statewide. Some people in Pittsburgh and upstate Pennsylvania cities were furious about our domination of the tax credit financing competitions, but they had only themselves to blame. Noel had mastered the system.

Since the cost of implementing great neighborhood reinvestment strategies is much higher than the level of funding that can be obtained from local, state, and federal sources, city governments need to craft and enforce sensible policies for allocating the limited funds available. Scarcity of resources is a critical issue affecting the reinvestment ambitions of neighborhoods and city governments, but the need for rational, consistent policy to guide the use of these resources is even more critical. Establishing and implementing a resource-allocation policy is as fundamentally important for local government as establishing and implementing a neighborhood strategic plan is for a local community. And the difficult task of defending this policy and responding to demands for funding has to be entrusted to fearless, capable people whose judgments are supported consistently by the city's political leadership.

City governments have a well-earned reputation for mismanaging public funds. During much of the first half of the twentieth century, big-city governments such as Philadelphia's existed primarily to service powerful political organizations and business interests. A late-1940s investigation of municipal corruption "revealed a huge catalog of scandalously haphazard and crooked city practices. . . . $40 million in city spending was found to be unaccounted for."[1] The misspending of funds awarded to cities under the Model Cities program of the Great Society era is well documented, as is the costly failure of the public housing system in many big cities during the final decades of the twentieth century.[2]

Although many of the progressive city administrations brought to office in the 1980s and 1990s achieved major improvements in overall fiscal management, municipal finance reforms have not always extended into the domain of neighborhood reinvestment policy. For several reasons, mayors and city budget directors tend to regard neighborhood reinvestment as secondary in importance to mainstream fiscal issues such as local tax policy and the cost of city-employee benefit packages. Because most money available for neighborhood reinvestment originates from sources other than the local tax base, neighborhood reinvestment doesn't have any direct relationship to hot-button political issues such as tax hikes or tax cuts. Little or none of the neighborhood reinvestment funding available to cities can be used to pay for local-government services such as trash collection or law enforcement, due to federal regulations prohibiting the use of HUD funds to support ongoing city-service responsibilities. And most mayors and fiscal managers don't have the time, desire, or ability to assess the potential costs and benefits of changing current policy. Because of these important differences between neighborhood reinvestment funding and other elements of the typical city budget, the leaders of the city's neighborhood reinvestment program have to commit themselves to make the best use of the limited dollars available, based on a sensible policy that is widely understood and accepted.

For more than a quarter-century, HUD funding programs have been the primary source of neighborhood reinvestment funding for most cities. The HUD-administered Community Development Block Grant (CDBG) program, which began in 1974 and has enjoyed a relatively high level of bipartisan support in Congress since that time, gives cities substantial funding for neighborhood reinvestment through an annual award, the amount of which is based on factors such as population, poverty, and age of housing. In

Philadelphia, a city with a 1990 population of 1.585 million, 20.3 percent of which lives in poverty, the Fiscal 1999 CDBG award was $68.3 million.

HUD funding through CDBG and the similar federal HOME program (authorized by Congress in 1992) brings potentially great benefits and potentially high risks. Both the benefits and the risks are related to two important characteristics of this funding: flexibility and local discretion. CDBG and HOME provide excellent illustrations of the value of replacing highly regulated federal "categorical" programs with annual lump-sum block grants of federal funding that can be used at the discretion of local government. (The fact that political advocacy for consolidating and block-granting federal programs often serves as a smokescreen for a policy of reducing net funding to cities has obscured this value.) With CDBG and HOME funding authorizations, a city government can set its own priorities and decide how to use available funding to address them. In any given program year, for example, a mayor and city council can decide to use the CDBG/HOME funding resource to:

☐ acquire a block of real estate for new-construction housing development;

☐ launch a neighborhood conservation program offering loans and grants for repairs, to help current residents maintain the homes where they are living now;

☐ replicate a nationally known job-training program that has succeeded in another city but has no local equivalent;

☐ support a housing-counseling program to help first-time homebuyers obtain mortgage financing for houses available in the private real estate market; or

☐ increase funding for a program that has exceeded performance goals, by taking funding from a program that has not delivered expected results.

CDBG and HOME dollars cannot be pledged in advance to support multiyear funding commitments (except through the Section 108 loan program, described below), because federal appropriations are made on a year-to-year basis. However, since HUD programs have received relatively consistent support from Congress, local governments can have some assurance that an activity which cannot be completed within a single year (such as a multiphase housing construction venture) will continue to be sustained by federal funding in subsequent years. However, the year-to-year nature of HUD funding makes it all the more important that local policy guiding the use of this funding be consistent and credible over the long term.

Some cities also receive state or local-government funding to support neighborhood reinvestment activities. Although some of this funding (such as the second-mortgage financing provided by some state governments for affordable housing development ventures) may be more restrictive than CDBG and HOME, local-government officials usually have significant, if not decisive, influence in directing the allocation of these funds to address city priorities.

The big risk associated with HUD money and the other relatively flexible and discretionary funding available for neighborhood reinvestment is that it will be misused—not spent illegally, but misspent, carved up into piecemeal awards that don't provide the greatest possible benefit to neighborhoods and the city as a whole. If city policy is not well led, organized, and managed, funding for neighborhood reinvestment becomes a "Christmas tree," a system for dispensing money to political insiders and "squeaky wheels," without real consideration for the general good.

The neighborhood reinvestment activity that consumes the most funding is housing production, the use of public money by developers to build new houses or rehabilitate vacant structures for residential occupancy. Although most of the following discussion focuses on resource-allocation policy for housing-production activities, many of the basic principles described below can also be made part of an approach for funding other development and service activities—from home weatherization grants to commercial development to employment/training programs—that involve commitments of public funds to nongovernment entities responsible for implementation.

The availability of public money in large quantities with relatively few restrictions can affect human behavior in unpredictable ways. Even the most honest and well-intentioned real estate developers, whether, private, nonprofit, or institutional entities, have a tendency to become blinded by the attraction of readily accessible public funds. A private developer with a long-standing reputation as a responsible businessperson will think nothing of encouraging a group of elected officials to gang up on housing agency staff in order to try to force the award of an excessive city subsidy for an overly costly development venture. A nonprofit group will publicly advocate for more rational, less fragmented neighborhood reinvestment policy; then, when the same organization's latest development proposal fails to meet financial underwriting standards (established, in part, as the basis for a more rational policy), the group will accuse the city of being insensitive to neighborhood needs and priorities.

Every constituency can produce an excellent rationale to explain why a development venture it favors should be given priority for city funding or granted waivers of project-underwriting requirements. Private developers (some of whom contribute to the campaigns of the mayor and other elected officials) insist that the policy waivers they are seeking will improve the city's business environment and enable the private sector to do its job without government interference—passing over the fact that the job they want to do is slated to be assisted with lots of government money. Private, nonprofit, and CDC developers that received city funding in the preceding program year maintain that continued funding of their proposals in current and future program years is necessary in order for the city to "move to scale" and establish an efficient "housing production system." Development organizations that have never received funding in past years complain that they have been forgotten, overlooked, or discriminated against and demand funding as compensation for this injustice—even though these organizations may never have previously submitted a financing proposal and may not be able to demonstrate capability to implement the development ventures they propose. Representatives of neighborhoods with significant low-income population feel that the development ventures they support should have priority because local government isn't doing enough for the city's neediest people. Representatives of neighborhoods with significant moderate- and middle-income population feel that the development ventures they support should have priority because the city isn't doing enough for working-class taxpayers, more of whom will move out to the suburbs if they feel left out of the city's funding program.

City governments have a responsibility to establish and enforce a good resource-allocation policy as a framework for mediating competing claims and demands for public money. Government leaders who abdicate this responsibility will start making haphazard commitments in reaction to external pressures and won't be able to stop. When this happens, people who really care about neighborhoods get dissatisfied and discouraged, and the city's program begins to lose credibility and value.

The two big responsibilities of the leaders of a city's neighborhood reinvestment program—getting the most value out of the limited funding available and allocating these resources effectively—can be met through a series of strategies, several of which address both of these responsibilities simultaneously.

Divest the city of its charitable-contributions program. Some city governments use HUD funding and other money available for neighborhood reinvestment to award grants to neighborhood-based service facilities and community centers, often to provide operating support for settlement houses, nonprofit health and human services providers, and civic groups not engaged in reinvestment-related activity. A policy of awarding funding to such organizations helps bolster a city's nonprofit service sector and can generate a lot of political good will for city officials, but this policy reduces the already limited neighborhood reinvestment budget. Nonprofit service organizations should be funded through a combination of contributions and memberships, charitable grants from foundations and corporations, and service fees, not from the city's reinvestment budget. To change this practice and expand the neighborhood reinvestment resource base, city governments have to manage a two-part transition from current policy: first, announce that the city will not fund any additional nonprofit service organizations; then phase out reinvestment funding currently being awarded to service organizations, preferably over a two- or three-year period. Lots of people will be unhappy with these changes; but if the city government really wants to make a serious commitment to neighborhood reinvestment, this draining of limited resources has to end.

Maximize borrowing capability. Through the HUD Section 108 program, a city government may borrow up to five times the amount of its annual CDBG award to support any CDBG-eligible activities, from housing development subsidies to construction financing for downtown hotels. This borrowing capability provides a major opportunity to expand the neighborhood reinvestment resource base. Based on its Fiscal 1999 CDBG funding level of $68.3 million, for example, Philadelphia's Section 108 borrowing capacity in that year was $341.5 million.

To support unsubsidized, market-rate ventures, such as the development of office buildings, hotels, and luxury housing, Section 108 financing can be used to provide developers with low-interest construction-period financing, made available in exchange for developer commitments to hire, subcontract with, and purchase from local and minority residents and businesses. As the development venture is built, the construction loan is paid back to the city from the developer's permanent financing, and the city, in turn, repays HUD. The city government gets substantial value at no cost, other than the relatively low expense associated with applying for and administering the Section 108 financing. Most, if not all, of the physical development occurs outside neighborhoods, but major economic benefits can be reaped for neighborhood residents and businesses through well-organized employment and procurement plans associated with these ventures (these plans are discussed further in chapter 7). Section 108 borrowing can also be used to finance the construction of subsidized housing for buyers and renters who can't afford market rents and sales prices. Drawing down Section 108 funds can give a city a big infusion of capital to support large-scale affordable-housing development in a targeted area or to expand a citywide housing production "pipeline" (the succession of city-supported ventures progressing toward financial settlement and construction start) and generate more housing development in a shorter time. For example, OHCD borrowed $18 million from HUD in order to support the development of 296 houses in the Cecil B. Moore area of North Philadelphia and fundamentally change the character of this very deteriorated neighborhood. In this use of Section 108 financing for affordable-housing development, the city is the sole borrower. The Section 108 debt-repayment obligation is not passed on to a developer with permanent financing, because city subsidy is the primary source of permanent financing in the deal. In ventures such as the Cecil B. Moore housing development, the market is so depressed and buyer incomes are so low that the sales price that can be charged for completed homes is much lower than development cost, and a substantial city subsidy is needed. In these situations, the city returns Section 108 principal and interest through commitments of funding from future CDBG budgets, payable in subsequent years of the program.

Although the annual loan repayments reduce the amount of CDBG funding that can be made available for other neighborhood reinvestment activities in future years, this disadvantage is often outweighed by the benefit of being able to mobilize high-priority, larger-scale housing development activities. For example the Cecil B. Moore housing venture would have taken more than a decade to develop, rather than five years, if Section 108 financing had not been available to Philadelphia. One special advantage of the Section 108 program is that the amount borrowed, once approved by HUD, doesn't need to be drawn down by the city until the money is actually needed for implementation activities. The city doesn't incur debt-repayment obligations until the Section 108 financing is actually being put to work.

Create underwriting standards. To direct and control the allocation of reinvestment funds, the city has to publish development-project underwriting standards and consistently enforce these standards as the sole gateway to city funding. What is the maximum city subsidy that will be awarded to any one development venture? What percentage of a project development budget can be allocated to "soft costs," such as developer fees and interim financing charges? Does the city give priority consideration to ventures proposed by community development corporations? To ventures located within an area that has established a neighborhood strategic plan recognized by the city as a reasonable reinvestment approach? Clear underwriting standards are the city's published response to these and other questions.

A developer who wants city funding should be made to show that the development team owns or can get ownership of the real estate to be developed, that the team has the capability to implement the proposal on time and on budget, that projected costs are realistic and appropriate, that the venture is well designed for the use proposed and for the community where it is located, that neighbors in the vicinity of the proposed development are being consulted about the proposal and that questions and concerns raised by neighbors are going to be addressed, and that the projected marketing results (for sales housing) and long-term operating results (for rental housing) are likely to materialize.

Exceptions to underwriting standards can be permitted, but granting of exceptions should be guided by city priorities, not by favoritism toward a developer or political constituency. OHCD authorized a development subsidy funding commitment of more than $2 million—substantially higher than the $1.5 million subsidy cap published in Philadelphia's CDBG plan—in order to support the Brentwood Apartments venture, a proposal to restore a century-old historic mansion, with interior space redesigned for subsidized apartments. Per-unit production costs associated with this venture were sky-high, but other variables decisively influenced the city's decision to make a commitment of funding at the level needed: (1) The site was a strategically important location, the centerpiece of a National Register Historic District across the street from Fairmount Park and the grounds of the 1876 Centennial Exposition. (2) The venture was led by a minority developer, James L. Brown, IV, who also happened to be a long-time neighborhood resident; the venture addressed a high city priority by generating neighborhood-based "special needs" housing, in the form of several apartments for people with chronic mental illness but capable of living independently. (Mr. Brown had demonstrated successful past performance in similar ventures, in which special-needs and market-rate rental units were integrated within a single apartment building). And (3) the reoccupancy of this centrally located, long-vacant property would create a new center of activity in a neighborhood that had experienced little publicly supported improvement in recent decades.

Never award development subsidy funding before underwriting is completed. The city should never specify the amount of development subsidy to be awarded to a particular venture until a thoroughly documented financing proposal has been reviewed and found satisfactory by city staff. Philadelphia used to take the opposite approach: OHCD would make dollar-specific commitments of funding based only on preliminary review of proposals that everyone agreed would be fully documented later. The agreed-upon city subsidy was published in the CDBG plan authorized by the mayor and City Council as part of the annual budget-approval process. This approach was intended to give everyone a feeling that city dollars committed to a development venture were secure, so that selected developers could concentrate on obtaining other financing and move more quickly to construction.

A practice of agreeing to dollar-specific development subsidy commitments up front, without substantive proposal underwriting, creates two big problems for the city. This approach surrenders all the leverage that city staff needs to use in order to negotiate design changes, insist on cost reductions, and extract other concessions and benefits from the development team responsible for the proposal. This approach also gives developers and their political supporters the impression that the city subsidy is "owned" by the development venture for which it was awarded and can never be taken away. This sense of ownership and entitlement can make it difficult, if not impossible, for a city housing agency to withdraw funding support from a development venture that proves too costly or from a developer that fails to demonstrate sufficient capacity to implement as proposed. The money doesn't get released, and no housing gets produced.

I began learning all about these disadvantages in 1992, at a meeting that took place in City Hall two days before my first CDBG budget was to be presented before City Council's Finance Committee. OHCD had proposed for inclusion in the budget a series of sales and rental housing development ventures, using the traditional dollars-up-front approach. A list including the name of each venture, location, number of units to be produced, name of the developer, and city subsidy amount had been prepared for inclusion in the CDBG plan document, to be published in final form following favorable City Council action. The list had been okayed by Mayor Rendell and reviewed in advance by key City Council members. I had asked to meet with two of these councilpersons, Anna C. Verna and Jannie L. Blackwell, who at the time were chair and vice chair, respectively, of the Finance Committee, in order to review a few outstanding issues related to the proposed subsidy-award list and to present what I felt was a constructive solution to the biggest outstanding issue: city funding for the Saint Anthony's School venture.

Saint Anthony's School was a nineteenth-century former parochial school, a multistory, historically noteworthy brick building that was the largest single deteriorated structure in an otherwise relatively stable residential section of Southwest Center City (several blocks away from the target area of Universal Community Homes' strategic plan). The site and the surrounding neighborhood were located within Councilwoman Verna's legislative district. Although developing this property with city subsidy support made sense, the development proposal submitted for this venture—by a development team that had acquired control of the Saint Anthony's property without city help—was so weak that city staff had ranked the proposal at the very bottom of the list of ventures proposed for subsidy funding. Their review of the proposal had produced findings that the development team was inexperienced, that the development budget was unrealistic and in need of substantial revision, and that the other financing needed to complement the city's subsidy was not in place and might never be secured. Some city staff wanted Saint Anthony's to be removed from the list altogether.

I had set forth my solution to this problem—to fund or not to fund Saint Anthony's—in a letter hand-delivered to Councilwoman Verna prior to the meeting. My recommendation: keep Saint Anthony's on the subsidy-award list, but give the development team a limited amount of time in which to resolve all outstanding issues. If the team proved unable to do so within the time specified, the subsidy award would be withdrawn from Saint Anthony's and transferred to a proposal that hadn't been included on the city subsidy list: another vacant-structure rehabilitation project that happened to be located in Councilwoman Blackwell's West Philadelphia legislative district.

We sat down in Councilwoman Verna's inner office—I and the two councilpersons, along with their aides and three members of City Council President John F. Street's staff—and I spent a few minutes walking everyone through my letter. From my perspective, the approach proposed should make sense to everyone. The Saint

Saint Anthony's School

Anthony's proposal, despite its weaknesses, would stay on the city subsidy list and the development team would be given a chance to prove itself, an outcome that I expected Councilwoman Verna to support. However, if the problems identified by city staff could not be resolved, the money would go to a venture that Councilwoman Blackwell supported. Everyone listened politely to my presentation. Councilwoman Verna, a lifelong South Philadelphia resident and a longtime council member, had built a successful career in the cutthroat Philadelphia political environment while maintaining a well-deserved reputation as a fundamentally fair and honest person. In a past era, her public demeanor would have been characterized as "ladylike."

I finished my remarks, and, to my surprise, Councilwoman Verna immediately expressed her disagreement with the approach I had proposed. Her exact words: "You must think that I'm a complete jackass." As she swept my letter back across her desk in my general direction, Councilwoman Verna let me know, in terms that left no room for misinterpretation, that a transfer of funds from Saint Anthony's to anywhere else would not be tolerated under any circumstances. Jannie Blackwell, a sympathetic expression on her face, just sat there. The councilpersons' staff people were silent. I felt shocked and, worse, clueless as to why my reasonable plan had been angrily dismissed.

What I didn't understand then was that Anna Verna, with Jannie Blackwell's tacit support, was just doing her job effectively: exercising political leadership. Once an award of city funding got committed to her district, it made no sense for her to allow it to be taken away, regardless of whatever fine points were being raised by a city staff critique of a particular development proposal. She had been elected by the voters to get and keep value for her district, not to engage in a discussion of high-minded principles of neighborhood reinvestment policy. Jannie Blackwell, much as she might have liked to see funding transferred to the rental venture located in her West Philadelphia district, was not going to take my side in a disagreement with another councilperson over an issue that I had created. Instead, she would try to find other ways of applying pressure to change the plan and get the West Philadelphia venture funded. From the moment, several weeks earlier, that I had decided to employ the traditional funding-up-front approach, I had unwittingly cemented the city's commitments in place and made substantive discussion impossible.

The result of our meeting in the inner office: the Saint Anthony's venture was included in the budget, with no contingent conditions. City Council approved the budget, and the CDBG plan was submitted to HUD. A funding commitment letter was issued to the

Saint Anthony's development team confirming the subsidy amount. It would be inaccurate to say that, because of my blunder, OHCD had surrendered all ability to apply underwriting standards and compel changes in the Saint Anthony's proposal as a condition for the ultimate release of funds. However, thanks to me, OHCD had given up its primary means of leverage to modify the city subsidy amount, influence the number and type of units to be developed, and demand other modifications from a position of strength.

In place of this approach, the city should publish generic, not project-specific, activity line items in the CDBG plan, with bland categorical names such as "Sales Housing Development," "Neighborhood-Based Rental Production," and "Special Needs Housing Ventures." Money needed to support individual development ventures should be drawn from these generic line items and committed only after underwriting has been completed, after an appropriate development subsidy amount has been determined, and after city staff are convinced that the venture is ready to move to financing settlement and construction start. Until these conditions are met, any city commitment to a particular development proposal should be made in a generalized form only, with the name and location of the venture published in the CDBG plan but without identification of city subsidy amount, location, and the number and type of units proposed. The basic rationale for this approach: if no money is specified as "set aside" for any particular venture until it has proven itself qualified, more money becomes available to support development that is ready to go to construction.

Developers, elected officials, and neighborhood advocates like to see published dollar commitments and dollar-specific funding award letters issued for activities they support. The uncertainty associated with budget line items that are generic and commitments that are not dollar-specific is going to upset them at first, but over the long term, the city is going to spend reinvestment funding faster and produce more housing. What good is a specific commitment of city subsidy dollars if the housing never gets developed?

The original Saint Anthony's development team was never able to get its venture organized in the months following the City Council's authorization of the CDBG plan in 1992. The deal documented in the 1992 development proposal fell apart. Over subsequent months, and then years, the OHCD funding award letter trailed us like a lost puppy, as a succession of development teams approached Councilwoman Verna and city housing agencies, seeking to recover the subsidy and develop the property. None of the proposals organized by these subsequent would-be developers managed to meet the minimum documentation requirements necessary to move to implementation. In the meantime, OHCD had succeeded in establishing a no-dollars-up-front, generic-line-item policy, had published this policy in subsequent CDBG plans authorized by City Council (initially with lots of misgivings on the part of some council members), and had enforced the policy, through Noel and his staff at the RDA. Soon it became evident that a lot more city-supported housing was getting developed in Southwest Center City under the new policy, while Saint Anthony's continued to remain vacant. In 1997, based on her recognition of this situation and her respect for the RDA's reliable post-1992 performance in delivering land and money to other development ventures within her legislative district, Councilwoman Verna agreed to support a different approach for Saint Anthony's: the RDA would use its eminent domain acquisition powers to acquire the building and would sponsor a competitive Request For Proposals to attract developers interested in obtaining both the building and a city development subsidy to support rehabilitation costs (with subsidy amount to be determined at the end of the underwriting process). In deciding to support this approach, Councilwoman Verna wasn't reversing the position she had taken during that meeting in which I had humiliated myself years earlier; she was simply acknowledging that OHCD and the RDA were now offering a more effective way to deliver value to her district.

As it turned out, the highest-ranking proposal received in response to the 1997 Saint Anthony's RFP was submitted by an experienced developer who succeeded in addressing all underwriting issues. The rehabilitation of the building began less than a year later.

Overcommit. Mayor Rendell called it his Economic Stimulus Program: millions of dollars of local-government funding (derived from one-time-only transactions, such as the sale of large city-owned properties) that he had decided to make available to support special neighborhood development and service projects, from the construction of new shopping centers to neighborhood-wide vacant lot cleanup campaigns. But Noel and I privately called it "Class 700" funding because, by our estimate, the mayor had committed the same dollars seven times over to various constituencies pursuing this much-sought-after money. In meeting after meeting in the mayor's cabinet room , following presentations of funding proposals by civic organizations, church groups, private developers, and neighborhood-based academic or health-care institutions, we would hear the mayor respond with a general expression of support, a request for further proposal review by city staff, and a statement like, "I think we could find two or three million in Economic Stimulus funding to help out with this, if everything else works out." Noel and I kept quiet. We knew that, in a similarly general way, Mayor Rendell had already pledged an amount substantially greater than the entire year's Economic Stimulus budget to other groups months ago.

From our perspective, Mayor Rendell wasn't doing anything wrong; he was just managing Economic Stimulus funding in the same way that we managed CDBG housing-production dollars, by tentatively committing to sponsors of affordable-housing development ventures a level of funding that, in the aggregate, substantially exceeded the city's housing-production budget. The mayor knew, and we had learned, that lots of affordable-housing development ventures (like many downtown and suburban development ventures) never reach financial settlement and construction start as projected, for a variety of reasons: the development concept proves infeasible; other sources of financing cannot be secured as proposed; the real estate to be developed cannot be acquired within the time period projected; neighborhood residents' questions and concerns cannot be resolved as quickly as anticipated; the development team falls apart because of internal conflicts or the withdrawal of a key member. With this consideration in mind, the mayor was taking a calculated risk that a significant amount of the Economic Stimulus dollars he was committing "if everything else works out" would never be needed—or at least not needed within the same program year. His approach worked; the mayor maintained a reasonable dollars-pledged to dollars-spent ratio (a ratio probably more like four to one than the seven-to-one spread Noel and I had joked about), and I never heard anyone complaining that the mayor had failed to come through when committed funding was needed to close a deal.

In a similar way, housing production dollars should be over-committed to developers of ventures that appear to be qualified for inclusion in the city's housing production pipeline. In some years, every housing production dollar in the city's CDBG budget can be promised twice. Does this mean that the mayor and the leaders of the city's neighborhood reinvestment program should, in effect, create a funding commitment structure that resembles a multimillion dollar chain letter or Ponzi scheme? In one sense, yes; the city's prospective commitments, all told, substantially exceed the amount of money available. In another important sense, however, this over-committing of housing production dollars is different from everybody-wins-the-jackpot scams. The city funding is committed in a general form and is not owed or due on demand to anyone. The condition for delivery of the funding is successful completion of the underwriting process, a condition which some would-be developers will not be able to achieve within the program year and that other developers will never achieve at all. Housing production funding is not the same as a foundation grant award or private funding that is escrowed or reserved and shouldn't be managed that way. Up-front funding commitments make bookkeeping easier, but this approach causes a lot of public dollars to remain unspent (when, following detailed review, some proposals are found not to qualify for release of city funds). A policy of up-front fund reservations also prevents a lot of housing from getting developed, by limiting the city's ability to take money from a venture that is not ready to go and award it to a venture that can move to construction without delay. If OHCD had not changed its resource-allocation policy after 1992, continuation of the preexisting policy would have meant that the million-dollar subsidy committed to the Saint Anthony's proposal in 1992 would have remained unspent for six years, until the venture finally reached construction start in 1998. Following OHCD's post-1992 policy change (discontinuing the practice of pledging and holding dollar-specific awards of city funding in advance of complete project underwriting), the city's commitment to fund Saint Anthony's remained unchanged, but the dollars previously reserved for the venture were spent on affordable housing ventures that were ready for construction start in 1993. When the time came to produce the city subsidy finally needed for Saint Anthony's construction start in 1998, the dollars were taken from the generic "Neighborhood Rental" line item in the CDBG budget a line item that contained funding for many rental ventures (never pledged in advance in specific amounts), some of which would never reach construction start in 1998, and others which would not be ready for years.

Overcommitting involves a certain degree of risk, and the leaders of the city's neighborhood reinvestment programs should be careful not to make so many commitments that money cannot be delivered on time when needed by development ventures that make it through the underwriting process and are ready to go. But some level of overcommitting is essential to a successful neighborhood reinvestment program, to ensure the timely expenditure of all funding available for ventures that need it.

Amend. The city should be prepared to amend the CDBG plan during the course of the program year in order to take money from budget line items that are underspending and add it to budget lines where productivity is higher than anticipated. Plan amendments enable the city to spend more money and deliver more results. If more transitional housing ventures for formerly homeless people are being brought to settlement and placed under construction earlier than anticipated, the opportunity to produce more transitional housing should not be delayed until the next year due to lack of funds. Instead, money should be taken from an activity that is not spending at the level anticipated and used to fund transitional housing development at full capacity. To amend its CDBG plan for a purpose such as this one, a city has to do little more than publish a legal notice in local newspapers. No local legislative action, mayoral authorization, or HUD approval is needed.

Housing units produced with government support are economic assets with market value that fluctuates over time, like the market value of a stock or a downtown office building. Government-supported housing also has a social value, defined in terms of city goals and priorities, such as developing targeted areas, producing more transitional housing, and leveraging Low Income Housing Tax

Credit investment equity. The social value of a publicly supported development venture also fluctuates over time, based on the extent to which it does or does not address these goals and priorities. Let's say , for example, that a new vacant-house rehabilitation plan, designed to leverage more private rehabilitation-loan financing and fix up more vacant houses within a designated community, is launched by a neighborhood organization and supported with a commitment of city subsidy funding to be made available over a five-year period. The plan is initially valued highly by everyone as an innovative approach with the potential to generate substantial new benefit in terms of funds leveraged and housing units produced. Two years later, however, the plan is still not delivering expected results because rehabilitation loan financing cannot be leveraged to the level originally projected, because the rehabilitation cost of the vacant houses in the target area has proven to be much higher than proposed (requiring greater city subsidy than anticipated), and because the houses that have been completed to date are taking a long time to sell. The social value of the rehabilitation plan has dropped significantly, and the plan and/or the implementation approach employed during the past two years has to be modified to improve performance and deliver better value. City and community representatives have to work together to determine what is wrong, assess alternative ways of improving the situation, and make changes before the next phase of development activity begins. If this does not occur, a proposal once highly valued is in danger of becoming reduced to a trophy, a token commitment of city funding extended to a weak plan that continues to be supported primarily because neighborhood sentiment favors it and the city lacks the political resolve to end it.

As with the market value of an asset, the social value of a city-supported development venture can be perceived differently by different individuals. Some city staff opposed the 1992 version of the Saint Anthony's proposal and wanted to see it removed from the list of ventures scheduled to receive subsidy funding. They viewed the proposal as a fundamentally flawed endeavor that was being proposed for inclusion in the city's development pipeline only because of the political influence of elected officials and community members, two constituencies of people who had chosen to overlook the inexperience of the development team, the poorly constructed financing plan, and other significant problems associated with the approach proposed. Other city staff supported inclusion of the 1992 Saint Anthony's venture on the city-subsidy list. While not unaware of the political pressure in support of the proposal, they viewed the plan as weak but capable of improvement. From their perspective, the development team could strengthen itself by joining forces with a more experienced co-developer or by learning more about city funding standards and the underwriting process; the development budget could be reconfigured into a more realistic financing approach; and design problems could be addressed through revisions of architectural plans. These changes would take time but would ultimately produce a result that everyone agreed was important: the rehabilitation of the last big vacant building in an otherwise relatively stable neighborhood.

The debate over the comparative social value of alternative forms of neighborhood reinvestment is exciting, challenging, and open-ended. Issues of social value linked to neighborhood reinvestment are easy for most citizens to understand, and no formal training or technical expertise is needed to qualify a person for participation in this debate. Although there are many examples of good and bad neighborhood reinvestment ventures, there is no single formula or cookie-cutter solution guaranteed to maximize social value in any given situation. People who have chosen to devote their energies to supporting the improvement of neighborhoods have to decide for themselves what approach will work in any given situation. Brilliant neighborhood reinvestment ideas can originate from the mind of a neighborhood activist, an architect, a block leader, a city government employee, a college student, or a lifelong resident of the suburbs. Local government has two key responsibilities related to the management of the debate over neighborhood reinvestment and social values: (1) to articulate and publish a reinvestment policy setting forth city-supported goals and priorities, which—because they are the city administration's position—are bound to become a primary focus of the debate; and (2) to establish and enforce a sensible, consistent resource-allocation approach based on this policy.

The city's resource-allocation policy should make passage through the reinvestment-funding gateway difficult for all sorts of trophy projects that support an individual or constituency without offering significant new value to the city or the community at large. A trophy project is one that has strong association with a politically favored individual, organization, or neighborhood but does not meet basic underwriting standards. A trophy project may also have one or more of the following characteristics: no linkage with a neighborhood strategic plan; no association with a strategically important development site or proximity to other reinvestment activity; lack of broad support in the community at large; and inadequacy with respect to development team qualifications, design features, and/or associated financial leveraging opportunities.

In the high-pressure political environment characteristic of all cities, it is inevitable that some trophy projects will find their way into the system and will eventually receive city funding. Like their counterparts in the suburbs and the region at large, big-city mayors and other elected officials, encounter and must deal with—and sometimes accommodate—people whose interest has relatively little identity with the philosophical ideal of the "general good." Even a consistently articulated and well-enforced resource-allocation policy will admit some trophy projects into the system, but when city policy is effective, trophy projects do not secure funding as quickly as more worthwhile ventures and will sometimes be stalled for months or years, if necessary to achieve compliance with underwriting standards, and often be forced to undergo significant modifications as they pass through the system.

Within the first eighteen months after taking office, a new mayor should identify a single housing production activity as a top community-development priority, the venture or program that will be specifically identified with the mayor's leadership and will be recognized as the mayor's "signature" venture for years to come. This top-priority activity can be a single development venture (such as a large housing construction plan that produces lots of new development on a big parcel of land), a citywide program (such as a purchase-and-rehabilitation financing plan that brings many new homebuyers to the sales housing market), or a series of interrelated development activities (such as the conversion of a deteriorated public housing site and nearby vacant properties into a mixed-use, mixed-income community). This top-priority activity, when successfully organized and executed, becomes a city landmark, a long-term asset that increases in both economic and social value over time and serves as convincing evidence that a big success has been achieved, that the city is improving, and that the neighborhood where the activity is being completed is becoming a center of renewed interest and energy.

A landmark venture should be selected with care and not until the mayor's administration has accumulated months of exposure to neighborhood reinvestment issues. The selection of a landmark venture should never be made during the political campaign or in the early months of the mayor's administration. The choice is not an easy one, in part because the venture selected is not likely to produce decisive results in a short time. The mayor should beware of those who lobby for a particular venture on the grounds that, when completed, it will influence many people to move into the city from the suburbs, will serve as a model for other cities, or will generate national publicity characterizing the mayor as a progressive leader. The likelihood of any of these results being achieved in the short term through the completion of any neighborhood reinvestment venture—even an outstanding neighborhood reinvestment venture—is small. The choice of a landmark venture has to be based on the mayor's personal interests and preferences, on the professional capability of city staff to produce the results desired, and on local political dynamics, the interaction between the mayor, elected officials, and neighborhood constituencies that can influence timing and results. Since the two most critical factors—city-government capability to implement and the nature of local political dynamics—take time to assess, the selection of a landmark venture should not be made prematurely.

Like other high-profile endeavors such as waterfront and convention center development, ambitious housing production ventures take a lot of time to organize, plan, and execute. For this reason, the selected landmark venture should, if at all possible, be built next to or near previously completed development, such as a neighborhood or business district that has undergone improvement as a result of past public investment. Using existing neighborhood assets as an anchor and building on the accomplishments of past mayoral administrations reduces risks and increases the likelihood that a landmark venture will succeed. Landmark ventures cut from whole cloth—involving new neighborhoods or untested development approaches—are less likely to be successful than ventures that build out from existing completed development and draw on the proven skills and capabilities of leaders and managers of the city's housing production network.

The Rendell Administration's landmark housing production venture, a comprehensive revitalization plan for a thirty-block area of Lower North Philadelphia, resulted in the production of more than one thousand sales and rental units, completed over a six-year period through development activities ranging from new town-house construction to historic housing restorations. The city's "Home in North Philadelphia" policy for Lower North Philadelphia, published by OHCD in 1993 and supported as a city priority for the remainder of the decade, gained widespread political and community support and generated lots of positive media coverage, including an upbeat *New York Times* article. Although the policy was praised as innovative and visionary, the reasons for the choice of location couldn't have been more prosaic. The Lower North Philadelphia area targeted for our landmark already contained many outstanding examples of publicly supported housing that was well maintained after years, sometimes decades, of occupancy. The selected area included the entire Yorktown community (described in chapter 1), which, thirty years after its construction, was in need of some home-improvement financing, along with rental townhouses, mid-rise housing for the elderly, and other development completed from the mid-1960s to the present. In two portions of the targeted area, community groups had spent years formulating large-scale housing development plans; one of these plans had already received a funding award in a HUD-sponsored national competition. In light of this history, all that OHCD staff needed to do was draw a boundary line around the area containing the successful previously completed development ventures, work with community representatives to modify current housing development plans to achieve consistency with city underwriting standards, target vacant sites in the area for small- and medium-sized development, and secure political backing for a sustained commitment of funding. No creative neighborhood planning approaches, customized financing programs, or innovative construction techniques were needed to make this large-scale, high-profile venture successful.

A good resource-allocation policy based on the approach described in this chapter addresses good-government and good-politics concerns simultaneously. When managed effectively over a period of years, the policy convinces people that the city is managing public funding in a fair and reasonable way and that tax dollars are well spent. At the same time, if the city uses strategies to increase funding available (through actions such as Section 108 borrowing) or to create an appearance that more funding is available (through overcommitting), elected officials and neighborhood advocates begin to believe that the city is becoming more responsive to their efforts to obtain funding for ventures they support. Well-managed resource-allocation policy moves the city toward a good-government ideal but never loses sight of the need to demonstrate responsiveness to people seeking economic and social value for their communities.

4

THE NEW
HOMEOWNERSHIP

Two incidents, little-noticed by the general public but unnerving to me, influenced Philadelphia's 1990s homeownership policy in a big way.

An African-American man had been promoted to a senior position with a big media company and was relocating to Philadelphia. He had been house-hunting in the city, and he asked a colleague, an African-American woman employed by the same company (a longtime Philadelphia resident), for her opinion of a particular neighborhood that he had visited recently, a community with many reasonably priced Victorian-era homes and excellent transportation access to the downtown and other areas of the city. Her response: the neighborhood's real estate market was trending downward, and the neighborhood's minority population was trending upward—so don't buy a house there. My interpretation of her assessment (an interpretation with which she disagreed): "Don't buy a house in that neighborhood; too many poor blacks live there." The community in question was Germantown, a Northwest Philadelphia neighborhood where OHCD had supported more housing development ventures and had maintained a closer working relationship with community-based organizations than nearly anywhere else in the city.

One evening during the same year, Mayor Rendell spoke at the opening reception for an architectural design exhibit cosponsored by

OHCD and the Foundation for Architecture. On the ground level of the Curtis Building atrium, a few steps away from the fountain, where streams of clear water flowed over a riverbed of smooth dark marble, stood a display of site plans and elevation drawings illustrating design solutions proposed for a group of vacant parcels located within North Philadelphia's Francisville neighborhood. Candlelight glowing up from tables of catered food and drink dissolved into the air beneath the darkened glass ceiling.

Standing before a group of several dozen architects, planners, community leaders, and city government managers, the mayor praised the work of all the participants in the design project and expressed appreciation for the cosponsoring organizations' initiative in organizing the exhibit. Then he kept talking. Mayor Rendell was very knowledgeable about many topics, from the city's marketing strategy for the decommissioned naval shipyard to the first-round draft picks of the nation's professional basketball teams, but urban design was not one of his primary interests. So he spent the next few minutes talking about another topic instead: his dismay over the high cost of producing affordable housing in Philadelphia. His astonishment that the city would participate in the rehabilitation of a vacant house that cost more than one hundred thousand dollars to bring back to life. His conviction that high-cost development made no sense in an urban environment where so many people needed government help in dealing with critical housing needs. In thinking-out-loud style, Mayor Rendell said that he sometimes felt that the city should end its participation in high-cost affordable-housing development altogether. My jaw began to clench. In fact, the mayor continued, he liked the idea of setting a per-unit ceiling on housing subsidies, prohibiting city agencies from spending more than, say, twenty-five thousand dollars on any single house. The executive director of the Foundation for Architecture clutched his press kit firmly and maintained an impassive demeanor; under the mayor's hypothetical policy, two-thirds of the Francisville plans on display that evening would go into the dumpster, and the development site would become long-term urban meadow. In a half-joking, half-serious way, the mayor said that he sometimes wished that the city could just give away money to people in need of housing, let them buy houses for sale on the private market, and forget about engaging in any housing production activity whatsoever. The charitable foundation executive next to me, who had helped underwrite the cost of the exhibit and who had channeled a lot of foundation dollars into Philadelphia housing development ventures, frowned and stared fixedly at Mayor Rendell's shoes. The mayor concluded his remarks, was applauded, shook hands, and dug into the catered finger food. The event regained its friendly, informal spirit, and everyone enjoyed themselves—except for me and the small cadre of people who had organized this project. One of my goals in launching this initiative had been to get elected officials excited about the ways in which good urban design could bring dramatic, positive change to Philadelphia neighborhoods. We had clearly succeeded in getting at least one elected official excited—about advocating for a point of view opposed to ours.

But these two incidents raised two even bigger questions. Was all the effort we had devoted to producing housing in neighborhoods such as Germantown and Francisville a colossal waste of money and time? And even if we, the designers and leaders of the city's reinvestment programs, felt that the time and money committed to these housing production activities was worthwhile, did our opinions on the subject really matter, in light of these unequivocally negative responses from two people whose opinions we cared about?

Mortgage lending practices, insurance underwriting standards, interest rates, down payment requirements, and financing charges are all important issues affecting homeownership in older urban communities. But the most important issue is race. City government leaders who don't understand the fundamental importance of race as it relates to homeownership are overlooking a major responsibility and missing a big opportunity.

African Americans represent 12.8 percent of the total U.S. population as of 1999, but the participation of African Americans in the ownership of key American economic assets continues to be disproportionately low. How low? Consider a sample of a dozen, or a few dozen, Fortune 500 companies. The representation of African Americans on the governing boards of directors of these companies is likely to be substantially lower than 12.8 percent, and a significant number of the firms in the sample are likely to have no African-American representation on their boards at all. A large proportion of the stock of companies such as these is owned by other private companies, and most of these companies are also likely to have few or no African Americans seated on their boards. African Americans hold some key positions in the largest and most profitable legal and accounting firms in the nation, but the overall representation of African Americans at partnership status within these firms is likely to be disproportionately low, relative to the number of African Americans living in the regions where these firms conduct business. Even in fields such as entertainment and sports, which traditionally have offered more opportunities for blacks, leading business enterprises are owned and governed by whites. Basketball teams, entertainment conglomerates, sporting-goods manufacturers, radio and television stations, and recording companies—even those largely or exclusively oriented to black consumers—are more likely than not to be owned and governed by whites. In large metropolitan areas, the individuals, partnerships, and corporations that own and control the most valuable nonpublic real estate are exclusively or predominantly white.

In the century and a half that followed the Emancipation Proclamation, the fundamental problem of African-American dispossession was never really resolved through either policy initiatives, legislation, or court action. Late-twentieth-century civil rights legislation and judicial mandates did not address the fact that blacks had been systematically denied opportunities to own and govern American economic assets—private goods, from suburban split-level houses to downtown department stores—in preceding decades. No decisive public action, equivalent to *Brown v. Board of Education* or the Voting Rights Act, was taken to deal with this basic problem. Public education reforms and affirmative action policies have improved the economic status of many blacks since 1950, but these improvements, by themselves, are not sufficient to address the issue of disparity in the ownership and governance of private assets.

Because more blacks were better educated and had better access to job opportunities in 1999 than they did in 1949, the number of blacks able to accumulate wealth, own businesses, and gain positions on corporate boards was orders-of-magnitude greater in 1999 than it was a half-century earlier. But despite this history of improvement, the current rate at which African Americans are moving into key ownership and governance positions is not fast enough to correct the problem of disproportionate ownership in the fore-seeable future. More than a "level playing field," to use the meta-phor employed in discourse about affirmative action policy, is needed. With respect to ownership and race, the present state of affairs is less like a playing field than a marathon for which both white and black athletes have received equal opportunity to train and equip themselves. Although the goal of every runner is to cross the designated finish line in the shortest period of time, the start-ing line for blacks has been placed a considerable distance behind the starting line for whites. Some of the stronger, better-trained African-American runners will overtake some of the weaker, less pre-pared white runners, but most of the top finishers are going to be whites. The handicap granted to the white runners is the network of family ties, social relationships, professional acquaintances, in-heritances, endowments, and trusts that have perpetuated, and will continue to perpetuate, a tradition of white ownership for many more years.

The most productive subsidized housing programs of the 1990s—the Low Income Housing Tax Credit and the HOPE VI pub-lic housing revitalization program—have provided great direct ben-efit to many African Americans and other citizens in the form of newly developed, affordable rental housing that was both well de-signed and well managed. But even these public programs perpetu-ate the tradition of disparity in ownership. Most tax credit and HOPE VI developers are white-owned businesses, often working in partnership with tenant councils, nonprofit organizations, or com-munity development corporations that usually hold a substantially smaller share in the ownership of the venture. The structure of the tax credit program itself provides a federal benefit, in the form of a federal income tax write-off to wealthy investors (more likely to be white than nonwhite) as an incentive for them to make equity investments in virtually risk-free subsidized rental housing ventures. The tax credit and HOPE VI programs have generated extraordi-nary benefit for minority-owned development firms, contractors, and suppliers, as well as for residents of many neighborhoods with predominantly nonwhite population, and these programs should continue to be authorized by Congress and expanded if possible.

But even these highly valued, neighborhood-oriented programs do not address the issue of disparity in ownership in any new way.

Neither of the two broad alternatives for remedying this problem, one asset-oriented, the other citizen-oriented, are likely to gain sufficient political support at the federal level to be considered realistic options in the current political environment. Government intervention to force racial proportionality in the ownership and governance of existing businesses and private assets is unlikely to occur as long as free enterprise remains the economic system favored by most Americans. A citizen-oriented approach, in the form of reparations paid to African Americans (comparable to benefits rendered to Native Americans and reparations paid to Japanese people held in detention camps during World War II) is probably more feasible in principle. A reparations initiative would probably produce broader benefits for the economy and for society as a whole than other one-time-only federal funding awards such as the $165 billion savings and loan bailout of the 1980s or the massive middle-class tax cut proposed by congressional Republicans during the late 1990s. However, the likelihood of a reparations program being authorized by the federal government is only somewhat less remote at present than the likelihood of government intervention to change the ownership structure of Fortune 500 companies. The view that African Americans can and should, despite the inequitable marathon, gain ownership of American assets through a "bootstraps" approach—taking advantage of opportunities in today's society to get a better education, find a better job, and consequently, accumulate more assets—seems likely to prevail for now.

A great city-government-administered homeownership policy is not going to resolve this fundamental problem and usher in a new era of racial harmony. No government-subsidized sales housing program is going to be regarded as the equivalent of "forty acres and a mule" or as a payback for a national history of racial injustice. However, local-government homeownership policy is still critically important, because the HUD funding available for neighborhood reinvestment (through CDBG and HOME) is by far the biggest and most accessible resource for addressing one important aspect of the problem of disproportionality—the disproportionately low level of homeownership among African Americans during past decades of American history—while simultaneously benefiting the city as a whole. An effective homeownership policy is not a grand solution to the problem of disproportionate ownership; however, such a policy is the only element of an overall solution that can be implemented now, on a local level, using existing federal funding and regulatory authorizations. The leaders of the city's reinvestment programs should make the fullest use of these available resources to promote homeownership through policy and programs that will generate maximum benefit to African-American citizens and to the public at large.

The overall aim of a city homeownership policy is to offer more opportunity and choice to citizens interested in owning their own homes. Offering more opportunity means helping people afford the cost of buying homes and gain the best possible access to mortgage financing. Offering more choice means giving people the ability to select a home from among a variety of house types and neighborhood locations throughout the city. Because older cities have substantial African-American population, the more effective the city's homeownership policy, the more likely that more African Americans will own their own homes. Simply by virtue of prevailing urban demographics, a good municipal homeownership policy increases African-American ownership and begins to address the problem of disproportionality without the use of set-asides or quotas.

The results of a national survey sponsored in 1998 by the Fannie Mae Foundation, *African American and Hispanic Attitudes on Homeownership*, confirm that homeownership is highly valued by nonwhite Americans, many of whom live in older urban communities. The vast majority of African-American and Latino respondents to this survey indicated that homeownership is a "very important to number-one priority" (67 percent of African-American respondents, 65 percent of Latino respondents); that homeownership would "have a positive impact" on the community (60 percent and 50 percent, respectively), on the country (64 percent and 64 percent), and on their families (68 percent and 75 percent); and that homeowners are a stable part of the community (71 percent and 52 percent).[1]

Most city homeownership programs involve the financing of

housing production ventures—construction projects that produce new or rehabilitated homes for sale at formerly vacant and abandoned sites. Using HUD funds, the city lowers the development cost of each of these ventures by paying the developer a subsidy, either in the form of a grant or a loan on which repayment is forgiven for each year in which the completed property is owned and occupied by people of low or moderate income. The city may also decide to subsidize mortgage interest rates, down payments, or settlement costs associated with the purchase of this housing.

City policy and neighborhood strategic planning determine the type and location of housing to be developed with local-government funding support. The scale of a city-subsidized sales housing venture may be as small as a single house or as large as a hundred houses or more. A variety of housing construction approaches may be considered, depending on city priorities and neighborhood strategic goals: vacant-house rehabilitation on relatively stable residential blocks with three or fewer vacant houses; the improvement of a neighborhood's worst residential blocks, where the vacant houses are so numerous and in such poor condition that the prospect of privately financed rehabilitation is nil; the development of new-construction "infill" housing on small vacant lots, many of them located between existing occupied houses; scattered-site rehabilitation or new construction, in which groups of houses dispersed over a broad geographic area are built or rehabilitated; or the construction of many brand-new houses on a group of city blocks or a large cleared parcel.

The characteristic shared by all these sales housing production ventures is the use of government funding to support a development project rather than to promote consumer choice. In the development-oriented approach to homeownership, city subsidies provide the *opportunity* for people to purchase housing produced with city support. However, a buyer's *choice* of housing type and neighborhood location is limited to a selection among the housing types and locations funded through the city's program. The development-oriented approach limits choice significantly, since the number of houses produced with city funding support is a relatively small portion of the total number of houses available for sale on the private real estate market throughout the city.

Promoting homeownership through sales housing production ventures makes sense, despite this significant limitation of housing choice. The public money spent on sales housing development ventures reduces vacancy and restabilizes residential communities struggling with disinvestment. Through sensible planning guided by common sense, city and neighborhood leaders can pick genuinely promising development sites where a reasonable expenditure of public money will produce attractive, sellable houses.

Large-scale sales housing development, the production of many houses on a big tract of land or within a designated target area, is an excellent way to reclaim a community that has experienced higher-than-average population loss and housing vacancy. The two most recent HUD programs promoting large-scale sales housing production—the 1980s Nehemiah program and the 1990s Homeownership Zone program—support an effective approach for restoring communities made bereft by disinvestment: acquire most or all of the vacant property and develop it with many attractive new or rehabilitated houses for sale. This approach worked in Yorktown during the 1960s and has succeeded in many other urban locations since then. When large-scale sales housing is done right, people buy the houses and stay in the neighborhood for a lifetime.

Philadelphia's experience in the West Poplar neighborhood during the 1990s reaffirmed the value of this approach. City staff and community organization members worked together for months to reach agreement on a sales housing construction plan for a twenty-five-acre tract in this Lower North Philadelphia community located seven or eight blocks north of the Convention Center and the downtown area and just south of Yorktown (an application of the "building from strength" principle recommended for landmark ventures, as described in chapter 3). The large-lot, low-density site plan that the city and neighborhood planners adopted for West Poplar was termed "suburban-style," but was actually patterned after older Philadelphia "streetcar suburb" communities like Mount Airy in Northwest Philadelphia. These older communities had bigger houses—both detached houses and twins sharing a party wall—built on lots large enough to provide space for a driveway and a yard. Although Mount Airy homes are more than twice the size of traditional Philadelphia rowhouses, a block full of these homes is still

Houses in Northwest Philadelphia "streetcar suburb." This photo was used in the planning sessions that led to the development of West Poplar townhouses with similar features.

sufficiently high in housing density to become a place where neighbors can readily get acquainted with one another, form friendships, and look out for one another. Hard-core advocates of "traditional neighborhood design" in architecture and planning might have called for higher density, little or no setback (i.e., bringing house fronts up to the sidewalk line), elimination of driveways, and integration of rental units and some retail uses into the West Poplar development plan. But the approach selected for the West Poplar tract represented another tradition in planning and design, one that had made Mount Airy and similar neighborhoods appealing to generations of homebuyers, and that the West Poplar planners felt could be effective in inner-ring new communities developed close to the downtown area as well.

Schoolteachers, police officers, nurses, restaurant chefs, and office workers—some of whom had grown up in the suburbs, others

West Poplar townhouses under construction

of whom had grown up in public housing—were attracted to larger older houses in places like Mount Airy, and people like them got interested in buying the newly developed houses in West Poplar as well. The first phase of West Poplar construction sold out quickly, at a rate of one house per day. The second phase sold out before construction start. A geographic area that had been marked as nearly all-vacant on city maps at the start of the decade had become all-occupied by the decade's end. A ragged fringe area north of Center City was transformed into an urban asset that complemented and reinforced the Convention Center and other downtown investment.

In cities that have been losing, or just maintaining, their level of population, large-scale new housing production ventures are not likely to change existing demographic trends and draw lots of buyers back into the city from suburban areas. Instead, the newly developed houses will, for the most part, attract buyers from other city neighborhoods. No significant net population gain will occur as the result of city-subsidized ventures producing hundreds of new homes: families will just move out of one city neighborhood—probably an older one—and into the new community where the houses are being built. The whole endeavor amounts to a big reshuffling of the same deck of cards, at substantial government expense. Despite this significant zero-sum factor, large-scale sales housing development should still be considered an important element of reinvestment policy for cities with shrinking population. Older cities need to address the effects of population loss in a systematic way and make use of public resources to redefine the city, remaking some devastated neighborhoods as new residential communities and allowing others to continue to be depopulated, creating opportunities for future conversion to industrial, commercial, or institutional uses that make sense in today's economy. A publicly funded depopulation strategy—in which government money is used to encourage people to get out of the neighborhood where they live now (by offering relocation payments or replacement housing elsewhere in the city)—is going to cost the city a great deal of money and is guaranteed to be very unpopular politically. No one wants to be the person who has to announce to any group of taxpayers and voters, "Your community has just been written off; it's time to leave," no matter how badly deteriorated the neighborhood or how small the number of remaining residents. The reverse approach, a repopulation strategy in which a lot of sales housing is produced in selected neighborhoods, builds up locations where the city wants to establish a strong, long-term residential presence. This strategy is particularly important as a possible option for neighborhoods which, though badly deteriorated, are located near the downtown core.

What about the future condition of the neighborhoods that buyers leave in order to move to the newly developed housing? By using public money to produce hundreds of attractive houses in designated areas, isn't the city undermining other neighborhoods, as hundreds of families move out of existing dwelling units in order to buy the new houses, thereby creating hundreds of vacancies? Some cities that have supported large-scale sales housing development can't evaluate the scope of this potential problem, because they never kept track of the prior addresses of people who bought the new houses the city helped finance. Philadelphia's experience, based on a review of buyers who purchased homes produced in large-scale, city-supported sales housing ventures during the 1990s, is that most buyers moved from housing in good condition on stable blocks with little or no vacancy, and that the dwelling units they vacated had been taken by someone else and were still occupied three to five years later. A smaller proportion of the buyers, about 25 percent, moved out of more deteriorated neighborhoods, from blocks containing vacant houses and lots. However, the housing units vacated by these families were all reoccupied at the time of the city's review. A few families moved from public housing sites that the Philadelphia Housing Authority wanted to depopulate anyway, in order to prepare for demolition, redesign, and new construction. These results suggest that large-scale sales housing production in Philadelphia did no harm to the existing neighborhoods from which families moved when they purchased city-subsidized houses. However, these results should not be accepted as universally applicable. Cities should assess the results of their large-scale housing development programs to learn more about the effect of public investment on existing residential communities.

Does large-scale, city-subsidized housing development reinforce existing patterns of racial and ethnic concentration? The answer is an unqualified yes. During the 1960s, the new houses built in Yorktown, on a development site located in the center of the highest existing concentration of African-American residency in the city, were purchased by African Americans. Decades later, the houses in the Villa de Esperanza venture developed by the Nueva Esperanza community development corporation were purchased by Latinos. When the Philadelphia Chinatown Development Corporation marketed the Chinatown North sales housing venture in the mid-1990s, the first buyers in line to sign agreements on the new houses were Chinese people. This outcome of inner-city sales housing development is predictable but, for the most part, it is not a bad outcome. The danger that cities need to avoid, and have avoided in most late-twentieth-century subsidized sales housing development, is reinforcing racial and ethnic concentration in economically disadvantaged locations—the combination that is characteristic of much of the public housing produced in the 1950s and 1960s. Unlike older public housing, city-supported sales housing tends to be developed at locations that are attractive and have good access to centers of employment, retail services, and public transportation. If the housing is well planned and designed, the chances are excellent that both the buyers and the city at large will benefit over both the short and long term. Most sales housing produced in Philadelphia since 1960 is intact, occupied, and part of a stable neighborhood, unlike many of the public housing units produced during the same period.

Some members of racial and ethnic groups that have suffered from discrimination—that is to say, some members of all racial and ethnic minorities represented in American cities today—want to live in good neighborhoods that are populated by many other people of their race or ethnicity. One member of the Universal Community Homes development team told me that the geographic area selected as the focus of UCH's housing development plans was the only remaining portion of South Philadelphia available for an expansion of African-American residency in a desirable neighborhood environment. African Americans had been displaced from Society Hill, the Rittenhouse Square area, and other neighborhoods within Center City as the result of 1950s and 1960s urban renewal and gentrification. Blacks had also been excluded for many years from the working-class South Philadelphia neighborhoods that extended from ten to fifteen blocks south of City Hall all the way to Veterans Stadium. The only remaining opportunity for substantial African-American population growth in this section of the city was a rectangular area located south of Center City (just below the upper-income Society Hill and Rittenhouse Square areas) and north of the fully developed South Philadelphia core. The UCH team was not interested in creating a racially segregated enclave in this area, which was also home to many whites. But the organization's development strategy had been shaped with an awareness of the relationship between this geographic band of real estate and the prospects for African-American population growth in this part of the city.

Although concentrated racial and ethnic residency is not necessarily harmful and can be beneficial, the fact remains that integration is a positive value that cities should promote—and, for the most part, city-supported sales housing development ventures do not promote this value at all. A lot of prospective homebuyers want to live in a diverse community, and most of these buyers are not going to find what they want in the products generated through city-supported sales housing development. The severe limitation on housing choice that is characteristic of the development-oriented approach to homeownership is a big disadvantage for these buyers and for the city in general. To overcome this disadvantage, the city has to support consumer-oriented approaches to homeownership that complement sales housing development ventures and enable people to choose a home from among many houses for sale in communities of all kinds across the city.

What's the best way to promote housing choice? We couldn't just give people twenty-five-thousand-dollar housing vouchers, in keeping with Mayor Rendell's off-the-cuff remarks at the reception. The HUD rule book wouldn't permit such a program, which would amount to terrible public policy anyway (one inevitable effect: rapid inflation in the sales prices of those houses most likely to be bought by people eligible to receive the vouchers). Mandates and incentives designed to promote racial integration had, in my experience, not been very effective. Despite strict HUD "site and neighborhood standards" intended to prevent public housing from being located in areas of racial or low-income concentration, most public housing produced during the late-twentieth-century decades in which the HUD standards were enforced was, if anything, more isolated and racially or economically "impacted" than most other housing in the city. Prior to my first term of employment at OHCD, I lived in one of three apartments in a house that had been purchased with a mortgage made available through a nonprofit organization. This organization provided low-interest financing to support home purchases that, in its view, had the effect of promoting racial integration in neighborhoods undergoing demographic changes. But shortly after settlement, the new owner, a white person, terminated the lease of a black family in order to move into one of the apartments. Mandates and incentives probably work effectively to promote integration under some circumstances, but they will never achieve big or widespread results. Germantown's African-American population grew substantially during the decades after 1950, as the African-American woman described at the beginning of this chapter recognized. During this period, the quality of public education and services declined, crime rose, and social problems increased. Would any city-sponsored incentive program have succeeded in keeping Germantown racially and economically integrated under these circumstances?

The approach OHCD took to promote housing choice was a major expansion of housing counseling services for first-time homebuyers, accompanied by city-funded settlement assistance grants. Housing counseling services have been available in most cities for decades, usually under the sponsorship of government agencies or nonprofit organizations (counseling offered by banks or real estate agencies has much less value, because, it is not "arms-length," disinterested assistance). A trained counselor helps a family interested in buying a home for the first time learn about the differences between renting and owning, about the responsibilities of homeownership (from repairing the heater to paying the property taxes), and about the variety of house types and neighborhood locations available in the city. The counselor helps the family review the agreement of sale prior to signing and can assist in questions about negotiating the purchase price or modifying the agreement before it is signed. With counseling support, the buyer learns about a variety of mortgage products available through lending institutions and gets help in applying for a mortgage and securing financing approval. For prospective buyers who are not "creditworthy" because of past delinquency or default on credit-card payments or personal loans, the counselor helps organize a credit-repair plan designed to address these obligations and clear the way for mortgage approval. Credit repair can take weeks, months, or years, depending on the seriousness of the problem and the capability of the prospective homebuyer to resolve it. Housing counseling services provide a structured approach for credit repair, linked to an ultimate reward—a home of your own—and many counseling clients make and keep a commitment to see this process through to conclusion, no matter how long it takes. For buyers that completed prepurchase counseling, OHCD funded a one-thousand-dollar settlement assistance grant, paid to the title company at closing, to offset financing fees and other charges payable by the buyer. OHCD's housing counseling approach was designed to produce buyers who understood what homeownership was all about, who had made a good selection of a house and a mortgage product, and who were starting their experience as homeowners on sound financial ground.

To advance this approach, OHCD issued a request for proposals, inviting nonprofit organizations and community development corporations to seek funding for housing counseling staff and related administrative expenses. We ended up funding more than two dozen organizations, most of them neighborhood groups, along with some larger nonprofit organizations that drew clients in from many areas of the city. Some agencies, such as Women Against Abuse and Intercultural Family Services Center, offered specialized services to specific groups. All counseling staff funded through OHCD received training through a program administered by a bank consortium, the Delaware Valley Mortgage Plan, and the performance of all the counseling agencies was monitored on a regular basis by OHCD staff and outside experts.

This expanded housing counseling initiative was called "Philadelphia 500," because I thought that our goal should be to help deliver 500 first-time homebuyers to the Philadelphia sales housing market annually. This goal was higher than the number of settlements that most OHCD staff felt could be reasonably achieved each year—300 or 400 by their estimate—and lower than the number of settlements that some of the more experienced housing counselors in the city felt could be achieved—about 700 or 750. The estimates and the goal I had set proved to be wrong. Demand for housing counseling and settlement assistance rose sharply within a few months after the start of the program and remained consistently high for years. Most counseling agency staff found themselves working at full capacity and maintaining waiting lists which grew as the program continued. More than 2,200 settlements were produced annually in both Fiscal 1996 and 1997. By mid-1999, OHCD's initiative had brought more than 10,000 first-time homebuyers to the Philadelphia real estate market. Many of the buyers whom our agencies counseled would not have been able to purchase a house readily—or at all—without the assistance provided through the counseling program. Most of the houses purchased by the counseled families were located in neighborhoods that hadn't had a strong real estate market in years. Many of these houses would have remained for sale and unoccupied for months or years if our program had not produced qualified buyers with approved financing. In some years, the buyers counseled through OHCD's program were estimated to represent 15 percent or more of the entire Philadelphia single-family sales market.

When it became clear that 10,000 settlements would be achieved in 1999, OHCD scheduled a press conference at City Hall to publicize the achievements of all the housing counselors from around the city. We distributed T-shirts with "10,000" printed on the front and "PHILADELPHIA HOUSING COUNSELING—AMERICA'S BIGGEST AND BEST" on the back, along with the names of all the organizations participating in the program. The extraordinary results of the program made lots of people in city government and in neighborhoods pleased and proud.

Because of the high performance of our housing counseling/ settlement assistance program and the extensive word-of-mouth communication that informed the general public about the availability of this resource, OHCD staff kept finding out that people they knew were participating in the program or had already bought a house with assistance through the program: a neighbor's brother-in-law, an ex-girlfriend's daughter, the woman who worked at the day-care center down the street. The traditional pattern, in which a City Hall insider helps close friends and family members get special access to a scarce public resource, was altered; instead, city staff were unexpectedly discovering that people they knew were among the many families obtaining access to this widely available resource.

OHCD maintained a data base containing detailed information about characteristics of the first-time homebuyers supported through city-funded counseling agencies. Because Philadelphia's program had become the nation's biggest housing counseling/settlement assistance initiative, this data base held the most extensive, most detailed information available anywhere about first-time homebuyers in older urban neighborhoods. The contents of the data base revealed key characteristics of the new homeownership, the kind of home buying patterns taking place in an older city in the 1990s. Four characteristics were especially noteworthy.[2]

☐ *Direction.* The direction of the old homeownership—the homebuying patterns of Philadelphia and other older cities in the post–World War II period—was outward, characterized by families moving out of older neighborhoods into newly built housing in outlying city neighborhoods or in the suburbs. The direction of the new homeownership, as evidenced by the transactions recorded in OHCD's data base, is inward, with most purchases involving houses built before 1950 and located in traditional working-class neighborhoods or Victorian-era communities once populated by middle- and upper-class families.

☐ *Race/ethnicity.* The new homeownership is much more racially and ethnically diverse than the homeownership demographic of the mid–twentieth century. Of 5,447 families assisted through OHCD's program between 1996 and 1998, 2,803 (51.5 percent) were African-American, 1,358 (24.9 percent) were Latino, and 314 (5.8 percent) were Asian.

☐ *Income.* The families participating in the OHCD program were not experiencing the order-of-magnitude income growth characteristic of 1950s homebuyers (a 96.6 percent increase in median income over twenty-three years, as cited in chapter 2). For example, the household income of most buyers assisted through the program in 1998 (980 of 997 buyers) was lower than the $46,200 "area median income" (for a three-member household) published by HUD. Homeownership in Philadelphia was within reach of families with incomes at this low level because of the traditionally low price of housing in the city. The average sales price for a home purchased by a family participating in the program in 1998 was $42,696. Cities with substantially higher housing sales prices can pursue the modified approach to consumer-oriented homeownership described later in this chapter.

☐ *Mobility.* A 1995 survey by Bryn Mawr College economics professor Harriet Newburger of 548 families that had participated in the program provides some interesting insights into the relationship between race/ethnicity and moves within and among neighborhoods. Newburger found that white buyers in the sample tended to buy houses in or near the neighborhoods where they had previously lived. Latino buyers bought houses in neighborhoods long recognized as traditional Latino "expansion corridors" (neighborhoods with a substantial concentration of Latino residency, bordered by areas in which Latino population, while lower, was on the rise), with higher-income families moving to corridor edges where Latino population was not as concentrated. African-American buyers in the sample tended to move farther than the other two groups, with a substantial number "jumping" from one traditional expansion corridor to another, often to purchase homes in neighborhoods that were more racially mixed than the neighborhoods they left (according to 1990 census data).[3] One conclusion that might be drawn from this study: most new homebuyers in the Philadelphia sample demonstrated a preference for racially or ethnically mixed communities.

These housing preference patterns could not have come to light through an analysis of purchases and prior residency among families that bought houses produced through Philadelphia's development-oriented homeownership program, because nearly all of these houses were located in areas of existing racial or ethnic concentration. Philadelphia's development-oriented approach offered no choices for African Americans who shared the perspective of the woman who advised against buying in Germantown, as well as other people who feel strongly that mostly-nonwhite residency and economic disadvantage tend to go hand in hand in some areas of the city.

As our program grew, OHCD staff heard from some real estate brokers who weren't very enthusiastic about the city's decision to get involved in prepurchase counseling in a big way. Some of these real estate professionals didn't understand or didn't care about the potential value of the program to consumers. They insisted that any prospective homebuyer who walked into a housing counseling agency with a signed agreement of sale should be considered eligible to receive the one-thousand-dollar settlement assistance grant. OHCD staff and housing counselors disagreed. An important part of the counseling process is learning about the choice of homes available for purchase and understanding the terms of an agreement of sale before making a commitment to purchase. Because a buyer who arrives at a counseling agency with an executed agreement of sale has missed the opportunity to consider these issues beforehand, the value of housing counseling for such a person is very limited. Besides, we didn't want to position OHCD in the role of a grant-dispensing government agency that, in effect, acted in response to referrals from real estate agencies. Counseling had to be respected as a resource that was closely linked to, but separate from, the business of transacting real estate in Philadelphia neighborhoods.

Other real estate brokers, including several who had been very helpful in advising us about the design and start-up of our program, expressed concern about the need to keep counseling removed from the real estate transaction process. These brokers felt that some counselors were interjecting themselves into negotiations over purchase price and sale terms—in effect, practicing real estate without a license. OHCD staff wanted to address this concern and make it clear to housing counselors that they had no legal authority to participate in real estate negotiations. But we also wanted counseling agencies to produce the greatest possible benefit for the first-time homebuyer, just as real estate agencies worked to achieve the greatest possible benefit for the seller.

In the course of dealing with this issue, we came upon a way to show responsiveness to the real estate brokers' concerns while bringing new value to the program: we gave counselors the opportunity to become licensed real estate professionals. With training and a license, there could be no question of a counselor's understanding of real estate transactions and respect for the roles of the parties in these transactions. Some of the city's veteran housing counselors had already completed course work and passed the state real estate licensing examination, years before the OHCD program began. One counseling agency director, Michelle Lewis of Northwest Counseling Service, Inc., was a licensed real estate broker. Why not help interested OHCD-supported counselors obtain these credentials?

After finding that many counselors wanted to pursue this opportunity, OHCD contracted with Temple University Real Estate Institute to underwrite tuition for counselors interested in completing course work needed as a prerequisite for licensing. The response to this opportunity was very strong and, within two years, most of the counselors in the OHCD program had completed basic courses in real estate principles and practices. Some of these counselors went on to take and pass the state examination and obtain their licenses. In a short time, most of the key participants in the city's program had established professional credentials recognized by the private sector. The need to keep counselors out of negotiations over price and sale terms remained an important issue, but no one questioned the professional qualifications of the counselors who had gained these credentials.

When it became clear that OHCD's program would influence many housing transactions during the course of each year (at its peak, the program influenced an average of one settlement every hour of every business day), we began to consider issues that we hadn't regarded as priorities when our expectation of program capacity was much lower. The most important of these issues was the quality and condition of the houses purchased by the buyers we counseled. The vast majority of these houses were built prior to 1950, and many were more than a century old. Counselors were not qualified to conduct inspections of houses being considered for purchase, and no city staff had been assigned to inspect these houses in order to determine whether or not they were in need of repair or had significant long-term maintenance problems.

To address this issue, we decided to do for each client what an informed buyer in the private market would do: secure the services of a qualified home inspector to look over the house and complete a write-up, so that repair needs could be identified and dealt with in advance as a condition of the sale. OHCD contracted with three private home inspection firms, staffed by inspectors certified by the American Society of Home Inspectors (ASHI). The inspectors were assigned to inspect and report on the condition of each house being purchased with OHCD counseling support; the assignment was made after the execution of the agreement of sale and was completed quickly enough to enable the parties involved to determine how any repair needs were to be addressed prior to settlement. The inspectors cost OHCD more money—a few hundred dollars for the initial inspection and, when needed, a reinspection to confirm completion of repairs—but the inspectors' work gave everyone assurance that houses bought with assistance through the city's program were worth buying. The completed inspection reports also provided the buyers with useful information about long-term maintenance and repair issues that needed to be dealt with in the years following settlement. As the program continued, OHCD accumulated, through these reports an extensive base of detailed information about the condition of thousands of older occupied houses in the city's neighborhoods.

Philadelphia's approach to consumer-oriented homeownership was particularly effective because of the very low single-family sales prices that traditionally prevailed throughout the city. In the 1990s, these sales prices, combined with single-digit mortgage interest rates and rising rent rates, made homeownership especially advantageous to lower-income purchasers. For many first-time buyers in Philadelphia, the difference between the monthly mortgage payment on a newly purchased house and the monthly rent on the property vacated at settlement amounted to a savings of thousands of dollars annually.

For many other cities, where housing sales prices are much higher, more than counseling and a $1,000 grant is going to be needed to help lower-income families become homeowners. In these cities, higher sales prices restrict opportunity, making it harder to afford homeownership and obtain mortgage financing. To expand opportunity in a higher-priced single-family market, the city can use some of its funding to do what is done in the development-oriented approach to homeownership: write down total housing cost through a subsidy award. In this program variation, the subsidy (in the form of a grant or a ten- to fifteen-year "soft" second mortgage, on which principal and interest payments are forgiven in each year that the family continues to own and live in the house) is awarded to the homebuyer rather than to a real estate developer or contractor undertaking a city-supported housing construction project. For example, a family qualified to obtain a $55,000 mortgage and prepared to make a $3,000 down payment could receive a $42,000 soft second mortgage from the city in order to purchase a $100,000 house which the family chose and was prequalified for during the counseling process. A soft second mortgage program can be designed in coordination with Fannie Mae or Freddie Mac to insure that the subsidy will not be a barrier to private mortgage lenders' ability to sell their portion of the financing on the secondary mortgage market.

The consumer-oriented and developer-oriented approaches to homeownership represent two ends of the public subsidy spectrum, constituting the lowest-cost and the highest-cost program approaches, respectively. For one thousand dollars each, plus the cost of counseling services, OHCD was able to help thousands of Philadelphia families achieve homeownership. On the other hand, because Philadelphia market values were so low, a particularly deep construction subsidy—sometimes approaching one hundred thousand dollars per house—was needed to make up the difference between the cost of building a new city-subsidized house and the relatively low sales price of the completed house. (In Philadephia's program, prices are always set at a level comparable to market values in the community where the house is located, in order to give neighborhood residents the opportunity to purchase.)

Mayor Rendell never followed through on his threat to get the city out of the housing-production business altogether or to cap city subsidy at twenty-five thousand dollars. As our consumer-oriented programs grew and generated thousands more homeowners than the traditional development-oriented approach, most of the city's homeownership program was delivering value at substantially less than twenty-five thousand dollars per unit.

However, the significantly lower cost of the consumer-oriented approach has to be weighed against the fact that the development-oriented approach has an additional goal: reducing vacancy and stabilizing a neighborhood through the completion of construction activity. This goal is critically important for neighborhoods, just as important as the completion of convention centers, hotels, stadiums, and waterfront projects supported with public funding are for downtown areas. In strategically located neighborhoods where vacancy and abandonment are widespread, the city has to establish a realistic policy linked to a commitment to undertake housing production. And sometimes this commitment is going to mean acceptance of relatively high development cost to produce new city assets—newly built or rehabilitated houses—in selected city neighborhoods. Cities should devote more attention to designing lower-cost consumer-oriented homeownership approaches, but should not lose sight of the long-term value of higher-cost housing production. The tension between the economic value of low per-unit cost and the social value of housing production takes different forms from city to city, based on differences in housing markets, the extent of vacancy, and local political considerations. Neighborhood supporters should learn more about this dynamic as it relates to their city and should seek to strike the balance between these values that works the best for the most neighborhoods.

5

CDCs ON
THE EDGE

The Mercado was a big failure—another one of those creative but hard-to-realize ideas spawned by the Norris Square Civic Association and aggressively promoted by its tireless director, Patricia DeCarlo. The civic association, a community development corporation with several years' experience as a housing developer, neighborhood planner, and manager of community service programs, wanted to acquire and develop a large, vacant, multistory building on Front Street, a former bank branch office that had been a community anchor back when the neighborhood was a thriving industrial zone packed with factories and rowhouses. The civic association was going to clean out the old building, then outfit it for reuse as a market hall for small retailers selling food products of particular interest to the neighborhood's Latino consumers: fruits and vegetables flown in from the Caribbean, along with baked goods and desserts prepared by local entrepreneurs. The cost of renting stall space or operating a vending cart would be set low enough for small neighborhood vendors to afford. The location of the big empty bank was perfect for this venture: it sat at a busy corner on a commercial corridor flanked by densely populated neighborhoods.

Pat DeCarlo supervised the drafting of a business plan for the Mercado. She had the building inspected, written up, redesigned, and cost-estimated. She got foundation grants to pay consultants to work on a financing plan and start-up strategy. She submitted proposals for development subsidy funding to government agencies and corporations, including the corporate descendant of the bank that had vacated the old branch office many years before.

Weeks of organizing and predevelopment planning turned to months. The venture began to encounter serious problems. The cost of adapting the building—even a basic clean-out and a refitting of utilities—was very high and required a level of grant funding or public subsidy that no one was offering. Operating expense projections—for building maintenance, utilities, taxes—were coming out much higher than the level of rental income that could be collected from the small vendors and retailers who needed to be attracted to the Mercado and who wanted to pay little or no rent. Some Front Street merchants, the retailers who one might expect to be standing in the front line of community support for a venture such as the Mercado, opposed the development plan, claiming that a new retail center would take business away from little grocery stores and restaurants on the corridor and would eventually drive these existing neighborhood retailers out of business.

DeCarlo had lots of experience with debate, disagreement, and conflict over neighborhood improvement issues. She was one of a group of community members who had reclaimed Norris Square park, a square-block green area, from drug dealers who had ruled it for years. She and the other neighborhood activists ignored the death threats, out-intimidated the drug gangs, and restored the park as a safe, attractive neighborhood amenity. DeCarlo organized a group of unemployed neighborhood residents, some of them recently out of prison, into a work crew and negotiated a joint-venture relationship with a suburban builder to get the crew working on Philadelphia construction contracts. She spearheaded the planning, design, organization, financing, and development strategy for Los Balcones, a new-construction rental housing development venture that replicated some Caribbean exterior design features: stucco fronts, balconies, terra-cotta roof tiles. The Los Balcones development proposal generated a lot of argument over the additional cost of these special design features, but the civic association prevailed. The completed venture was an attractive new community asset that illustrated the new identity of the community as effectively as the reclamation of the park had reaffirmed the community's respected past.

As months passed, a modified approach to the Mercado venture took shape. The Norris Square Civic Association organizers knew that a key attraction of the Mercado would be fresh produce flown in overnight from Puerto Rico: plantains, papayas, chironja (a citrus fruit), chayote (a squash), and calabaza (West Indian pumpkin). In the past, produce was often sold in Norris Square, as in many Philadelphia neighborhoods, from the sidewalk, from carts, cars, trucks, from houses, garages, and warehouses.Why wait for the bank building to get developed? Why not start importing and selling now?

In midsummer 1997 the first shipment arrived, was loaded onto an old yellow school bus and transported to Norris Square. The Mercado opened in an old former mansion facing the park. The produce was displayed in cartons and crates and spread out on long folding tables. People from the neighborhood brought over homemade products for sale: yellow rice and sausage, *sofrito*, mango cheesecake, *flan de vainilla,* and more.

The market quickly attracted an enthusiastic neighborhood clientele. To supplement this base of neighborhood shoppers, the Mercado was promoted to specialty restaurants located downtown and in trendy neighborhoods. Chefs began stopping by, and coming back; the Mercado's fruits and vegetables were the freshest Caribbean products available in the region. Business continued to grow. On warm days, the Mercado spilled over into the park across the street. The size of the air-freight shipment from Puerto Rico grew nearly threefold. Norris Square Civic Association hadn't abandoned the ambitious bank building renovation plan or the market hall concept. The organization was just demonstrating its skill in adapting its plan to achieve tangible short-term benefits. The approach was working. The Mercado was a big success.[1]

Let's organize a little community development venture together. A headquarters location won't be hard to find: we can rent one of those empty storefronts on the avenue. We'll buy vacant houses, fix them up, sell them, make a little profit on every sale. We'll stay in business for a long time; this neighborhood needs a lot of fixing up.

First, we'll get some government seed money or a foundation grant and put together a development package, a group of houses to rehabilitate. We'll meet with community members, let them decide what houses they want to see completed first, and make plans to employ local residents and neighborhood-based contractors as our construction workforce. We'll set aside some of our profits each year to help pay for neighborhood-supported activities and investments, like hiring a community organizer or building a new day care center. Anyone who believes in neighborhood improvement will applaud our endeavors.

Let's start a small business enterprise together. We'll locate and transact all our business in one of the worst neighborhoods in the city—one of the places where the real estate market and business climate are weakest. We'll try to make money acquiring, fixing up, and selling houses, even though there is no evidence that steadily declining property values will start rising anytime soon. Rather than "cherry-picking" foreclosure properties and other recently vacated houses in reasonably good condition—which could be rehabilitated faster and at lower cost—our business is going to select some of the most deteriorated houses in the community: the boarded-up, fire-damaged, nearly collapsing vacant properties that take lots of time and money to develop. Given these operating parameters, most of our development ventures are going to be money losers, financially infeasible without a government subsidy to make up the difference between development cost and sales price.

Delays in the public land acquisition and development financing process will force us to move ahead much more slowly than anticipated. As the months pass, costs will go up and we'll start drawing from our not-yet-earned developer fees to offset increased expenses. Due in large part to circumstances beyond our control, we'll complete each development package behind schedule and over budget. If we're lucky, our ventures will break even; not infrequently, they'll produce a net loss. When a development package does turn a profit, most or all of the money will be used as working capital to fund predevelopment costs for the next development package. Anyone who believes in sound business practice will raise serious questions about the feasibility and long-term viability of our endeavors.

Reconciling neighborhood improvement goals with the realities of operating what is, in effect, a small company is a difficult challenge for all community development corporations (known as CDCs). CDCs, usually located in and associated with a particular neighborhood, are created to improve physical conditions and provide community members with better access to human services. Sometimes founded by or affiliated with local nonprofit civic associations, many CDCs plan, build, manage, and/or sell affordable housing and other kinds of real estate, such as shopping centers or community service facilities. Most successful CDCs are skilled at assembling funding from government, private, and charitable sources to support an array of development and service activities, from the construction of new supermarkets to the operation of job-training programs.

Any neighborhood-based or neighborhood-oriented organization that starts influencing physical development or other forms of reinvestment activity should be entitled to call itself a CDC. Although CDCs sometimes have been defined as neighborhood groups that engage in construction activity, well-organized groups with no construction capacity can coordinate, plan, and supervise the implementation of development activity as well as, and sometimes better than, groups that take on development-implementation responsibilities.

Nearly everyone likes CDCs, because, at their best, these organizations represent the principle of neighborhood self-help in a very tangible way. A completed CDC venture such as the rehabilitation and reoccupancy of a deteriorated, long-vacant apartment building proves that community members can get together to address serious problems and, when their initiative is sustained, generate a sequence of reinvestment activities that could return a distressed neighborhood to economic stability. CDCs dare to take on development challenges that private developers reject as too complicated or risky. CDCs can find creative ways to use available resources to address neighborhood needs, and an innovation crafted by one CDC often can be replicated in other communities. CDCs are likely to know more about neighborhood needs and existing conditions than even the best-informed government employees and, for this reason, a successful CDC-sponsored development venture or service program is likely to deliver greater overall value to the neighborhood than the same activity completed by an outsider. When a capable CDC is the driving force behind a development venture, the construction work gets done properly, qualified community members have opportunities to work for or subcontract with the development team, and the completed venture is responsibly maintained for years to come.

But starting and managing a CDC is a risky endeavor, comparable to getting up on ice skates for the first time. One skate blade is ambition, the other is capacity. After lacing up, you can carefully maneuver yourself into a standing position and hover there, with blades parallel, ankles and knees in an unsteady holding position. But to move ahead, you have to learn how to push forward with one blade while setting and holding your direction with the other. Every move brings the risk of slipping, losing balance, and collapsing.

In their desire to praise the positive results of CDC ambition and endeavor, some CDC supporters create the impression that, if only sufficient resources and political support were forthcoming, neighborhood groups could accomplish almost anything. In "Neighborhoods First: Communities Revive from the Bottom Up," part of a 1995 report on the Greater Philadelphia region produced for the *Philadelphia Inquirer*, Neal R. Peirce and Curtis W. Johnson maintain that "the transfer of power and responsibility to neighborhoods and individuals is the final needed step" in realizing the fullest potential value of the 1990s trend toward "devolution" of federal responsibilities to states. According to Peirce and Johnson, "the overall goal would be to send directly to the neighborhood the money that now flows through the bureaucracies that oversee social services, recreation, health, welfare, even police protection." The authors of the "Peirce Report" approvingly cite the remarks of a U.S. Department of Health and Human Services official: "Our whole system of governance, of services, has failed . . . it can't be screwed up any worse. So we must let neighborhoods have the resources now controlled by state and local governments . . . it's time to be bold, throw out the rule book and say we believe in empowerment of neighborhoods and families."[2] In *Reinventing Government*, David Osborne and Ted Gaebler devote a chapter to "community-owned government," citing neighborhood-oriented innovations from parent involvement in the Head Start program to the establishment of community boards for the resolution of civil disputes previously referred to the court system.[3]

But just because some CDCs can perform some responsibilities well doesn't mean that all CDCs can do everything well or that CDCs should be assigned the functions of local government. Some CDCs have established strong track records as developers of houses, retail centers, and service facilities, but most CDCs in cities such as Philadelphia lack sufficient organizational capacity and experience to produce reliably from one year to the next or to develop at larger scale. Private developers with affordable-housing expertise can easily outperform most CDCs. Giving community organizations more money and the authorization to take over local-government responsibilities wouldn't automatically bestow increased capacity upon these groups. It would just create a neighborhood-level bureaucracy that would actually slow down the pace of development.

One limited form of local governance, the practice of "contracting out" to neighborhood groups some service activities previously managed only by city government agencies, seems to have grown substantially during the 1980s and 1990s. In Philadelphia prior to 1990, for example, most city-funded housing counseling services for first-time homebuyers (the homeownership program described in chapter 4) had been provided through a city government agency located downtown. Although the city's counseling program at that time was staffed with capable professionals who delivered reliable service, consumers received substantially more benefit through Philadelphia's modified counseling approach in the 1990s, when the city began contracting with many community organizations to make counseling services available at the neighborhood level. Although the city's increased funding commitment to housing counseling in the 1990s was a critical factor in enhancing the performance of this program, the greatest gain came through the placement of this resource in neighborhoods rather than downtown and through the delivery of counseling services by trained neighborhood residents, people with first-hand knowledge of neighborhood housing conditions and local consumer preferences.

Even a successful contracting-out experience of this kind doesn't prove that all sorts of other government-managed programs can be contracted out as well. The success of Philadelphia's housing counseling program was due in large measure to the leadership and commitment of a capable city staff—not a government bureaucracy, but a handful of overworked people who efficiently managed the delivery of funding and technical support to the organizations under contract with OHCD. Laying off these city staff and handing over to neighborhood-based organizations the HUD funding and associated, federally mandated administrative responsibilities would have brought Philadelphia's program to a standstill.

Some of the greatest achievements cited by community organization supporters are, on closer examination, successful government-neighborhood collaborations, in which initiative and leadership is exercised by both public agencies and community groups. Community policing is a a good example of a successful collaboration of this kind. Some of the most effective community policing strategies of the 1990s were initiated by police officers, others by neighborhood volunteers. Police department and neighborhood organization collaboration in testing, refining, and managing these strategies made community policing successful in many urban neighborhoods. However, this experience does not support an argument for turning over police powers to community groups, just as the success of community boards in resolving civil disputes doesn't mean that neighborhood groups should take over the judicial system.

The Kenilworth-Parkside public housing resident management initiative, described at great length in Osborne and Gaebler's *Reinventing Government*, was spearheaded by a capable tenant leader; but this endeavor succeeded only as the result of sustained collaboration between resident leaders and government officials over an extended period. Despite the national recognition earned by Kenilworth-Parkside, relatively few replications of this venture have been successfully undertaken in cities across the country. Why not? Because resident management is a difficult, complicated responsibility for which most resident groups, local housing authorities, and HUD decision makers are not prepared. A change from housing authority management to resident management, followed by resident ownership, requires years of mutual support by resident leaders and public officials, and most resident groups, housing authority managers, and HUD administrators aren't willing or able to sustain elsewhere the level of commitment that made Kenilworth-Parkside succeed.

More recent resident management and ownership initiatives in public housing also illustrate the value of sustained collaborative effort. In Philadelphia, a public housing resident council established a development entity that negotiated the acquisition of Southwark Plaza, a 470–unit public housing site, and obtained financing through the National Equity Fund and other sources to support an extensive demolition and reconstruction program. Although the tenant group provided leadership and applied the political pressure needed to drive this complicated venture to a successful conclusion, the group had no experience in real estate finance, construction management, or rental property management. The resident ownership plan succeeded only because of the high level of participation by nonprofit service organizations, consultants, government agency staff, and funding source representatives associated with the venture. Like Kenilworth-Parkside, Southwark Plaza is a model of successful government-community collaboration, not "government by community."

These observations are not intended to downgrade the role of CDCs but to emphasize the overriding importance of a government-neighborhood dynamic in advancing neighborhood reinvestment. The mayor and other elected government leaders are empowered by the city's voters to take responsibility for crafting and executing public policy that is rational, fair, and relevant to neighborhood needs and interests. Local-government agencies are legally responsible for administering HUD money awarded to the city and for the management of most other resources available to support neighborhoods. City leaders and managers can't and shouldn't abdicate these responsibilities. For their part, good neighborhood organizations know how to assess community strengths and weaknesses better than anyone else, and the best neighborhood organizations know how to draw on public resources to build up community assets and respond to problems and deficiencies. Government and community leaders need to recognize their respective responsibilities, get better acquainted with one another, and establish collaborative working relationships in order to ensure that public policy and neighborhood initiative are joined in ways that produce the best value for the city's communities.

The fact is that the three activities described above—real estate development ventures executed by community organizations, the delivery of services by neighborhood groups under contract with government, and joint endeavors between community and government interests—all represent varying forms of this government-neighborhood dynamic. The interplay between public and community interests can be handled well or badly, depending on the values and capabilities of public agency and neighborhood organization leaders at any given time. In this decade, as in the past, well-intentioned government officials can generate either good or bad policy, and ambitious community groups can use their influence either to mobilize support for constructive reinvestment activities or to politically force commitments of public resources to unproductive and wasteful activities. However, when the government-neighborhood dynamic is managed right, the city's approach to neighborhood reinvestment becomes genuinely collaborative and delivers the most value.

The conventional wisdom about the history of government-community relationships in urban areas is that cities have progressed from a "top-down," authoritarian, 1960s urban renewal approach toward neighborhoods to a "bottom-up," "devolved," community empowerment approach in which policy is increasingly guided by enlightened neighborhood residents. This view differs substantially from the actual history of urban areas since World War II: top-down, bottom-up, and collaborative approaches each have had significant influence on city neighborhoods. The majority of rental and sales housing development produced during the purportedly top-down 1960s and 1970s—through the HUD Section 235, 236, and Section 8 new-construction and substantial-rehabilitation programs (the latter of which differ significantly from the present-day Section 8 program)—were developed or sponsored by community groups, nonprofit organizations, or religious congregations. In most cities, these ventures are still some of the most attractive, best-maintained affordable housing in existence. The 1960s Model Cities program was far more "devolved" and "empowering" of community organizations than any 1990s counterpart. Even the Clinton Administration's Empowerment Zone program, designed to make public resources more accessible to neighborhoods, is far more restrictive than Model Cities. For example, Empowerment Zone funds are awarded to city governments, which are legally responsible for compliance with federal regulations; in contrast, Model Cities money was allocated directly to community organizations, bypassing local government.

Today's environment does differ fundamentally from that of past decades in two important respects: first, several key funding resources that were readily available in past decades (the public assistance payment programs available prior to the enactment of welfare reform legislation, for example) have now dried up considerably or entirely. At the same time, there are more opportunities now than ever before to replicate past successes and to reinforce and expand current ones: good reinvestment policies, development programs, contractual relationships, and specialized collaborations. Knowing about models of success in neighborhood reinvestment doesn't compensate for the major reduction of federal supports that cities experienced during the 1990s. But, in the best-managed cities, the recognition that resources are very limited influences government and neighborhood leaders to be disciplined and sensible in setting public policy goals and creating workable structures for the realization of neighborhood ambitions. Such cities are the places where neighborhood reinvestment is most likely to succeed during the coming decades.

Anyone interested in strengthening CDC participation in neighborhood reinvestment needs to know more about several inherent CDC weaknesses and limitations which must be addressed if CDCs are to succeed over the long term.

CDCs are not broad-based, inclusive organizations. CDCs aren't like block groups, civic associations, or community coalitions that encourage broad community participation in meetings and organization-sponsored events. Instead, CDCs, like other small business ventures, need to be governed by a relatively compact, close-knit group that can make decisions and address problems quickly and efficiently. Because CDCs are, of necessity, closely held organizations, it is important that each CDC establish a means of communicating with, reporting to, and demonstrating accountability to the community at large. This linkage to the broader community can be achieved through the inclusion of local civic association representatives on the CDC governing board; through the scheduling of well-publicized annual meetings, where CDC leaders report on current activities and solicit community comments and advice on future plans; or through an understanding that each CDC venture must be formally supported by the civic association or block group in the area adjacent to the development site. Some clear and consistent link between CDC activities and broader community review and approval is essential. CDC leaders and staff should not be expected to play community-organizing roles; and local civic groups that want to support the work of CDCs in their neighborhoods need to commit themselves to publicizing and promoting CDC activities and to mobilizing support for future CDC plans.

CDCs are led by very small groups. Nearly every CDC is dependent on one key individual or a very small number of individuals (rarely more than four people) who control the group, take most of the responsibility for organizational operation and management, and play the critical role in securing funding and support resources. Many CDCs are vehicles for fulfilling the dreams and ambitions of inspired, energetic individuals, who dominate the organizations they lead or manage. The strength and vitality of a CDC often derives entirely from a single person or a handful of determined individuals; this characteristic of CDCs is not different from leadership patterns found in other small businesses and is not an inherently bad quality (as long as a relationship of accountability to the broader community is maintained). However, CDCs and their supporters fear the day when a "key person" associated with a CDC resigns, moves out of the community, dies, or engages in a bitter dispute with another key person in the organization. To reduce the risk of CDC failure caused by the unexpected loss of a key person, CDC participation in neighborhood reinvestment has to be accompanied by a strengthening of internal organizational capacity.

CDCs can't afford to be "holistic"; they need to stay focused on a restricted scope of activity. How can we improve the neighborhood without organizing neighborhood residents? What good is it to build housing if the schools are in deplorable condition? Why spend time on real estate development when the real issue is jobs for community residents? How can we consider any other activity as being higher in priority than services to young children and their mothers? Reversing disinvestment and restoring economic stability in the most devastated neighborhoods means overcoming a combination of complicated, serious problems, from housing abandonment to unemployment, and meeting a multiplicity of pressing neighborhood needs, from child care to quality public education. Someone has to be devoting a lot of energy, organizing skills, and political influence to addressing each of these problems, but most CDCs are not sufficiently funded to address more than a few of them effectively. Some CDCs, in fact, have to limit themselves to a single issue as their exclusive focus of activity.

Consider, for example, real estate development as an area of CDC activity. A CDC that wants to engage in real estate development has to learn how to perform as well as or better than a private development firm, but usually must do so in a "flat" or declining real estate market with far less profit potential than the markets in which mainstream private development firms are active. The availability of public and foundation funding for CDCs does not make up for this disadvantage. Even the best-qualified, most efficiently managed CDC will not ever be as successful as a reasonably well-managed private development company working in a profitable market. To establish a reliable real estate development capability under these conditions, a CDC needs, at a minimum, to be able to employ two full-time staff: one person devoted exclusively to development financing responsibilities (such as applying for funding, handling coordination with project-funding sources, managing construction-period payouts to contractors), the other devoted exclusively to construction responsibilities (such as supervising the completion of work write-ups and cost estimates, preparing construction bid documents, and managing contractor and subcontractor activity during the construction period). In addition, the CDC executive director has to make a major commitment of time to supervising and promoting the real estate development activities undertaken by the organization. Developer fee income, the profits earned through the completion of real estate development ventures, will not be substantial enough to support these staff positions. CDCs that don't have multiyear commitments of grant funding from government, corporate, or foundation sources to support CDC operating expenses will not succeed in producing reliably from one year to the next or in "moving to scale," that is, increasing substantially the number of housing units or retail square footage produced every year. In addition, most CDCs are going to have trouble finding good people to staff the two key full-time positions necessary to support a real estate development role. The most qualified candidates for jobs such as these make a lot more money and enjoy a lot more job security in private-sector work.

Each CDC has to decide on a primary focus of activity and devote most or all organizational energy and resources to the pursuit of that activity, whether it be housing production, energy conservation, homeless housing and services, job training, or services to children. CDC supporters have to decide how they are going to address the fundamental need for multiyear operating support, for without this CDCs will not be able to sustain their organizational focus for the extended period required to organize plans and produce results. Both CDCs and their supporters have to evaluate the costs and benefits of CDC activities on a regular basis and refine plans as needed to keep expenses under control.

Most CDC ventures are not money makers. In the short term, most CDC ventures will not generate a significant level of net cash flow or trigger short-term "spinoffs" or "ripple effects" that produce additional benefits for the CDC and the community. Unless public agencies deliberately pay inflated developer fees or contractual service fees to community-based organizations, most CDC activities will not earn significant profits or generate funds that can be used to pay for general organizational overhead or for other community improvement activities. Most CDCs working as real estate developers find that they have to use developer fee income to pay for unanticipated construction-period expenses, to deepen subsidy in order to make an apartment-construction venture more affordable for lower-income renters, or to serve as working capital for predevelopment activities associated with the organization's next project. For most CDCs, fee income from managing rental property doesn't generate significant profits until the organization has at least two hundred rental units under management—and even then the profits are not large. Most service contracts held by CDCs (for activities such as job training programs) don't provide "extra" money for general administrative costs unrelated to the services being performed; any savings achieved through CDC cost-efficiency in delivering the services go back to the funding source.

Because nearly all CDCs operate in communities where the business climate and real estate market are weak, most CDC ventures are not going to attract consumers of unsubsidized, "market-rate" housing or "private pay" services. As described above, this characteristic of the CDC working environment means that most or all CDC activity has to be subsidized, limiting economic benefit to the CDC organization. But another equally important implication of operating in a weak economic environment is that most CDC ventures, no matter how well organized and executed, are not going to immediately influence other development and improvement in the community. The construction of a successful new retail center in a previously declining commercial corridor is not necessarily going to encourage private developers and retailers to reexamine their perceptions of the corridor as a place to do business and consider opening stores there, at least not in the short term. The operation of an outstanding job-training program to qualify neighborhood residents for good jobs at fast-growing "data intensive" companies (i.e., firms that specialize in the performance of computerized data-processing tasks) is probably not, by itself, going to attract data-intensive industries to the neighborhood; the trained residents will have to find jobs outside the community.

This limitation has to be recognized by those who fund CDCs and evaluate their performance. In many urban neighborhoods where the economic environment is weakest, CDC activity cannot realistically be expected to have the effect of pumping up property values, bringing housing abandonment to a halt, or attracting private businesses back to the neighborhood. Because no one can predict what it will take to reverse disinvestment in the most devastated urban neighborhoods, both CDCs and their supporters have to be sure that each activity undertaken by a CDC has a significant value of its own and must recognize that even the best CDC endeavors are not likely to generate a chain reaction of private-sector interest, at least not in the short run. Specific performance standards have to be established for evaluating CDC activity, and each activity has to possess a stand-alone value that produces significant benefit for the community, even in the absence of spinoffs or ripple effects.

None of these limitations should be regarded as deficiencies or shortcomings; they are some of the defining characteristics of community-based organizations that, with adequate support, have the potential to bring major benefits to distressed neighborhoods. People who want to help CDCs realize this potential and advance neighborhood reinvestment have to find the best ways to address these issues. Below is a description of three essential elements of a CDC support approach, with recommendations for related actions.

OPERATING SUPPORT

Working CDCs need a reliable source of multiyear core operating support to pay for general administration and front-end expenses associated with new development and service activities. A commitment of multiyear operating support provides job security to CDC program staff and allows the executive director to spend time and energy on implementation tasks rather than fund-raising activities.

Some cities make annual commitments of CDBG funding to provide operating grants to CDC organizations. This approach directly addresses CDC operating needs, but reduces the already limited budget available for bricks-and-mortar production activities: as more CDCs are funded for operations, fewer houses get built or fixed up. A city policy of granting operating support to CDCs also may become politicized and make it impossible to link city funding to CDC performance. For example, if a city has ten city council members representing specified geographic districts (as Philadelphia does), each council member may well feel entitled to demand an operating contract for at least one community-based organization in each district. What if the organization for which the councilperson is advocating isn't a well-managed working CDC? And once the city starts awarding grants to community organizations favored by the local legislature, will it be politically possible to cut off funding to an organization that is performing substantially below par? City governments that fund CDC operations have to determine whether these potentially difficult political problems can be managed effectively without loss of city administration control over neighborhood reinvestment policy.

Philadelphia was able to address the issue of CDC operating support through the creation of an innovative state tax credit program initially known as the Philadelphia Plan and legislatively authorized as the Neighborhood Assistance Program/Comprehensive Service Program (CSP) in 1994. The fact that I had no role in designing the program was probably advantageous, because I never would have imagined that government and the private sector could organize such a progressive approach to this central issue, and my skepticism probably would have slowed down the creation of this new resource.

The CSP legislation allows a 70 percent business tax credit to a business that establishes a ten-year "partnership" with a community-based organization. (Most organizations supported through the program to date have been CDCs, and the neighborhood-improvement orientation of the program makes it likely that this pattern will continue.) The business–community organization relationship, which has to be documented in a proposal to the state and formally approved by the state's Department of Community and Economic Development (DCED) calls for the business to make annual contributions of up to $250,000 to the community organization with which it has associated itself. Based on the value of the tax credit, the real cost of this contribution is as little as twelve cents on the dollar.

This approach represents much more than a tax break for private-sector charity. The CSP program is specifically designed to promote substantive, ongoing working relationships between businesses and CDCs, to the benefit of both parties. The business is expected to take advantage of opportunities to provide the community organization with a variety of in-kind goods and services, which may range from printing a CDC brochure to donating technical assistance from corporate legal counsel. Through its link with the community-based organization, the business can establish a stronger presence in the neighborhood and more effectively market itself to community consumers. (In the first twelve CSP partnerships established in Philadelphia, eight of the participating business entities were banks or insurance companies; another was the Philadelphia Electric Company.)

The CSP legislation also requires that the business-community partnership be linked to a "strategic neighborhood revitalization plan" that is designed to "assess community/neighborhood needs, identify resources, assign priorities and determine an appropriate course of action."[4] The link between the business-community partnership and a strategic plan establishes specific neighborhood improvement goals and priorities as an integral part of the relationship and creates a context for evaluating CDC performance and identifying opportunities for the business to provide supplemental support as needed to address plan-related tasks.

The experience of Mellon Bank and Greater Germantown Housing Development Corporation (GGHDC), two CSP partners that had already enjoyed a close working relationship prior to the enactment of the CSP legislation, illustrates how the state program provided significant added benefit. Through the tax credit, Mellon was able to leverage its post-1994 corporate contributions to GGHDC, bringing substantially more dollars to the CDC at lower cost to the bank. Prior to the 1994 legislation, a $250,000 contribution to GGHDC would have cost the bank $250,000; following enactment of the CSP legislation, the same contribution cost the bank less than $50,000. The formalization of the Mellon/GGHDC relationship through CSP also established a rationale for the bank to make associated contributions of service to the CDC. A manager from Mellon served as a GGHDC board member and assisted with financial oversight tasks. The bank's legal counsel provided some legal services to GGHDC. Mellon's human relations department assisted GGHDC's executive director in working through a difficult personnel problem. None of these activities alone "counted" as a CSP-eligible contribution, but all of them were forms of assistance that Mellon wanted to provide to GGHDC to help nurture and support the link established through CSP. CSP also gave the bank's corporate contributions managers a better opportunity to enlist the volunteer participation of other Mellon staff in GGHDC- and Germantown-related activities; some of these Mellon employees might not have been interested or made themselves available if the special link between the bank and the CDC had not existed.

Every city interested in creating a resource base for CDC core operating support should consider pursuing the enactment of similar state legislation. An initiative based on the CSP model provides an excellent structure for corporate participation in neighborhood reinvestment and creates a major new funding resource for CDCs. Because corporate leadership was probably the single most important factor in the successful organization and implementation of CSP-type legislation, business leaders should be fully involved in the exploration of the opportunity to establish a CSP approach. In Pennsylvania, a long-standing corporation–community organization relationship between the Tasty Baking Company and the community-based Allegheny West Foundation served as a model for the state program. Nelson Harris, a retired Tasty Baking executive, played the primary role in supervising the drafting of the legislation, enlisting corporate support for it, and promoting the program following enactment. A Philadelphia CSP program manager, funded through a state contract, maintains an office at the Greater Philadelphia Chamber of Commerce, further underscoring business leadership of this program.

DEVELOPMENT

Between 1990 and 1995, a scary trend began to emerge among Philadelphia community development corporations. During these years, more resources became available to support CDCs engaged in housing production, but the number of housing units completed or financed by CDCs remained level or decreased. Grant funding, technical assistance, board and staff training, working capital financing and other forms of assistance to CDCs seemed to be having little or no positive effect in advancing their housing production. Different organizations had different explanations for why housing production was falling short of expectations. One high-performance CDC lost its development director and didn't find a suitable replacement for nearly two years. Another CDC committed itself to the pursuit of a large-scale housing venture which, as it subsequently turned out, required several years' effort in order to secure full development financing. Still another CDC found that the cost of rehabilitating recently acquired vacant houses was substantially higher than projected, necessitating a revision of development financing plans and a request for more city subsidy; then the marketing of the houses took longer than anticipated, delaying other plans that had been scheduled to start as the rehab package was completed. All CDCs were adversely affected by an administrative reorganization of city housing programs that involved an eighteen-month transition period, during which all production slowed down; however, production by private developers participating in the city's programs still moved substantially faster than CDC production during this time.

The overriding reason why CDC housing production didn't increase as anticipated during these years was that, after a certain point, no amount of funding or technical support can transform more than a few CDCs into successful real estate development firms. Strong real estate markets downtown or in rising neighborhoods can fuel the for-profit activities of lots of private development firms. But to overcome the significant disadvantage of weak real estate markets in distressed neighborhoods, CDCs need a combination of mature board leadership, timely access to sufficient bricks-and-mortar development funding, capable people to fill CDC housing production staff positions, and available real estate that has been acquired and prepared for construction—a combination not likely to be found by more than a handful of CDCs in any city.

During the past two or three decades in the history of the community development movement, most CDCs and their supporters have assumed without question that a fundamental goal for every CDC was to develop the internal capacity to operate as a real estate developer, with housing production as one of its major activities. More recently, however, there has been a growing recognition that real estate development requires an operating budget and an internal organizational capacity that most CDCs don't have and can't get in the short term. As important, some CDCs have decided that other activities have higher priority than housing development—activities such as business support services and job training programs—and that most CDC resources should be devoted to the pursuit of these higher priorities.

The physical improvement of neighborhoods is important in most communities represented by CDCs, and the need to develop vacant property and produce new community assets has to be addressed in some manner in each such neighborhood. However, a one-size-fits-all approach to CDC participation in development won't work. Every community-based organization needs to evaluate different ways of participating in development and to decide on a form of participation that matches its ambitions and capacity. City government can help an organization find its place by providing varying levels of staff support, technical assistance, and direct funding, based on organizational capacity.

☐ For a civic association, block organization, or other group that has no development ambitions, the city can assign staff to attend meetings and provide information about city-funded programs and services.

☐ For a community group that has no development staff but has organized a housing committee or development committee, the city can provide some training or consultant services to help the group learn more about neighborhood planning, identify key neighborhood reinvestment issues, and consider how these issues should be addressed.

☐ For a community group that has completed basic neighborhood planning and wants to be a developer or serve as a catalyst for development, the city can provide predevelopment grant funds to support the completion of architectural plans, engineering studies, environmental assessments, and feasibility analysis for a particular development venture. OHCD often funded predevelopment grants jointly with the Philadelphia Local Initiatives Support Corporation (LISC), the local office of a national foundation that provides financing for neighborhood reinvestment and community organization capacity building and has a presence in many cities.

☐ For a community group that wants to become a CDC with internal real estate development capacity, the city can offer a modest subsidy as a test of the organization's development capability. OHCD's approach to this initial testing of development capacity was to challenge any newly formed group with development ambitions to rehabilitate one or two houses through the RDA's moderate-rehabilitation financing program (a resource which was available at any time to provide funding for eligible development financing proposals) as a way of demonstrating the group's capability to organize and complete its first development venture.

☐ For a CDC with demonstrated real estate development capability, the city can make development subsidy funding available for larger-scale ventures on a priority basis. Before public funding is committed and released, every developer should be required to compete for development financing or, in the absence of a competitive process, to demonstrate compliance with city underwriting standards. However, cities can and should give higher-priority consideration to development financing proposals submitted by CDCs.

These city supports, most of which cost relatively little, can help community groups interested in development move through a series of activities involving increasing levels of responsibility and opportunity. A key decision that every CDC needs to make is whether to try to establish itself as a real estate developer or to instead limit itself to the role of catalyst for development activity. More CDCs, particularly those organizations that have key goals and priorities unrelated to housing, need to restrict themselves to a catalyst role in order to avoid overextending themselves. As a catalyst for development, a CDC identifies and completes predevelopment planning: organizing the development team, acquiring the real estate, completing basic planning and design work, and securing community support for the development venture. The CDC then selects an established development firm (often a for profit developer with expertise in subsidized housing or an experienced, well-staffed citywide nonprofit development organization) to obtain financing, carry out construction, and earn most or all of the associated developer fee. This approach allows a CDC to retain control over development activity in its service area without having to engage in time-consuming efforts to build an "in-house" real estate development capacity, efforts which may ultimately be unsuccessful. A "catalyst" CDC earns little or no developer fee, but a developer fee has no real value when a CDC's participation in development proves costly or damaging to the organization.

PERFORMANCE STANDARDS

CDCs and their supporters in every city have to get together to establish ways of evaluating the extent to which CDCs are succeeding in the pursuit of their goals. Measuring CDC success in terms of the number of housing units produced each year can be misleading and inappropriate. Developing a unit of special-needs housing for a formerly homeless family is much more complicated than using a city subsidy and a rehabilitation loan to turn around a recently vacated single-family foreclosure property. In addition, a traditional, count-the-houses approach to CDC performance has no relevance to groups that are devoting their energies to goals such as job training and business development.

CDCs and their supporters should create performance standards to guide their evaluation of CDC accomplishments. Because every CDC has a different history, direction, and capacity, CDC performance standards have to be tailored to take these differences into account. However, all CDC performance evaluations can start from common points of departure. The traditional approach, counting units of housing produced each year, is one such point of departure; another is evaluating performance in terms of the achievement of specific goals set forth in a neighborhood strategic plan, including nonhousing goals, such as developing a new day care center or implementing a landscaping program for unimproved vacant lots; another is evaluating performance in terms of the fulfillment of the requirements of a contract for a key CDC activity (for example, a contract for job training or housing counseling services). Performance standards also have to change as CDC plans shift, so that midcourse adjustments (such as the Norris Square Civic Association's adjustment of the Mercado plans) are recognized and assigned appropriate credit.

CDCs themselves, not just CDC funders, should participate in the design and use of performance standards. The first comprehensive performance standards for Philadelphia CDCs were established through a joint effort involving representatives of the Philadelphia Plan, the Philadelphia Association of Community Development Corporations (a coalition of CDC organizations), and the Philadelphia Neighborhood Development Collaborative (a consortium of corporations and foundations that provided selected CDCs with multiyear operating support grants). CDC commitment to and participation in the evaluation process is essential.

The participation of community organizations in neighborhood reinvestment is not a new phenomenon. Community organizations have been engaging in many forms of neighborhood improvement activity for decades—long before the term "community development corporation" became widely known—and many community groups long ago established records of performance that rival the accomplishments of today's most highly regarded CDCs. But today more community-based organizations than ever before are interested in and participating in neighborhood reinvestment activity, and more people—in government, business, the news media, and the community at large—are taking CDCs seriously. Even people who aren't knowledgeable about or interested in working with community organizations acknowledge that CDCs have some measure of political standing—that is, some recognition as legitimate participants in policymaking and in the delivery of public goods and services and as interest groups that have to be dealt with at some level. The most important task for CDCs during the coming years is to secure and broaden this standing in order to insure that reinvestment policy produces the greatest value for the people who live and work in the neighborhoods where these organizations are active. A sustained focus on basic CDC survival and performance concerns will greatly improve the prospects for CDCs and their supporters to further improve CDC standing and bring more benefits to residential communities during the coming years.

6

SECOND-GENERATION SEGREGATION

Take a good look at that woman sitting next to you, that tenant council leader. As you get acquainted with her, you'll come to admire her extraordinary skill at getting and keeping political power within her domain. At the public housing development where she lives, she'll rule for life. Her access to the system and familiarity with the players give her a big advantage over her neighbors and make them dependent on her. Want the work order for your leaking sink to be processed quickly? Want your kid to get into the summer camp? Want a job at the housing authority site office or in a maintenance crew? If she helps you out, your chances are better than most; if you can't get it together with her, you might be out of luck.

She's no Ph.D., but she has this way of talking that lets you know that she understands public housing, knows the workings of the system in the greatest detail, and can use this knowledge to best advantage. She'll refer to policies and regulations that the average person in the neighborhood, in local government, or in the political system never heard of, but which have make-or-break significance in the public housing world because they relate to issues as basic as getting a phone call returned or getting a heater restarted. Sometimes she'll show her power to disrupt a dialogue by interrupting and persistently hammering another participant with hard-to-answer technical questions. At other times, she'll portray herself as an uneducated, disadvantaged person dependent on a system over which she and other residents have little control.

Take a close look at her. She's got a pager in her pocketbook. She's carrying her own cell phone. The housing authority makes sure she gets her share of free tickets to dinners, shows, and sports events. She and a group of other Philadelphia tenant council leaders are going to fly to the West Coast later this week to participate in a four-day conference about public housing issues. They'll get together with their counterparts from other cities, and they'll spend a lot of time talking politics and comparing strategies for getting the most out of the system. In the broad scheme of things, equipping and accommodating her is a relatively small expense but—to be honest—the money paying for her perks and comps could be used to improve living conditions for other public housing tenants. So who's the chump who's picking up the tab for this largesse? Me! the American taxpayer. My federal taxes make her lifestyle possible—and, because I'm not part of the public housing system, there's nothing I can do to change this perverse state of affairs.

Believe me, this woman is a person you could really get to dislike.

By way of contrast, check out the tenant council leader over there. She's no fashion plate, and she doesn't drive a Cadillac; in fact, she doesn't drive at all. She's raised two generations of kids in the past three decades, her own sons and daughters, then a second group of little survivors of the drug scourges of the 1980s and 1990s, their parents adrift, jailed, or dead.

She's not well educated, but she has taken the time to teach herself the intricacies of the public housing system—the rules and procedures that housing authority managers learn at conferences and training seminars. Her knowledge and her ability to work the system help the public housing residents she represents make their way in an environment of hardship and adversity.

Will she use her political power to bump someone up to the top of the plumbing-repair list, get a kid into summer camp, jump a neighbor to the front of the line for a job opportunity? You bet—but is her exercise of power more deserving of criticism than the influence of the more advantaged players in the politically charged public housing system, the elected officials and political appointees who have their fingers on everything from the size of a line item in the modernization budget to the entries in the appointment book of the housing authority's executive director? Her prodding, her pressure tactics, her wheeling and dealing give some residents a clear advantage over others; but the power she's using is linked to human need and is guided by an understanding of the realities of life in public housing, an existence that the vast majority of the elected and appointed officials have never experienced and that many of them don't even care about.

She'll go to that four-day conference, and she'll stay up late talking political tactics with resident leaders from other cities. To continue to be effective, she needs to use every opportunity to expand her understanding of the nuances of the system and to get better acquainted with the cast of characters who populate it, especially those people who have the power to shape policy in Washington and in the big cities.

She knows how to disrupt a meeting, talk tough, and play dumb when these tactics suit her purposes. But no one who's seen her in action will question her credibility or integrity when she says, "I'm doing these things for the residents; I just want the residents to get their fair share." She's bringing value to a hard environment, using a special combination of experience and knowledge that no one else possesses.

Trust me, this woman is a person you could really get to admire and respect.

Despite their differences in character and temperament, these tenant council leaders have a lot in common. In fact, they're the same person.[1]

The worst thing about America's public housing system is not the oppressive environment of the badly designed, deteriorating megaprojects, not the waste and inefficiencies of the local and federal bureaucracies that dispense funding and manage poorly performing programs, not the patronage-ridden housing authority organizations or the politically guided contract awards. The worst thing about public housing and the root cause of all the system's problems is the fundamental segregation of public housing from the social, economic, and political mainstream of urban neighborhood activity. This characteristic of public housing creates unlimited potential for problems, misunderstandings, and conflicts and insures that most residents of public housing in larger cities will live in worse conditions than other citizens.

The public housing system is the second-largest affordable-housing program in the nation, funded at a level of $17 billion in Fiscal 1999.[2] America's largest affordable-housing program is the mortgage interest deduction for homeowners, which cost $58.3 billion in forgone tax revenues in 1995. Both programs are fundamentally inequitable to lower-income citizens, but they deliver inequity in different ways. The mortgage interest deduction, an American institution as venerated and as politically unassailable as Social Security or the Federal Highway Act, provides greatest value to people on the high end of the economy and no value to people in greatest economic need: the citizens who can't afford to buy houses and don't make enough money to itemize deductions. In 1994, 49.6 percent of the total tax savings achieved by Americans taking advantage of the mortgage interest deduction benefited families with incomes of $100,000 and over; another 21 percent benefited families with incomes between $75,000 and $99,999.[3]

In contrast, the public housing system is designed for people at the low end of the economy, from destitute individuals with no income to "working poor" families that don't earn enough to afford good market-rate housing. The public housing system is also an American institution of sorts, but one very different from the mortgage interest deduction. While the mortgage interest deduction is delivered privately and unobtrusively through a tax filing, the public housing system is highly visible, particularly for Americans who live in or near big cities. Many public housing sites are readily distinguishable from other housing because of their poor design, lower-quality construction, and physical isolation from adjacent residential communities. Because urban public housing is readily distinguishable as such, the direct beneficiaries of the public housing system—the people who can be seen entering, leaving, and congregating near the assets developed and maintained through this system—are also readily identifiable, unlike the tax filers who benefit from the mortgage interest deduction.

In concept, the basic principle underlying the public housing system is easy to understand and resembles one of the core elements of the CDBG program: tax dollars pay for the construction and operation of affordable rental housing for some of the nation's neediest households. A local public agency—a housing authority—uses the federal money to develop and manage the rental housing. However, the governance of the public housing system is fundamentally different from the governance of the CDBG program. A city's CDBG program is authorized by the city's mayor and local legislative body, elected officials who are accountable to the voters and who bear legal responsibility for the proper management of this resource. A city housing authority and its programs are governed by an independent board which does not necessarily have a relationship of direct accountability to either local government or the voters. Cities use various methods of selecting housing authority board members. Depending on the wording of state enabling legislation for a particular housing authority, board members may be appointed by the mayor, by the local or state legislature, or by each other. What many board members of city housing authorities do have in common are high visibility in the local political system and a relatively limited understanding of the mechanics of the public housing system.

To receive CDBG funding, a city government must prepare an annual plan describing programs and services proposed for the coming fiscal year and explaining how these activities are going to be coordinated with locally funded government programs such as health and welfare services. The proposed plan has to be advertised, and two public hearings must be held to allow citizens the opportunity to raise questions and offer comments. Following the hearings, the plan must be authorized by the mayor and the local legislative body prior to submission to HUD and receipt of funding. In contrast, a city housing authority does not have to prepare an annual plan for detailed review and authorization by anyone except the authority's board and a relatively small number of HUD officials. A housing authority does not have to demonstrate that public housing programs and services are connecting with and supporting other local-government activities, and the budget for the upcoming fiscal year—incorporated into an "Annual Contributions Contract" (ACC) between the housing authority and HUD—is not subject to approval by the mayor and local legislature, except in the relatively few cities where the housing authority is controlled by city government.

The public housing system is as complicated, restrictive, and inflexible as the CDBG program is straightforward and discretionary. Consider the following differences between CDBG and public housing programs.

☐ CDBG funding can be used to produce new housing anywhere in the city, and the CDBG budget is an especially valuable resource for supporting new construction in economically depressed neighborhoods. In contrast, most public housing production in past decades has been subject to congressionally mandated "site and neighborhood standards," which can make it impossible to develop public housing in locations termed "impacted"—that is, in economically depressed or nonwhite neighborhoods in need of reinvestment.

☐ If a property purchased years ago with CDBG funding—a house or an apartment building—is now deteriorated, vacant, and infeasible to rehabilitate (a situation that rarely occurs), a city housing director can use currently available CDBG money to demolish the property and convey the resulting cleared site to a private or nonprofit entity. In contrast, if a property purchased years ago with public housing funding is now deteriorated, vacant, and infeasible to rehabilitate (a situation that frequently occurs in larger cities), a housing authority director who wants to demolish and convey the property must prepare a written proposal for submission to a national HUD clearinghouse, and then wait for approval or rejection. The process takes months, and approval is not guaranteed.

☐ City government leaders and managers can use their own judgment to determine how much CDBG funding should be committed to support the development of a particular affordable-housing venture, can establish restrictions on the amount of public subsidy to be devoted to any one development venture, and can waive these restrictions if they feel that exceptions should be made under special circumstances. In contrast, the development of public housing is governed by HUD-mandated "total development cost" (TDC) standards which impose strict limitations on the amount of money that can be committed to a public housing development venture. The imposition of TDC standards makes it hard for local housing authorities to develop public housing with amenities comparable to those found in market-rate housing (such as porches and yards) and builds in an incentive to produce higher-density public housing as the best way to keep costs down. The result: the poorly designed high-rises and barracks-style low-rises that distinguish public housing sites in many cities, conveying a message of inadequacy and failure.

These characteristics give public housing two more serious disadvantages that are readily apparent in larger cities. First, housing authority pay scales are higher than those of other local public agencies. The best housing authority executive directors and managers, the people who really understand how to deal with the complexities of the public housing system, have to be paid substantially higher salaries than most other city government officials, because their knowledge and expertise is a relatively scarce commodity. Second, most available housing authority resources have to be devoted to maintaining the authority's weak asset base, the unattractive, hard-to-manage public housing sites developed under past HUD policies. No other public entity at the local level—not even a publicly owned hospital or utility system—is saddled with a comparable combination of restrictive regulations, limited local discretion, and low-value, poorly performing assets.

The public housing system is particularly resistant to fundamental structural change, because, although almost anyone can be blamed for the current failings of the system, no single party can be held solely and ultimately responsible for the task of reform and long-term improvement.

For example, *Congress* might be blamed for not amending public housing legislation to eliminate burdensome statutory requirements and to provide more local discretion and flexibility. But one could also maintain the opposite: that Congress has done its share to try to correct underlying systemic problems. "Home rule" legislation included in the 1998 housing act promotes local discretion by giving city governments the opportunity to actually take charge of and assume full responsibility for public housing resources. More radical congressional actions would produce bad results. A congressionally authorized giveaway of public housing funds, with few or no strings attached, to local housing authorities or local governments would guarantee local misspending.

Critics of Congress's role in maintaining the public housing status quo need to understand that, like all forms of legislation, congressional action is a "blunt instrument";[4] it cannot be fine-tuned to fit a variety of local circumstances. For example, the "site and neighborhood standards," described above as a serious limitation on flexibility and local discretion, were enacted by Congress for a good purpose: to prevent the ghettoizing of public housing residents. Rather than asking Congress to abolish these standards, shouldn't local housing authorities do more to promote the development of public housing in racially and economically mixed neighborhoods?

HUD could be blamed for not reforming the flawed administrative structure of the public housing system and for not giving local housing authorities more power to manage their own resources. But HUD leadership has made substantial efforts to do just that. In 1993, HUD secretary Henry Cisneros challenged Mayor Rendell to appoint himself and City Council president John Street to the board of the Philadelphia Housing Authority and take direct responsibility for the governance of PHA, at the time one of the nation's most poorly managed housing authorities. In return, Cisneros offered a package of funding awards, waivers of administrative regulations, and commitments of HUD staff support for Philadelphia public housing initiatives. Mayor Rendell accepted the challenge, and the city/HUD collaboration produced many benefits for Philadelphia during the remainder of the Clinton Administration.

But even this extraordinary initiative did not fundamentally change Philadelphia's public housing system, because it did not provide relief from congressionally imposed burdens such as the regulations described earlier. The changes that resulted from Cisneros's action produced great value for selected public housing sites but did not produce substantive systemic reform. During the 1990s, HUD implemented new programs and regulatory changes that promoted mixing of public housing and market-rate housing, removed disincentives that had previously discouraged public housing residents from getting off welfare and seeking employment, and cracked down on public housing–related fraud. HUD probably could have done even more during the 1990s, had agency leadership and staff not needed to devote so much time to defending themselves against congressional attempts to eliminate HUD altogether, to abolish the 1937 enabling legislation for public housing, and to apply other meat-cleaver solutions to public housing problems.

City governments might be blamed for not lobbying for more effective HUD and congressional action to reform public housing and for not taking more initiative to seize control of local public housing systems. But lobbying and advocacy have their limits—and predominantly Democratic city mayors and legislators could not be expected to have substantial influence over the Republican, predominantly suburban and rural legislators who controlled Congress during most of the 1990s. Furthermore, most city government leaders are not well versed in the regulatory and administrative complexities of the public housing system. A city government takeover of local public housing could very likely have the same effect that HUD takeovers had in Philadelphia and other cities during the 1980s and 1990s—they made conditions even worse. Why would any mayor want to accept responsibility for all the disadvantages of public housing in its current condition—the deteriorated assets, the burdensome regulations, the political claims on the system? Why not wait till the federal government has made at least some headway in straightening out the whole mess?

One could blame the *board members* of local housing authorities for not leading a reform effort. But in many cities board members are appointed for the express purpose of representing specific constituencies who have a stake in the status quo—a racial or ethnic group, a trade union, or a political interest; they have no mandate or incentive to launch a reform campaign. The *executive director and staff* of the housing authority could be faulted for not cleaning house of political dead weight and for not collaborating more extensively with city government agencies; but, in the absence of strong political support from the authority's board or the city's mayor, such staff initiatives would lead nowhere. Housing authority *resident leaders* could be criticized for their aggressive pursuit of their own self-interest and for their unwillingness to advocate for structural reform to improve the system as a whole. But why should resident leaders be the first to give away political power to support reform? Before residents are asked to give up anything, shouldn't the other, more influential players in the system take the lead, to demonstrate that—this time—the proposed reform will actually be implemented and benefit all concerned (unlike the failed efforts of past years)? And the *general public* could be blamed for not ad-

vocating more strongly for fundamental changes in the public housing system, for not generating a level of citizen outrage that would
compel improvement. But the general public has little or no knowledge of what the public housing system is or how it works: the average person can't distinguish an ACC from a TDC. How could the
general public reasonably be expected to mobilize effectively for a
comprehensive change in the nation's public housing system?

One element of the system, the Section 8 rental assistance program, was designed to overcome the isolation of public housing–
assisted residents and promote the integration of assisted families
into stable residential communities—in effect, to provide a benefit
for lower-income families in a way that would be as unobtrusive
as the mortgage interest deduction. The Section 8 program gives
an income-eligible individual or family rental assistance, a government payment to make up the funding gap between the "fair market" rent of a privately owned and managed apartment and the
amount that the person or family can afford to pay. The Section 8
subsidy pays the difference between the resident's share of the rent,
an amount not exceeding 30 percent of income (the HUD affordability standard), and the actual rent amount. The housing authority commits its share of the rent through the execution of a contract
with the owner or manager of the rental property where the resident lives. For example, a three-person family with an annual income of $12,000 can lease a two-bedroom apartment renting at
$450 a month (an amount well within the 1998 $700–per-month
maximum "fair market rent" established by HUD for two-bedroom
units located in the Philadelphia area). The family's share of the
rent is $300 per month, or 30 percent of the family's $1,000
monthly income. The Section 8 subsidy, made available through a
contract between the housing authority and the landlord, pays the
$150 difference between the family's payment and the $450 rent.

Most Section 8 assistance takes the form of "tenant-based" subsidy. When an individual or family reaches the top of the Section
8 waiting list, the housing authority issues a certificate of eligibility
to receive rental assistance. The resident then looks for suitable housing in a neighborhood of the resident's own choosing. A landlord
willing to rent to a Section 8 tenant must be found; landlords are

not legally obligated to rent to Section 8 recipients, and many land-lords won't even consider Section 8 certificate holders.

Section 8 rental assistance may also be site-based; that is, linked with a specific rental property rather than issued to a tenant. In site-based rental assistance (ineptly termed "project-based" in HUD regulations), the subsidy is awarded to a specific rental apartment and remains associated with that dwelling unit for the length of the funding contract; any income-eligible tenant leasing the apart-ment receives the rental assistance benefit. Site-based assistance is particularly useful in complementing CDBG funding for affordable–rental housing development ventures: the CDBG subsidy helps pay for bricks-and-mortar construction costs, and the Section 8 rental assistance (often awarded to a small proportion of the total num-ber of units being developed, in order to avoid creating Section 8 enclaves) helps support operations by assuring a reliable flow of rental income for as long as the Section 8 contract remains in effect.

The disadvantages of the Section 8 program have become in-creasingly apparent in recent years. Some of these disadvantages are federally imposed; others are home-grown at the local level. The program's most serious problem is the use of Section 8 rental as-sistance to address the housing needs of formerly homeless people and others with very little income. In 1988 HUD instituted a re-quirement that preference be given to applicants for Section 8 and other HUD-funded programs who were homeless or experiencing some other form of housing crisis. This federally imposed prefer-ence system was discontinued in 1994, but some cities (including Philadelphia) retained for years afterward, in some form, a Section 8 priority for homeless people. The problem with this use of Sec-tion 8 subsidy is that former residents of homeless shelters and other impoverished people have a high level of need for support-ive services—services as varied as literacy training, child care, job placement, and drug/alcohol treatment—along with a need for case management to make the delivery of these services as effective as possible. But most properties available for rent to residents with tenant-based Section 8 certificates are not operated by settlement houses or other human services providers; they're operated by profit-motivated landlords or rental agents who—like most people in the real estate business in any metropolitan area—are not interested in or capable of providing human services to their tenants. As a result, although many formerly homeless people or other citizens with critical economic needs obtain housing with the help of Section 8 rental assistance, the health, social, or economic problems which caused or contributed to their need for affordable housing are not addressed.

The absence of supportive services and case management for holders of Section 8 tenant-based certificates is one cause of neighborhood complaints about the conduct of renters living in Section 8–supported properties: the kids don't attend school, the adults don't have jobs, housekeeping and maintenance of the front steps and walk are poor or nonexistent; loud music is heard late at night; the residents just don't fit in. Racism underlies many, but not all, such complaints. But even after discounting for racism and other forms of "not in my back yard" (NIMBY) antagonism to subsidized housing, the fact remains that formerly homeless people and very low-income people are going to need service support in order to become responsible tenants and valued neighbors, and this support is not an integral part of the Section 8 program.

In theory, the need for supportive services and case management could be addressed by referring formerly homeless people and other very low-income people to rental units owned and managed by CDCs, nonprofit groups, and private development organizations possessing in-house service delivery and case management capability. These service-linked rental units could be awarded Section 8 site-based assistance contracts. However, a housing authority's ability to forge this link is very limited. HUD regulations prohibit a housing authority from awarding more than 15 percent of its total Section 8 budget for site-based assistance; 85 percent or more must go toward tenant-based assistance. As a result, the developers and rental property managers best able to provide service support to Section 8–assisted residents have relatively little opportunity to do so; conversely, the Section 8 residents most in need of services often end up signing leases with rental agents or landlords who have no service orientation or commitment.

Some housing advocates strongly oppose proposals to allow housing authorities to increase site-based assistance to a level above the 15 percent limit. In Philadelphia, an initiative by Mayor Rendell to pursue this change and introduce other elements of flexibility into the Section 8 program was labeled "clustering" by a local newspaper[5] and denounced by housing advocates as an attempt to force people into "projects"—notwithstanding the fact that all of the proposed increase in site-based assistance would be awarded to community development corporation ventures or other housing integrated with existing neighborhood fabric and supported by local residents. At the same time, advocates for the homeless insisted that PHA not change its local "homeless preference" and continue to give first priority in the award of tenant-based Section 8 certificates to people referred out of the city's emergency shelter system—the people most in need of the services that could be made available in association with site-based rental assistance. In the view of these advocates, giving Section 8 renters maximum freedom of choice in seeking a place to live was a higher priority than linking these residents with available service support.

The homeless advocates weren't wrong in pressing for priority use of Section 8 as a resource to benefit formerly homeless people. Getting people out of shelter housing and back into a community environment is a critically important element of any effective strategy for addressing homelessness, and rental assistance is the most direct way to achieve this result. What was wrong about this advocacy was that it promoted a policy of sending thousands of people from shelters to neighborhoods without requiring any commitment to a plan of action—a plan centered on education, training, and job placement, with associated service support—to give them the best opportunity to reduce dependency on public resources and move toward self-sufficiency. Neither Philadelphia's housing authority nor the city government, any more than their counterparts elsewhere, had enough funding to launch a comprehensive program of supportive services and case management for all former shelter residents. And HUD regulations did not provide sufficient opportunity to modify the local Section 8 budget to achieve a better blend of rental assistance and services.

These limitations and restrictions force local government and neighborhood leadership to make a difficult choice between two unfair alternatives: is it better to press for the relocation of people from shelters to neighborhoods with little or no service support, based on the assumption that any neighborhood-based housing is preferable to a shelter (besides being less costly than shelter housing) and that Section 8–related complaints amount to little more than racism, NIMBYism, or a need for more tolerance and mutual respect? Or does it make more sense to pursue Mayor Rendell's position, reducing housing choice for Section 8–assisted citizens in order to insure their relocation to rental properties with on-site services that could provide more direct benefit? Neither party was entirely right or wrong—but a more flexible Section 8 regulatory structure, allowing greater local discretion in allocating rental assistance and associated services, would have offered the parties engaged in Philadelphia's Section 8 debate the best opportunity to resolve their differences and do more for people receiving Section 8 assistance.

The problem of the regulatory inflexibility of the Section 8 program became particularly evident in Philadelphia in 1996–1997, when the city tried to support a proposal by HELP, a New York–based developer of transitional and permanent housing for formerly homeless people, to build a ninety-unit complex at a West Philadelphia site. HELP had been successful in New York in part because New York City was able to provide funding from the municipal budget to underwrite the organization's service-intensive approach to homelessness. No comparable funding source existed in Philadelphia's city budget, and Section 8 regulations did not give the Philadelphia Housing Authority the ability to use public housing funds to support the mix of subsidized rents and associated services that had made HELP a national model. As a result, the city and the housing authority had to painstakingly assemble a combination of resources—including short-term rental vouchers funded through the city's federal HOME allocation, several rental assistance certificates funded through the city's federal Housing Opportunities for People with AIDS (HOPWA) award, and other funding—to make the HELP venture feasible. Ironically, HELP's founder and executive director through 1993 was Andrew Cuomo, who subsequently left the organization to become secretary of HUD. With more flexibility and local discretion over Section 8 funding, replicating a successful model imported from another city would be relatively easy, but it is often hard, if not impossible, under the current Section 8 regulations.

Efforts to change the public housing system during the past decade have brought some benefits but have not decisively addressed the conditions of isolation and segregation to which most participants in the system are subject. In addition, most 1990s public housing reform initiatives have actually had the effect of substantially reducing public housing as a resource for urban residents. Preventing further reduction of a city's supply of public housing should be a priority concern for supporters of neighborhood reinvestment, because no other resource is available to help a city's lowest-income residents.

By the end of the 1990s, the term of most Section 8 rental assistance contracts had been reduced from five years to one as the result of congressional and HUD belt tightening. (Congress has continued to renew existing Section 8 contracts every year as part of its authorization of the federal housing budget, but this annual renewal of contract authority is not guaranteed and could be reduced or discontinued in any future year). Prior to this change in the Section 8 contract term, housing developers, local and state government housing finance agencies (such as RDA and PHFA), and private lenders felt safe in assuming that, based on past congressional practice, Section 8 contract renewals would occur automatically, replenishing funding for existing contracts indefinitely. Based on this shared assumption, Section 8 site-based assistance had been a key element in financing affordable–rental housing development ventures. Because a Section 8 contract associated with a particular rental venture was assumed to guarantee a steady stream of income linked to the rent-assisted units, the developer of such a venture could use the expectation of this income stream to obtain mortgage financing. Because many mortgage lenders shared this view of the Section 8 contract as an assured source of income—more specifically, as income available for payment of debt service—a lot of mortgage money was available for Section 8–assisted ventures. The mortgage financing awarded to these ventures, in turn, reduced the amount of city development subsidy needed as a source of development financing, leaving more subsidy available to fund other housing production. The expected availability of Section 8 as a long-term financing resource assured developers that their operating position was strong, made private lenders feel confident that debt would be repaid, and enabled cities to hold down the level of subsidy needed to support rental housing development ventures. All of these favorable consequences associated with the expectation of automatic Section 8 contract renewals and long-term Section 8 availability were undermined when Section 8 contract terms were reduced to one year. The result: developers could no longer obtain mortgage financing based on Section 8 as a debt service repayment source, and in consequence already-scarce city development subsidy funding had to be used to make up for the loss.

The Clinton Administration's major new capital investment program for public housing, known as HOPE VI, provided large subsidies (often tens of millions of dollars) to support the transformation of deteriorated or obsolete public housing sites into well-designed, mixed-income communities. The HOPE VI subsidy finances a portion of the cost of demolishing high-rise towers, bulldozing low-rise barracks, and developing new site plans with attractive townhouses for sale and rent within a network of streets and green spaces. A HOPE VI site becomes a new neighborhood, in which public housing is integrated with market-rate sales and rental housing. Development ventures financed through HOPE VI are among the best-designed subsidized housing produced in urban neighborhoods in years.

But HOPE VI has two serious limitations. The selection process for HOPE VI projects is highly competitive, and only a portion of the development proposals submitted to HUD each year will be funded. Because the HOPE VI budget line item is a relatively small portion of the overall public housing budget, the vast majority of run-down, badly designed public housing sites are never going to receive HOPE VI funding. An even more significant problem is the fact that all HOPE VI–funded development involves a substantial reduction in value for lower-income residents of a city to which this funding is awarded. Reducing density and producing mixed-income housing through implementation of a HOPE VI plan means drastically cutting back the number of subsidized rental units. In Philadelphia's Schuylkill Falls HOPE VI venture, for example, a former 714–unit conventional public housing site completed in 1955 is being transformed into a community containing 304 newly constructed units of sales and rental housing, 150 of which will be available to public housing residents—a net loss of 564 public housing units. In the Martin Luther King Plaza HOPE VI venture, for which a Philadelphia development team received a $25.2 million funding award in 1998, a 537–unit site is being converted to 330 sales and rental units. A total of 85 of the newly developed units will be public housing, resulting in a net reduction of 452 public housing units. King Plaza residents who don't move into the newly developed housing are given one-year Section 8 certificates, as is customary at other HOPE VI sites across the nation when the new venture results in a downsizing of public housing. But, in light of the shortened duration of Section 8 contracts, this offset amounts to one year's worth of value, not a replacement of the asset lost as the result of the HOPE VI–funded venture. Some people say that Congress's annual renewal of Section 8 certificate funding is all but guaranteed. But a lot of people thought that Congress would never legislate an end to welfare; by comparison, congressional cutbacks or discontinuation of Section 8 funding would be relatively easy.

What's wrong with using federal money to support the development of outstanding mixed-income communities in degraded urban areas? Isn't it about time that more federal housing money was spent on attracting middle-class people back to the city? The answer is that, while supporting middle-class residency in the city should be a high priority for everyone, the funding used to promote this priority should not be taken from the only resource available to house a city's lowest-income citizens—and that is exactly how HOPE VI works. The trade-off for millions of subsidy dollars spent to attract a higher-income class of residents to a former public housing site is the reduction of potentially valuable subsidized housing resources for low-income citizens. One could argue that, under the existing public housing system, these resources are being squandered on the "modernization" and maintenance of failed public housing sites, sites that should be leveled and refashioned as new communities through the award of HOPE VI funding. But doesn't everyone share responsibility for the severely flawed public housing system that produced these failures? And shouldn't we also share responsibility for reforming the system, rather than acquiesce in the depletion of affordable-housing resources that accompanies every HOPE VI award?

In 1996 Congress passed the Omnibus Consolidated Recissions and Appropriations Act (OCRA), containing a provision that, in effect, compelled housing authorities to demolish deteriorated older public housing sites without providing capital funding to replace the demolished units. Section 202 of OCRA requires local housing authorities to downsize or completely eliminate public housing sites of three hundred units or more which have a vacancy rate of 10 percent or more and which cannot be "reasonably revitalized" with existing HUD funding. If the cost of making the occupied rental units at these sites "viable," based on HUD standards, exceeds the cost of providing rental assistance, the nonviable units must be removed from the public housing inventory and replaced with Section 8 certificates.

Section 202 standards defining what constitutes "viability" insure that many large, older, city-based public housing sites will be demolished. To be viable, revitalization costs must not exceed 90 percent of the TDC standard and must be lower than the cost of replacing rental units with Section 8 certificates. Funding to support revitalization must be available in the housing authority's budget. Housing density at the affected sites must be reduced to a level "approaching that which prevails in the community for similar types of housing (typically family), or a lower density," and the income mix of residents must be broadened.[6]

Sites that fail the Section 202 viability test get downsized or demolished, with one-year Section 8 certificates issued to departing residents. The result is a substantial loss of the public housing asset. For example, a Section 202 assessment of Cambridge Plaza, a 372–unit North Philadelphia site first occupied in 1957 called for demolition of two high-rise towers containing a total of 248 apartments. Residents of the approximately 200 still-occupied units in these high-rises would get Section 8 certificates and move out. The remaining 124 units at the site, located in low-rise townhouses, would be rehabilitated or reconstructed, but none of the 248 high-rise units would be replaced with new public housing. The overall result of these activities: a downsizing of the public housing asset at Cambridge Plaza from 372 units to 124, a 69 percent cutback.[7]

People who aren't well acquainted with public housing may feel that the Section 202 requirements represent a positive, pragmatic approach, in which HUD tells housing authorities to either fix up now or go out of business. This view overlooks the fact that regulations imposed on housing authorities by Congress and HUD during past decades played a significant role in making older public housing sites as bad as they are today. TDC standards compelled local housing authorities to develop public housing at densities substantially higher than "that which prevails in the community." The poor design of many public housing sites, strongly influenced by the TDC standards and other HUD-imposed limitations, helps insure that, for many older sites, revitalization costs are going to be substantially higher than the cost of issuing Section 8 certificates. The Section 202 assessment stacks the deck, leaving local housing authorities no real chance to develop an orderly exit strategy from the old system (in which HUD regulations allowed little opportunity to do more than "modernize" and maintain bad public housing sites) and to reposition themselves to comply with completely new HUD standards.

The big losers in the Section 202 game are the residents of older public housing sites who have committed themselves to working with their local housing authority to improve the places where they live, based on the expectation that resources available under the pre–Section 202 HUD funding system would be provided to support these improvements. The Section 202 regulations, in effect, inform these residents that all bets are off, that the sites where they live are now nonviable and that there is no alternative to downsizing or elimination. The *Philadelphia Inquirer* quoted Virginia Wilks, tenant council leader at Richard Allen Homes, as saying, "If we have to barricade ourselves within these projects, we will do that," upon implementation of Section 202 measures at Richard Allen.[8] The Section 202 approach unfairly puts resident leaders like Wilks in an untenable position, setting them up to be characterized as defenders of failed past policies. Section 202 takes resources from these residents without providing any opportunity to effect a transition from long-standing federal policies to the new mandates.

The "home rule" provision of the 1998 federal housing act, allowing a city government to get permission from HUD to take over its local housing authority, is not really a comprehensive solution to the problem of public housing, because, as indicated above, this measure simply transfers to local government a larger share of the burden of responsibility for the flawed existing system. Exercising home rule gives a city political control of a housing authority—but also imposes on city government all the disadvantages of the system. By linking itself formally with the local housing authority, a city government exposes itself to legal liability for public housing problems and positions itself as a "deep pocket" for claims against the public housing system. Home rule does not offer a package of funding and regulatory relief comparable to that offered Mayor Rendell by Secretary Cisneros in 1993—only an opportunity to shoulder more responsibility for public housing. Home rule may be a good option for cities where public housing is functioning reasonably well. But exercising this option is the wrong choice for cities with housing authorities on the HUD "troubled" list or housing authorities with significant capital or operating problems of any kind.

A really effective solution for public housing has to offer everyone better value than the existing system provides, while also requiring everyone to take greater responsibility for making the system work. A new and better approach to public housing reform has to be oriented toward big cities where public housing conditions are worst, and has to deliver several values simultaneously: more flexibility, discretion, and control at the city level; no reduction in benefits for current public housing residents; more effective use of public housing as a resource for formerly homeless people and others with specialized housing and service needs; less waste of funds on administrative expenses and overhead costs; and more direct accountability to the general public.

All of these issues can be addressed to everyone's advantage if local city governments and their housing authorities are given an opportunity to begin converting public housing funds into funding that has a level of flexibility and local discretion similar to CDBG. Such an approach could be implemented in the following manner.

First, *Congress* enacts legislation authorizing HUD to allow cities and local housing authorities to convert up to twenty percent of their annual public housing funding to "value-added" funding no longer governed by public housing regulations. Subject to HUD approval of an application for conversion of funds, the affected funding is made subject to the more flexible, less restrictive CDBG regulations (with one change, noted below).

Then *HUD* publishes regulations inviting city governments and local housing authorities to apply for this benefit through submission of a joint proposal authorized by the board of the city's local housing authority and by the mayor and local legislative body. HUD requires its Community Planning and Development division, currently responsible for the administration of CDBG funding and its Public and Indian [sic] Housing division, currently responsible for the administration of public housing, to collaborate in managing this new approach.

In any city where there is interest in pursuing this approach, *city government and the local housing authority* then work together to organize their city's plan for the conversion of public housing funds. The plan is made part of a housing authority board resolution and is published in the city's *Consolidated Plan* application, submitted to HUD as part of the annual CDBG funding process. The conversion plan includes the following elements.

☐ All public housing funds proposed for conversion to value-added funds are used to support one or more of the following activities: new construction and vacant property rehabilitation, to produce housing for low- and very low-income residency; supportive services and case management for people eligible for public housing; short- and long-term rental assistance; and operating reserves to support affordable–rental housing ventures. (The last two activities are not eligible for funding under CDBG regulations but would be permitted uses of value-added funds.)

☐ Each dollar of public housing funds proposed for conversion to value-added funds is matched by a dollar of city funding committed to the activities proposed; the source of the local funding match may be

CDBG, HOME, or other federal funding awarded to the city, or the city's operating or capital budget.

☐ The plan submitted to HUD documents specific ways in which the value-added funds used to support the proposed activities will produce greater benefit for low- and very-low-income residents than would be possible if these funds remained subject to public housing regulations and controls. The plan shows that every housing unit produced with value-added funding supports at least two of the following goals: racial/ethnic integration; income mixing; and/or implementation of a neighborhood strategic plan.

☐ Neither public housing funds proposed for conversion to value-added funds nor the local funding used as the required one-for-one match may be used to support administrative expenses. Existing HUD "caps" limiting the use of CDBG and HOME funds for general administration are held in place.

☐ All residents currently participating in the existing public housing system are protected against displacement associated with activities supported by the value-added funds or the local funding match. The plan submitted to HUD is required to show that any replacement housing proposed for residents of existing public housing sites offers equal or greater housing quality and housing choice than the units to be vacated.

Who controls and administers the converted public housing funding and the local matching funds the housing authority or the city government? Each city can address this question in its own way, based on local preferences and existing management capabilities. All of the funding can be consolidated and managed by one entity; or, alternatively, funding can be distributed or mixed, based on whether a city agency or a housing authority department is going to take primary responsibility for a particular funded activity.

After five years of successful performance, HUD may authorize a city and its housing authority to apply for the conversion of a larger portion of the public housing award—perhaps up to 50 percent—to value-added funding.

Implementation of this approach would create a new resource to support the financing of suitably located affordable housing, managed by capable private and nonprofit development organizations. Decisions about where to locate the housing, how much to spend on developing it, and how to blend subsidized and market-rate units would be made at the local level. Some rental assistance could be made available in the form of fifteen-year contracts with housing developers interested in leveraging debt financing. Other rental assistance could be provided in shorter-term increments, for use as an incentive in association with transitional programs for formerly homeless people or with welfare-to-work initiatives. Residents of failing older public housing sites would be offered a wider variety of housing options, and these deteriorated sites would be depopulated more systematically, with minimal disruption. Tenant councils would position themselves to work more effectively with private and nonprofit developers to redesign and upgrade existing public housing sites or to develop and manage replacement housing built at better locations. The whole Annual Contributions Contract system of yearly funding for the modernization and maintenance of poorly performing existing assets would be transformed into an investment program supported by long-term financing.

One key element of this investment program, not possible under the existing system, would be the use of value-added funding to create operating reserves, "endowments" that generate interest and dividend income and thus, over an extended period, reduce rent levels at housing sites operated by private, nonprofit, or CDC development organizations. One example of the "endowment" approach that could be replicated widely with value-added funding was pioneered by Women's Community Revitalization Project (WCRP), a Philadelphia CDC committed to addressing the housing and service needs of low-income, female-headed households. For each WCRP rental venture, the organization used a portion of its developer fee to capitalize a reserve fund, invest the fund principal, and, through payouts of fund principal and earned interest, write down rents for low- and very-low-income tenants for up to fifteen years. For example, a person with a disability who was dependent on public assistance might have $140 available to spend on housing per month (i.e., 30 percent of a public assistance payment of about $466). A one-bedroom apartment developed by WCRP would ordinarily cost about $355. By capitalizing a reserve of $36,605 and investing the principal for a 5 percent annual return, WCRP could generate an income stream to subsidize this

tenant's $215–per-month "affordability gap" (the difference be-
tween the apartment rent and the amount this tenant could afford)
through payouts of fund principal and earned interest over a
fifteen-year period. With access to more flexible public housing
funds, an organization like WCRP could produce more supportive
housing and would not need to sacrifice its developer fees in order
to address the housing affordability needs of the members of its
primary beneficiary population.

The value-added approach would transform the existing public housing budget into a readily usable neighborhood reinvestment
resource. All the participants in the existing system would gain substantial benefit through the implementation of this approach. Congress and HUD would have a workable exit strategy from the
existing public housing system into a new one that provides much
greater overall value at no additional cost. HUD would retain its
supervisory authority but would refocus this authority more con-
structively: on the creation of more housing like the currently scarce
HOPE VI–funded development ventures rather than on continued
oversight of the distribution of federal money to prop up the flawed
existing system. City governments would have access to a valuable
new funding resource and an opportunity to link city government
and public housing interests without having to commit to a city
takeover strategy, a strategy that many public housing residents (as
well as other citizens) would oppose and that would expose the city
unnecessarily to legal liability for the problems of the existing public housing system. Public housing board members would be able
to deliver more benefit to the constituencies they represent, because
value-added funding would produce faster and better results. Currently, for example, there isn't much value in holding a housing
authority board position as an advocate for a constituency such as
the city's Latino population under circumstances in which the existing public housing system isn't producing and maintaining housing reliably for Latinos or anyone else. Under the new structure,
housing authority staff would be given a mandate to collaborate
with their city agency counterparts and could use the increased access this relationship brings to influence the flow of city resources
to address public housing concerns. Public housing tenant councils would not lose any of their political power and would posi-

tion themselves much more effectively to participate in housing development and property management joint ventures than is possible under the existing system. And the general public would finally have a direct relationship to a restructured, improved public housing system, accompanied by a real opportunity to influence plans for the delivery of this renewed resource, to the benefit of citizens and neighborhoods. Within five years, a city government and a local housing authority could be sharing responsibility for as much as 70 percent of a city's public housing resources and, through their collaboration in the value-added approach, each party could achieve a one-for-one leveraging of dollars committed to this endeavor, in the form of readily accessible, readily usable funds.

Not every city and housing authority will be ready and willing to take advantage of the value-added approach. Some city governments will not be prepared to make the substantial commitment of matching funds that this approach requires. Some housing authorities will not be willing to enter into collaborative working relationships with their respective city governments. Some cities and housing authorities will not be able to accept the managerial self-discipline needed to assume responsibility for the delivery of substantial new resources while holding down administrative costs. And some neighborhood organizations and public housing tenant councils are not going to favor a departure from the existing public housing system. But, for those who pursue it, this approach provides an orderly, honorable departure from the current highly restrictive and inequitable system and offers a real opportunity to establish a stronger base of resources to meet the most pressing housing needs of urban neighborhoods.

7

WORKING THE
ECONOMY

The YouthBuild program was just starting up in Ludlow, a community termed "the forgotten neighborhood" by some of its long-time residents. The place had known a generation of desertion and downgrading. "Marlboro Country" was what a neighborhood leader had called it back in the seventies, reflecting disparagingly on the community's substantial vacant-land acreage. Ludlow's vacant lots ranged in size from twenty-by-forty parcels where sheds or rowhouses had once stood to block-sized urban prairie, broad expanses of dried yellow grass, tall weeds, and trash.

The leaders and managers of the YouthBuild organization knew how to prepare for the Ludlow start-up. They formed a working relationship with the local civic group, the Ludlow Community Association (LCA) and carved out their respective responsibilities: YouthBuild and LCA would work together to recruit young people to participate in the program; YouthBuild would develop the housing; LCA would promote the sale of the houses to first-time homebuyers. Then representatives from both organizations met with and explained the program to Darrell Clarke, aide to City Council President John Street, and got Clarke's endorsement. They made an appointment with State Senator Shirley Kitchen, briefed her on the program, and got her seal of approval. Then they asked OHCD for funding to expand the YouthBuild program,

already operating successfully in South Philadelphia's Point Breeze community. OHCD agreed to the expansion, and an increased YouthBuild
line item was proposed in the CDBG budget, okayed by Mayor Rendell,
and authorized by City Council.

Most neighborhoods in the city had an ample supply of young people
who could qualify for entry into the YouthBuild program: eighteen-to-
twenty-one-year-olds who had left school and now wanted to go back,
to complete their education and set a direction in their lives. LCA's
president, Marvin Louis, knew plenty of out-of-schoolers who were eligible for the program and who might be interested. A lot of young
people walked in to apply. Referrals were called in or sent over by
staffers from the offices of Council President Street and Senator
Kitchen. Some of the applicants began calling LCA and YouthBuild every day to find out if they had made it into this year's program.

Ludlow's first YouthBuild recruits and staff got together near the
corner of Eighth and Oxford one afternoon to clean up the area surrounding the work site. They cleared the vacant lots of weeds and
debris. They picked up trash from the sidewalks and street corners.
They teamed up at an intersection and began sweeping down the entire length of the block. People inside the houses heard the activity
on the street, peered out of their windows, then opened their front
doors. What they saw was, in one sense, no big deal but, in another
sense, an activity that had no precedent in the community's history:
an organized group of young people from North Philadelphia systematically cleaning up Ludlow's streets and open spaces. The residents
came out of their houses and met the members of the YouthBuild
group on the sidewalks and in the street. The YouthBuild participants
explained the program and told the residents where the first housing
construction would begin later that month. By the end of the afternoon, both the YouthBuild group and the residents had gained an understanding of each other and of their shared future in Ludlow.

On another day, meeting with a block leader in her dining room,
the construction supervisor explained how YouthBuild could change a
young person's point of view. The dining room table was covered with
a lace tablecloth. The chair seats were vinyl-covered. Gold-framed
graduation and wedding photos occupied all the available space on a
polished sideboard nearby. The muted sounds of a television program
drifted in from the next room.

The young people who come into the YouthBuild program are used to failing, he said. They feel as though they've never done anything worthwhile, never succeeded at anything worth doing. They enter the program without a lot of expectations. To an outsider, the work site wouldn't inspire high expectations either. When the tin is pulled away from the window of the first vacant house to be rehabilitated, what you see is a water-damaged ceiling, crumbling plaster walls, a collapsed stair, and a front room filled with trash and broken glass. Confronted with this sight, you might draw an immediate conclusion: they'll never be able to fix up this place.

But everyone picks up tools and gets to work. The members of the group unseal the front door and step inside carefully, window glass and crack vials crunching under their feet. All the litter and any other thing that is broken, decayed, or failing goes out the window and into a dumpster. The place is cleared out. And then the real work begins.

Not everyone stays with it, he said. During the first weeks, some of the young people don't keep pace with the program and drop out. Attendance and punctuality rules are strictly enforced. The recruits who leave the program are replaced by applicants who have been waiting to get in, and, within a few weeks, a permanent group takes shape. The rules of the program are demanding, but the young people who stick with it graduate with an attendance record of 97 percent or higher at the end of nine months.

Soon the participants are learning carpentry skills as they work on framing, stairways, floors, drywall. They're getting used to sharing responsibilities and they're beginning to appreciate what an organized group can accomplish. They go home tired at the end of the day, but they're back on time the next morning. As the house changes and improves, they start to share their pride in what they're accomplishing: We built that two-story addition in back, we replaced those stairs and laid the carpet, we installed that kitchen. The spirit of teamwork and mutual support grows.

And then the day comes when the members of the group, now graduating from the program, hand over the keys of the just-completed house to the family who will live there. The graduates are going to move on, enroll in community college or take a job, but that house will remain as evidence of value they created and passed on to the neighborhood. Oxford Street was closed to traffic for the grand opening event celebrating the completion of the Ludlow YouthBuild rehabs. The street and sidewalk area was filled with YouthBuild graduates, parents, and neighbors, and people from agencies and organizations that had supported the program. The front entrance of one house in the center of the block was decorated with ribbons and balloons. Inside, a busy group was preparing refreshments in the kitchen and dining area. I walked up the stairs, feeling the silence of the newly carpeted landings and hallways, passing through open doorways into sunlit bedrooms. On the third floor, I encountered an older woman from the neighborhood. We didn't know each other, but we looked over the master bedroom together, examining the freshly painted drywall, the new lighting, the closet space. We looked out the double window facing south and saw the towers of Center City rising up twenty blocks away. "This really is very nice," she said softly.

The first year of the YouthBuild program in Ludlow was ending. The Oxford Street rehabs were completed. Next year's YouthBuild recruits would be starting new construction, building new houses on a big vacant lot nearby. The young woman selected as valedictorian for the graduating class stood at the top of the steps leading to the open front door and spoke to the group out on the street. She described the accomplishments of the class during the past months and spoke about their future. Her own job was starting next week. She had just passed the test for entry into the carpenters' union apprenticeship program.

Other graduates expressed their feelings in the yearbook. "I would like to thank my fellow trainees for helping me through the year. To Mr. Vince and Mr. Dwayne, I appreciate everything you taught me." "This has been a hard year, but I made it. All I want to say is thank God, and everyone who stood by my side." "Life is on the up and up, and I'm up and out."[1]

Like every nation, state, region, and city, every neighborhood has an economy with a distinctive structure and a life of its own. Although the characteristics that define the neighborhood economy, its current status, and its future potential can differ greatly from place to place, all neighborhood economies have two primary elements in common: houses and people. A major goal of reinvestment policy for urban neighborhoods is to increase the value and usefulness of the houses by fixing them up, by producing more of them where feasible, and by improving the surrounding physical environment through activities as varied as demolishing factory buildings and planting street trees. But what about the people?

Many of the urban neighborhood residents who moved out during the peak years of late-twentieth-century disinvestment were jobholders, some of whom began commuting to work in the city, while others found new work closer to their homes in the rapidly growing metropolitan region. Unlike this ex-resident population, a large number of the residents who stayed in urban neighborhoods or moved there during the same period were unemployed, under-employed, uneducated, or undereducated people lacking sufficient work experience to compete successfully for better jobs in the metropolitan economy. Neighborhood reinvestment policy has to be designed to help these community residents become jobhold-ers and to provide the best opportunities for them to move up from poverty.

The task of helping neighborhood residents find and keep good jobs has an important racial aspect that should be taken seriously. In every metropolitan region, older urban neighborhoods are the dwelling places for most of the region's nonwhite residents, as well as for the region's most economically disadvantaged residents. The more effectively the benefits of employment, training, and job readiness programs (referred to collectively in this chapter as "jobs programs") are managed and promoted at the neighborhood level, the better able these residents will be to pursue available opportu-nities. Some of these opportunities are linked with the transforma-tion of race described in chapter 2, the growing movement of nonwhites, particularly African Americans, into government, insti-tutional, and corporate middle-management and senior leadership positions from which they had previously been excluded. Although many resources to which nonwhites and/or low-income people need to gain access—resources such as schools, community colleges, training centers, and jobs themselves—are going to be located out-side neighborhood boundaries, the neighborhood has to be the place where people in need of good jobs gain a basic understand-ing of the value of these resources and learn how to make an ini-tial connection with a program or service that can deliver results.

Without effective connection at the neighborhood level, the fundamental problems of racial isolation and the distancing of non-whites from opportunities for economic success are never going to be solved.

This connection between neighborhood residents and the economy is what makes jobs programs different from human service activities such as health care, child care, and substance abuse programs. Although these human service activities have an important relationship to work readiness, they are ongoing responsibilities of government and local institutions, not a core element of a neighborhood reinvestment policy designed to bring economic stability and success to distressed communities. As indicated in chapter 3, neighborhood reinvestment funding should not be used to support human service activities, because every dollar committed to these activities reduces the already limited resources available to pursue reinvestment goals and priorities. Neighborhood reinvestment funding can and should be committed to jobs programs, however, when such commitments can produce beneficial results for both neighborhood residents and the neighborhood economy.

Leaders and managers of organizations participating in neighborhood reinvestment activities, from government agencies to civic groups, understand the overriding importance of the jobs issue. They know very well how participants in a community meeting anywhere in the city would respond if asked, "Would you rather have a house or a job? If you had to make the choice, would you rather have a good job and no home, or a good place to live and no job?" But the task of leading and directing jobs programs poses a serious managerial problem for most of these organizations, because the available resources and the associated implementation strategies for delivering these resources are so different from the resources and implementation strategies associated with physical development. Most of the public funding available for jobs programs originates from federal and state agencies that are not closely linked to HUD or other development funding agencies, and this money is often managed at the local level by public agencies that are different from the local-government agencies that administer development programs. In some cities, the jobs programs are run by nonprofit or quasi-public agencies (such as Philadelphia's Pri-

vate Industry Council, or PIC) that don't have direct accountability to local elected officials and historically have not been accus-
tomed to maintaining day-to-day working relationships with city
agencies. And, at the neighborhood level, implementation of jobs
programs requires a base of knowledge and skills that differs fundamentally from those needed to fix up a house or create a reuse plan for a run-down retail commercial corridor.

To address this managerial problem and make sensible strategic choices about how to pursue opportunities to link residents with
the best job-training and job-finding resources, and ultimately, the
best jobs, supporters of neighborhood reinvestment have to recognize some key principles on which all planning for jobs programs
should be based. The most important principle is that *jobs programs
are most effective when they are designed as a response to the current
condition of either the city's public school system or the city's system for
disbursing state and federal money for employment/training activities,
or both.* In a city where the school system and the local employ-
ment/training system are both operating at maximum effectiveness
and are producing the best possible results at the neighborhood
level—a condition that probably does not exist in any American
city—there is no need for special consideration to be given to jobs
programs as an element of neighborhood reinvestment policy. In
a city where the school system and the local employment/training
system are improving and producing better results than in previous years, the jobs programs supported as an element of overall
neighborhood reinvestment policy should be designed to build up
areas of strong performance in order to benefit more people or to
address areas of weak performance by replicating programs that
have succeeded elsewhere. In a city where the school system and
the local employment/training system are performing poorly, jobs
programs should be made a major element of overall reinvestment
policy and should be designed to either circumvent existing programs or to compete with and eventually replace them.

In the latter two instances, engagement in the jobs issue to promote neighborhood reinvestment is an intervention that parallels
but is distinct from development activity. Development strategies
are a physical intervention, a form of investment designed to improve
the neighborhood environment. Jobs strategies are a programmatic

intervention, a form of investment designed to improve or, in some cases, take the place of the local public education system or the local employment/training system.

People who want to design and implement jobs programs as an element of neighborhood reinvestment policy should be aware of two other important principles. First, *most job opportunities for neighborhood residents are not located in the neighborhood; instead, they are located downtown, in clusters of big institutions and businesses, or in the suburbs.* The location of jobs in Philadelphia illustrates this situation, which is also characteristic of many other cities. The downtown area, occupying about 2 percent of the city's total acreage, is the location for half the city's jobs.[2] Philadelphia's largest employer is the University of Pennsylvania (with about sixteen thousand full-time jobs in the city in 1998), an institution with a residential neighborhood at its western edge but bordered on the other three sides by other institutions and businesses belonging to the "University City" district.[3] All of Philadelphia's top ten employers, including Bell Atlantic Corporation, Thomas Jefferson University Hospitals, Independence Blue Cross, and US Airways, are located downtown or within geographically concentrated groupings of businesses and institutions. None is located within a neighborhood, and most are not even adjacent to residential neighborhoods.

In addition, most business expansion and job growth are not taking place within urban neighborhoods but across broad metropolitan regions, and these activities are associated with product and service categories that grew in importance after 1950 and have no historic or strategic connection with urban neighborhoods. A 1995 study by Greater Philadelphia First (GPF), a business leadership organization, defines five "industry clusters" as the strongest prospects for future economic growth in the metropolitan area: health care services and products, "data-intensive" services (involving computer-related jobs in fields such as finance and insurance), professional services, hospitality, and precision manufacturing.[4] The fastest-growing businesses in these categories have chosen and will continue to choose suburban and exurban locations that are totally unlike the urban neighborhood locations favored by Industrial-Age manufacturing firms. The largest privately held Greater Philadelphia companies that, according to the *Philadelphia Business*

Journal, grew fastest in 1995–1997 illustrate this difference. These companies include Cybertech International, an information technology consulting company located in Trevose (an inner-ring suburb linked to the Pennsylvania Turnpike); Complete Care Services, a provider of long-term care and assisted-living management and development services, based in Horsham (another turnpike-linked inner-ring suburb); CoreTech Consulting Group, an information technology consulting firm based in the King of Prussia/Route 202 "edge city"; ACC, a retailer of cellular telephones, located in Newtown (an older community with a traditional suburban/rural blend); and other companies of similar types in similar locations.[5]

The designers and implementers of jobs programs must also bear in mind that *the key employment issue confronting urban neighborhoods is not a need for more jobs but a need for more job readiness.* The big question is not whether there are enough jobs in or near the city for neighborhood residents but whether there are enough neighborhood residents who qualify for current entry-level job opportunities. Hundreds of thousands of factory jobs that had been available for unskilled and semiskilled workers prior to 1950 have left urban neighborhoods and vanished from the metropolitan economy for good. Some of the key business sectors that had defined the city's jobs base in previous decades are still a strong presence, but the nature of the work available within these sectors has changed fundamentally. Factory-based heavy industry has been replaced by specialty manufacturing. Hospital-based health care has been replaced by managed services. The newer business sectors that have redefined the employment base of the city and region in recent decades—such as the data-intensive, biotech, and hospitality sectors—are a major source of new jobs. However, the number, location, and duration of these jobs are constantly changing, as investors, lenders, government, businesses, and institutions expand, downsize, diversify, consolidate, or relocate to adapt to changes in the regional, national, and international economy.

Most of the biggest or fastest-growing businesses in the city and metropolitan region share a need for entry-level workers possessing the same two basic qualifications: literacy and "soft skills." Literacy means a middle-school-level reading and writing aptitude, sometimes accompanied by an elementary knowledge of arithmetic.

Soft skills are a combination of qualities: consistent, punctual attendance; appropriate dress and personal appearance; the ability to communicate, listen, and observe; willingness to take direction; and the ability to either work in a team or complete a task alone, as needed. These two basic qualifications are far more important than computer literacy or advanced technical training. Employers can and will train work-ready jobseekers—but employers can't make jobseekers work-ready.

Because the urban and regional economic landscape is constantly changing, no one can calculate with certainty the number of entry-level positions that are available for work-ready neighborhood residents at any given moment. However, one thing is certain: if neighborhood residents are not work-ready, the job opportunities in the local and regional economy will shrink and vanish.

A jobs program founded on these principles will have several distinguishing features. Such a program will offer opportunities not readily available through the public schools or the local employment/training system. The program will help get participants used to the necessity of traveling to work and making public transit a part of their job-search and employment plans. The program will either "cream" applicants in order to select only those who have an acceptable level of education, or else will commit to providing schooling as a key element of the program. And, most important, the program will focus on the development of "soft skills" and their application in the workplace.

Jobs programs possessing these characteristics differ significantly from traditional, mainstream employment/training approaches, in which job placement—finding any job that matches a jobseeker's existing qualifications—is the overriding priority. Historically, these conventional employment/training approaches have been most successful in helping experienced, displaced workers (such as those laid-off by a downsized company) find new jobs or in channeling inexperienced, unskilled people into low-paying positions (such as minimum-wage nurse's aide jobs) with little opportunity for advancement. When the Comprehensive Employment and Training Act (CETA) was in effect during the 1970s and early 1980s, many hard-core unemployed people could also be placed in public-service jobs such as street cleaning, providing them with income but rarely offering an opportunity to improve their employ-ment potential. Many of the recent welfare-to-work jobs programs have a similar orientation to placement as the highest priority. The measure of success for welfare reform in any state is the number of people who have been removed from the welfare rolls, not the state's performance in producing jobholders who can succeed as participants in the private-sector workforce. This "work first" prin-ciple, a key welfare reform theme, requires state caseworkers to seek quick-placement opportunities for their clients. Education and skills development, though available through some programs, are a lower priority.

Unemployed residents of the most distressed urban neighbor-hoods are not well served by either the traditional programs or the more recent welfare-to-work approach. The residents who need help most are not laid-off workers who can be retrained for good jobs in the regional economy, and the low educational and skill level of many neighborhood residents makes them the people least likely to succeed in a "work first" environment that places on them the obligation to work while they pursue education or training to im-prove their qualifications for better employment. Public-service employment programs established as part of some welfare-to-work approaches create the potential for a repetition of the biggest dis-advantage of the CETA program: the absence of a link between pub-lic service workers and a future in the private-sector workforce.

Because reinvestment resources are limited, available funding should only be used to support programs operated by existing, ex-perienced service providers, agencies currently operating training and readiness programs that produce work-ready candidates for jobs. These agencies should have staff, classroom and/or computer-lab facilities, access to other equipment used in the workplace, and a base of experience in preparing urban residents for jobs. Most CDCs and nonprofit organizations should not try to develop an in-house capability to deliver jobs programs, because these organi-zations don't have sufficient resources to make such an effort suc-cessful. Instead, most CDCs and nonprofits should participate as clearinghouses, as information/referral centers directing jobseekers to the best resources. An organization that wants to develop jobs program service-delivery capability as a core activity should seek foundation or corporation funding to pursue this goal; a start-up endeavor is too expensive and too risky to be funded from the neighborhood reinvestment budget. The use of reinvestment funding for jobs programs should be directed toward several kinds of activities: a contract between a government agency and an experienced service provider; the expansion or modification of an existing program to enhance productivity or address a specialized need; or the importing and replication of a jobs program that has succeeded in another place.

The jobs programs that best illustrate the positive characteristics described above are programs that are designed, implemented, and monitored with strong participation by private-sector businesses who want to hire qualified workers in the field for which training is being provided. An excellent model of a jobs program with this employer orientation was developed in Philadelphia during the 1990s by Campus Boulevard Corporation (CBC), a nonprofit consortium of ten Northwest Philadelphia academic and medical institutions, including Albert Einstein Healthcare Network, La Salle University, and Pennsylvania College of Optometry.[6] All of the CBC member institutions are located adjacent to or in close proximity to northwest Philadelphia residential communities. Most of the people who live in these communities are African Americans of low or moderate income. Housing in the area consists of older rowhouse blocks, with some mid-rise rental buildings and "garden apartment" complexes. This surrounding residential area is reasonably stable, with many attractive, well-maintained, tree-lined blocks. Some of these blocks, however, have conspicuously vacant or abandoned houses.

Following a period in which most of CBC's organizational energies were devoted to planning for the development of a new transit center located at a key intersection in the area, CBC's board hired a new executive director, Barbara Coscarello, and began considering a future direction for the organization. Coscarello interviewed representatives of the participating institutions and members of the community and found that many people were interested in doing more to help neighborhood residents obtain jobs. But while personnel officers at the institutions all were willing to make neighborhood hiring a priority, they did not want to have to hire job applicants who did not meet minimum qualifications. No one wanted to downgrade job specifications and accept less qualified workers simply for the sake of meeting a neighborhood-hiring priority.

Coscarello found that all the CBC member institutions had a need for workers in medical office, computer-related positions and that a wide range of opportunities were available: a receptionist could earn $9.45 an hour, a patient billing representative $11.55, a claims processor $13.04. During the course of a year, more than enough job opportunities became available in these and other positions to provide work for dozens of qualified neighborhood residents.

With the CBC board's approval, Coscarello hired a core staff to design and supervise a training program and recruit neighborhood jobseekers. Based on information that she had obtained from the member institutions, CBC's program model identified specific skills that trainees needed to gain in order to graduate from the program, including technical skills, such as typing fifty words a minute, as well as a bundle of soft skills, such as good attendance, punctuality, flexibility, willingness to work alone or in a group, and ability to get along with others. The overall goal of the CBC training program was skill training, specifically tailored to the hiring standards of the CBC member institutions. If the CBC program was effective, graduates would qualify for jobs at these institutions.

Because CBC had no classroom space, computer labs, or other training facilities, the organization decided to engage an experienced outside agency to provide training services, based on the program model CBC had designed. After visits to and interviews with several training providers, Coscarello and her staff found a training agency that was well staffed and well equipped, ready to manage a class of CBC trainees and willing to implement an eight-month training course based on the model designed by CBC. However, this training agency was located downtown, at least a half-hour commute from CBC's service area. After considering the alternatives—requiring trainees to travel every day or engaging a more accessible but less qualified provider—CBC decided to contract with the downtown agency. CBC staff concluded that establishing a high-quality training standard was a paramount value that should not be compromised and that participants in the program would benefit from the experience of travel outside the neighborhood every day, since their future jobs (including many of the jobs available at the CBC member institutions), were likely to require a commute of some kind.

Admission to the program, which began in 1994, is not conducted on an open-enrollment or first-come basis but through a careful screening and selection of recruits by CBC staff to identify applicants who meet literacy standards, pass drug tests and police background checks, and demonstrate willingness to make a commitment to remain in the program. This CBC screening has the effect of excluding the least-educated, least-prepared neighborhood residents—those who, it might be argued, have the greatest economic need for steady work. But this approach reflects CBC's highest priority: efficiently linking work-ready residents with job opportunities at CBC institutions. Although this priority is different from a serve-the-neediest-first priority, all of the recruits to the CBC program had incomes substantially below the Philadelphia citywide median, and 98 percent of the participants in the program between 1994 and 1999 (when welfare-reform policies took effect) were receiving public assistance.

The linkage between the CBC organization and private-sector employers gives the CBC program special advantages, in addition to the prospect of job opportunities following graduation. Managers and supervisors from CBC member institutions visit the trainees during classroom sessions to talk about jobs and the work environment that participants will be entering after graduation. Following the start-up year of the program, visitors to the classroom included prior-year graduates who described how they had made the transition from training to employment to successful performance in their current jobs. One of the most valuable aspects of the CBC-employer connection is an eight-week internship phase of the training, a temporary job at one of the institutions after twenty-eight weeks of classroom training. The internship gives trainees hands-on familiarity with the work for which they are preparing themselves, as well as work experience and an employer reference to include in future job applications. In many cases, these short-term internships are followed by offers of permanent employment, scheduled to start immediately after graduation from the CBC program.

OHCD provided funding to support CBC administrative staff, supplementing the Title II funds made available for program costs through the Private Industry Council. The availability of funding from OHCD over a period of years made it possible for CBC to build its capacity and expand the program from thirty-four participants in 1994 to seventy-eight in 1995.

By the end of the decade, the CBC program had become widely known as one of the nation's most successful employer-linked training initiatives. CBC won the Council for Urban Economic Development (CUED) Economic Development Program Award in 1997. A summary of program results published in early 1998 showed that the average annual salary of the graduates was $22,090, with some earning as much as $27,000; that nearly all had full employer-funded benefits packages; and that they were earning between three and a half to fourteen times as much as they had previously received from public assistance programs. A year after graduation, 93 percent of the people who had completed the training were still employed, and 63 percent had received promotions or raises.

The comments of the 1997 graduating class convey a clear message about the effectiveness of CBC's approach: "I would recommend the program to anyone so that they can better themselves and rid their life of the rigmarole of welfare." "Ms. Argo taught me how to type and be a person again. She felt like a mother, someone stern, yet loving." "Ms. Brinkley [CBC case manager Belinda Brinkley] is always very helpful and concise with the information you need to assist you with personal matters." "Bill [instructor Bill Ansel] made the software as simple as eating cake and ice cream." "Everything Ms. Brinkley and Ms. Simpkins said was true about going to work. [I was] taught how the real world works, learned the importance of being organized. [I had a] supportive atmosphere and learned how to work well independently."[7]

A key participant in the design of the CBC program was Jerome L. Kolker, an employee of the Greater Philadelphia First business organization who possessed decades' worth of experience in designing and managing jobs programs. In light of Kolker's expertise, GPF's standing in the business community, and its advocacy for an economic development strategy focused on the five key "industry clusters" identified in the organization's 1995 report (described earlier in this chapter), I asked GPF, through Kolker, to design more CBC-style, employer-oriented training programs to link other Philadelphia neighborhood residents with key employers in the local and regional economy.

GPF agreed to launch an OHCD-funded demonstration project led by Kolker, in which employer-oriented programs would be designed for two industry sectors: precision manufacturing and data-intensive services. The precision manufacturing model was designed in coordination with the Frankford Group Ministries CDC and with owners of manufacturing firms in the Frankford community. Although the Frankford neighborhood had experienced a substantial loss of manufacturing jobs since 1950, the many small- and medium-sized companies remaining in the community, taken together, represented a significant number of job opportunities. The data-intensive services model was designed in coordination with West Philadelphia Partnership, a CBC-like nonprofit organization governed by the combined leadership of University City institutions (such as the University of Pennsylvania) and West Philadelphia neighborhood organizations.

The OHCD/GPF demonstration project was the first major attempt to use private-sector strategic planning resources to link Philadelphia neighborhoods with good job opportunities in the current economy. The project was intended to deal with a key concern cited in the 1995 GPF report: the "shortage of employment-focused technical training programs beyond the high school level."[8] This concern was to be addressed through pursuing a five-part mission.

☐ Model an innovative partnership between the private-sector, community-based organizations, and the region's publicly-funded job-training and education systems;

☐ Articulate a private-sector perspective in the design and delivery of demonstration training programs tied to the strategic economic development objectives of the region;

☐ Organize the region's education and training resources to meet a more clearly defined demand for qualified workers;

☐ Provide a business service to participating companies by helping them find and retain qualified workers; and

☐ Improve the region's competitive advantage by building the world-class workforce the region needs to compete regionally and internationally.[9]

Previous analysis of the manufacturing sector by GPF found that the industrial firms remaining in the Greater Philadelphia region employed more than two hundred thousand workers and paid comparatively high wages.[10] Subsequent GPF staff interviews with forty-four manufacturers in the Frankford area revealed that employers were "dissatisfied with the availability of qualified labor, and found the process of attracting, screening, hiring, and retaining labor cumbersome and expensive."[11] In addition, many long-time workers at these firms were retiring, opening up new opportunities for qualified jobseekers. The GPF interviews also disclosed that most employers were looking for workers who possessed three categories of skills: basic (such as legible handwriting and the ability to read repair manuals), soft (such as the ability to take direction and work in teams), and technical (such as blueprint reading and forklift operation).[12]

After completing this evaluation of the needs of Frankford-area manufacturing firms, GPF designed a training program to help neighborhood residents develop the skills identified by these employers. Private-sector leaders, including representatives of Frankford-based manufacturing firms as well as of the big corporations represented on GPF's board of directors, supervised the initial evaluation, oversaw the subsequent program design process, and participated in the selection of an outside organization to provide the training services specified in the program design. The provider selected by GPF was a Northwest Philadelphia–based facility known as Philadelphia Area Accelerated Manufacturing Education, Inc. (PhAME). PhAME was the creation of a local community development corporation, Ogontz Avenue Revitalization Corporation (OARC), with strong ongoing leadership provided by the area's state representative, Dwight Evans. PhAME is an excellent example of how a successful jobs program can be imported from another city. The PhAME program and the facility where it operated were modeled after Detroit's successful Focus: HOPE program. Directors and managers of the Detroit program provided substantial assistance during PhAME's initial planning and start-up to insure that the Philadelphia replication would accurately mirror the original. Following the selection of PhAME as training provider, the private-sector leaders convened by GPF monitored the training activities to insure that the results specified in the GPF design would be achieved by program graduates, qualifying them for available manufacturing jobs. The PIC provided funding to implement the training program, and an initial class of trainees was recruited in 1997.

Although the CBC data-intensive training model, the GPF manufacturing training model, and PhAME all directly address a key regional economic development problem—the shortage of jobseekers possessing the qualifications needed to fill vacancies in the region's strategically important industry clusters—these organizations could not have obtained from existing mainstream employment/training or economic development programs the level and type of funding they needed to support their respective contributions to solving the problem. Rather, these solutions were made possible through special CDBG funding awards. During the coming years, funding turned over to states by the federal government as part of welfare-reform "devolution" should be regarded as the primary resource for jobs initiatives such as these. Metropolitan-area government and business leaders should advocate on behalf of employer-oriented training initiatives to insure that these effective responses to the regional workforce problem are made a priority.

In contrast to employer-oriented programs, the primary focus of programs such as YouthBuild is job readiness in general, not training for a specified placement. The mission of job-readiness programs is to provide participants with a foundation of basic education and skills needed for the successful pursuit of many of the jobs available in the regional economy. Job-readiness activities are interventions in the city's public education system, initiatives that compensate for the limitations and failings of local public schools. Some of the participants in these programs are young people who are in school but are encountering problems that threaten their future there, problems such as domestic abuse, homelessness, and

teen pregnancy, as well as academic difficulties and frustrations—
and who need help in order to emerge from the school system with
a diploma and some marketable skills. Other participants in job-
readiness programs are people who left school and need to find a
route back, a way to get a diploma and acquire the skills needed
for success in jobseeking.

YouthBuild Philadelphia initially worked in coordination with
the School District of Philadelphia, which assigned teachers to the
program in order to help participants complete coursework needed
to obtain their high school degrees. After the Commonwealth of
Pennsylvania enacted legislation permitting the establishment of
charter schools as an alternative to the existing public education
system, YouthBuild Philadelphia discontinued its link with the
school district and formed its own charter school—in effect, cir-
cumventing the existing public school system and competing with
the school district for a share of the public education funding
awarded to Philadelphia by the commonwealth.

Although some YouthBuild graduates pursue construction work
as a career, many decide to continue their education by entering a
community college or a training program, while others find jobs
in fields other than construction. From YouthBuild's organizational
perspective, fixing up houses is just a work model, a learning activity rather than a training scheme aimed at placements in the
construction industry. This focus on learning activities is what all
the best job-readiness programs have in common. Job-readiness activities are different from the "school to career" programs that some
schools offer as a way to help students learn about and prepare for
specific career opportunities. Many students from distressed urban
neighborhoods aren't sufficiently well equipped to benefit from
school-to-career programs; before career-track programs will have
any value for them, they will need to achieve literacy and complete a core middle- and high-school curriculum, as well as deal
with social problems that create barriers to achievement and
success.

As with employer-oriented jobs programs, job-readiness programs
depend on the expertise of a capable service provider responsible
for training and skills-development activities. As with the employer-
oriented programs, a provider model can be home-grown or

imported from another city. In Philadelphia, OHCD's collaborator in many job-readiness activities was Communities In Schools of Philadelphia (CISP), the local branch of a nationwide network of nonprofit organizations that manage specialized programs and services for public school students with social needs. CISP characterizes participants in its activities as "those students whose needs have not been met by the traditional education system and who have been deemed unlikely to succeed without intervention and support." For such students CISP provides "a personal, one-on-one relationship with a caring adult; a safe place to learn and grow; a marketable skill to use upon graduation; and a chance to give back to peers and the community."[13]

OHCD and CISP initially joint-ventured in implementing an OHCD-sponsored summer jobs program for middle- and high-school students. The program provided summer employment at OHCD, at other city agencies, and at community organizations that OHCD staff knew could provide adequate supervision and a good work experience. For some students with a particular career interest, match-ups could be found: one student interested in child care was placed at a nonprofit service agency that operated a day care center; for a student interested in becoming a lawyer, a position was found at a nonprofit legal aid agency.

Following this successful experience, OHCD and CISP decided to offer students who had done well in the summer program internship opportunities: part-time, after-school jobs at the place where they had worked during the summer months. Some students who needed to make up course work in order to obtain credits needed for graduation participated in Saturday School, a weekend tutorial program. The Saturday School participants included a number of young women who had missed school due to pregnancy and childbirth.

Cities have big opportunities to place qualified neighborhood residents in construction-related jobs financed with public money (in the form of construction-loan financing and development-subsidy funding that pays for bricks and mortar, equipment and supplies, and the employment of many skilled and semiskilled workers). A typical CDBG-financed housing development venture in Philadelphia, where the level of city subsidy rarely exceeded $1.5

million, had the potential to generate construction-period jobs for as many as 150 workers. Downtown Philadelphia development ventures financed through the HUD Section 108 loan program—hotels, office buildings, retail stores, and other projects—produced construction jobs for thousands of workers during the 1990s. For reinvestment policy to be successful, publicly financed job opportunities such as these have to be linked with qualified neighborhood residents, including the graduates of training and job-readiness programs.

In past years, some local governments tried to make this benefit available through the creation of racial and/or ethnic quotas or set-asides associated with city contracts. For example, a 1982 Philadelphia law called for 15 percent of all city contract awards to be set aside for businesses owned by African Americans. However, following a 1989 Supreme Court revision of the rules governing minority set-asides, many local-government mandates of this kind were found unconstitutional. For example, the 1982 Philadelphia law was struck down in 1995 by a federal judge who concluded that city officials had failed to prove that past racial discrimination justified the set-aside.[14] More to the point, however, a quota/set-aside approach doesn't necessarily produce significant value for urban neighborhoods, because these measures focus on race and ethnicity, not neighborhood residency.

A better approach for delivering development-related benefit to community residents, particularly nonwhite residents, is a creative application of Section 3 of the Housing and Urban Development Act of 1968. This section of the act requires that economic opportunities generated by HUD-funded housing and community development projects will, "to the greatest extent feasible, be given to low and very-low income persons residing in the area in which the project is located, and to area businesses which provide economic opportunities to low- and very-low-income persons."[15] Since the vast majority of CDBG-financed development ventures in Philadelphia, as in many other cities, are located in predominantly nonwhite, low-income communities, African Americans and other racial and ethnic minorities of low income automatically become the greatest beneficiaries of an aggressive Section 3–oriented hiring and contracting policy.

Philadelphia began to pursue a more aggressive Section 3

approach in 1995, through Mayor Rendell's issuance of an executive order calling for every developer receiving CDBG funding to work with city agencies to pursue a goal of returning at least half the value of the development venture to the community, through hiring neighborhood residents and contracting with or purchasing from neighborhood-based businesses. The means of pursuing this goal is the formulation of a "neighborhood benefit strategy" in which a developer selected to receive CDBG funding is expected to give first consideration to hiring qualified workers living in the same zip code as the development site or executing contracts for services or purchases of supplies with businesses located in this zip code. If needed, housing agency staff can assist by providing the developer with computer-generated lists of individuals and businesses within the zip code that have participated in other CDBG- and city-funded development ventures. After the developer has identified and pursued hiring and contracting opportunities within this zip code, workforce and business resources in zip codes adjacent to that of the development site are evaluated. This evaluation is followed by an assessment of opportunities for hiring and contracting elsewhere in the city. The evaluation process takes place before consideration is given to any hiring or contracting involving people or businesses at addresses outside the city.

No developer is categorically ordered to hire neighborhood residents or transact business with neighborhood-based firms, but every developer is required to give first consideration to qualified, work-ready neighborhood residents and to neighborhood-based businesses that can provide products and services relevant to the development venture. The 50–percent standard is a goal, not a mandate—but it is a goal that developers are required to take seriously and to pursue diligently. The executive order states that developers "are not to set aside or reserve fifty percent," but that meeting the goal constitutes a "safe harbor" with respect to compliance with the order.[16] The order also provides that failure to meet the goal may result in lower ranking or rejection of the developer's future bids on city work.

This approach creates a link between public money, civic advocacy, and existing community labor and business resources— identified through computerized city records—and encourages supporters of neighborhood reinvestment in city government and the community to work with developers to identify qualified local workers and businesses, in order to achieve maximum compliance with the order and deliver greatest benefit to the neighborhood. In some of the city's most distressed neighborhoods, there may be relatively few qualified workers and few or no firms ready and able to contract with or sell to a developer. The analysis of adjacent zip codes may also yield much less than optimal results, producing an overall economic benefit that falls far short of the 50–percent goal. But a requirement to look to the immediate neighborhood first, when properly supported and enforced by the city and when pursued diligently by a developer, produces far better results for the city and its residents—particularly for nonwhite residents—than a quota/set-aside policy.

In some cities where organized labor is strong, the unions can be the wild card in the jobs-for-residents game. How wild? Consider a flare-up that occurred in the West Poplar neighborhood during the second phase of the new-construction sales housing development there. After construction start, the building trades threatened to shut down the job, because they were opposed to the nonunion sheet-metal subcontractor selected by the builder. From a neighborhood-benefit standpoint, the profile of the selected subcontractor was ideal: a minority-owned business located in the same zip code as the construction site. Why couldn't the sheet-metal work have been awarded to a union subcontractor? Because no union subcontractors bid on the work. (The picketers were not concerned about the fact that, even if a union subcontractor *had* bid on the work, the mayor's executive order would have required the developer to give priority to the neighborhood subcontractor.) The picketing continued and the shut-down threats escalated. Sheet-metal work was rescheduled for late-afternoon and evening hours to reduce the possibility of a really ugly confrontation. The builder offered a compromise in an attempt to resolve the problem: the sheet-metal workforce would be mixed, half union, half nonunion. The building trades rejected the offer. A second compromise was proposed: the selected subcontractor—the minority-owned, neighborhood-based contractor—would give up half the dollar value of the contract to a union subcontractor. The building trades rejected this offer too.

Why are are the building trades so unyielding, so unwilling to negotiate and compromise? Neighborhood reinvestment could be a lot more effective—both in its physical-improvement aspect and its resident-employment aspect—if building trades, neighborhood organizations, and local government could establish policy-level consensus on hiring and subcontracting issues. The reason why such a consensus rarely gets achieved is easy to explain from the union perspective: no policy, no matter how skillfully organized and painstakingly drafted, can ever guarantee delivery of the unions' fundamental, bottom-line value: long-term, continuous employment for union members. A mixed union/nonunion workforce might be a fine idea during an economic boom period, when work is available for everyone; but union leaders fear, with justification, that when the inevitable economic downturn or recession hits, the union contractors and their workers will be the first casualties of the cost-cutting strategies that will inevitably ensue.

The building trades aren't inherently racist or antineighborhood; union apprenticeship programs and union participation in many community development initiatives across the country have provided a gateway to good jobs for many minorities and urban neighborhood residents. Nor is the federal Davis-Bacon Act, the law that requires union-scale wage rates to be paid to construction workers on certain HUD-funded projects, the root cause of these labor problems. Although Davis-Bacon is a significant obstacle to contracting with minority and neighborhood-based firms, many of which pay lower than union-scale wages, the fact that Davis-Bacon requirements don't apply to any CDBG-funded sales housing development ventures or to small-scale rental ventures (fewer than eight units) gives cities a lot of latitude in structuring opportunities for Davis-Bacon–free construction work. The fundamental union-related problem is the mismatch between building-trades imperatives and government-resource limitations. What do the unions want? All-union work crews on all construction jobs. Will the unions admit more neighborhood residents into their apprenticeship programs? Certainly—as long as the government promises to provide enough continuous work to guarantee employment for both apprentices and long-term union members, so that veteran members with seniority aren't denied work as the result of the union's commitment to an apprenticeship initiative. No union leader can be expected to formally endorse a policy that provides less than the guarantee of all-union crews and continuous work. Conversely, no government leader can possibly pledge to maintain an all-union workforce policy or commit enough public money to keep all union workers employed indefinitely.

The effect of this stalemate at the policy level is that significant construction-workforce issues such as the West Poplar crisis get resolved on an ad hoc, episodic, personalized basis by individuals whose past working relationships with one another give them the ability to apply pressure, offer or extract concessions, and negotiate tradeoffs. A suburban builder with strong union ties gets the building trades to grudgingly agree to allow a mixed union/nonunion workforce on a city-funded job in an urban neighborhood. Because Mayor Rendell brings the city many downtown development projects, producing a wealth of jobs for union members, the building trades contribute thousands of hours of donated labor for charitable projects that the mayor needs to get done quickly or inexpensively. Flare-ups such as the West Poplar incident get resolved through an intervention at the mayor's-office level. Attempts at negotiation or conflict resolution by someone like me don't get taken seriously. From the building-trades perspective, I never produced any significant new benefit for the unions in the past—I just administered one of a number of public programs already existing in the city—and my capability to offer any added value to the building trades in the future was questionable at best.

None of these considerations justify union misconduct or constitute an apology for union-created barriers to progressive neighborhood reinvestment policy. However, in a strong-union town, neighborhood supporters have to take these issues seriously and understand that progress is more likely to be achieved through a series of personalized, ad hoc, handshake deals among political allies than through the framing of a universal new policy that everyone supports. Neighborhood advocates, including agency staff and private-sector neighborhood supporters as well as community organization representatives, need to pick their priorities and enlist the help of allies who can advance these priorities in the current political environment. Some pro-union political leaders also represent substantial neighborhood constituencies consisting of people who, for the most part, have no union ties. These political figures are the ones who, given the right issue and the right circumstances, can persuade union leaders to back off, compromise, and get involved in resolving a crisis or addressing a problem.

Our jobs-program initiatives didn't solve the regional workforce problem overnight or decisively change economic conditions in the neighborhoods we supported. But these initiatives did produce higher-quality job-related opportunities and benefits for more neighborhood residents than most of the jobs programs that had been available before OHCD got involved. The stories I heard convinced me that OHCD's approach was starting to have an effect.

One afternoon a newspaper writer phoned Kevin Brooks, OHCD's director of employment and training. All the construction activity in North Philadelphia is great, he said, but why aren't minorities getting their fair share of contracts and jobs? An extended conversation about changes in OHCD policy and our current neighborhood-benefit approach ensued. That all sounds fine, the writer said, but why aren't we seeing better results out at the construction sites? Rather than spend more time on the phone, Kevin and the writer decided to go out right away and take a look at some of the city-supported construction work currently in progress. They drove to Nineteenth and Master Streets, the site of a new-construction sales housing venture being developed through a partnership between Tenth Memorial Baptist Church and the Philadelphia Housing Development Corporation. They pulled up and parked near the corner. The new houses, recently framed out, spanned the length of the block across from Tenth Memorial, an old stone church building. Work had stopped for a midafternoon break. Because the day was sunny and warm, Kevin and the writer got a clear view of the entire construction workforce; everyone was arrayed along the pavement at curbside in groups of twos and threes, smoking and drinking soda from plastic bottles. Every one of them was a person of color.

Earlier that year I went on a drive with the owner of a suburban construction company who wanted to show me some of the unsubsidized projects his firm had completed at sites outside Philadelphia. On the drive from one site to another, we talked for a while about his experience in Philadelphia, where his company had won the bid for the first phase of a big city-supported sales housing construction venture two years earlier. The contract award gave his company the opportunity to produce dozens of houses and generated many months of business. However, the owner was unhappy that his firm had subsequently been outbid on the second phase of this development. He had wanted, and felt that he deserved, to be awarded the second-phase work on a "sole-source" basis, without competitive bidding. OHCD and the RDA had refused to support this approach, and the job was bid competitively, with unfavorable results for his company. We drove on, past strip malls at busy intersections, through residential subdivisions and office campuses. "Thanks to your community employment policy, I hired a crew of workers from North Philadelphia," he said, "and now they're working on my jobs out here." "Are they all qualified?" I asked. "Of course," he answered, "they're all really good workers—and now they're all working in the suburbs." The conversation moved on, but I had heard enough. His complaint was the clearest indicator of our success.

8

THE UNFINISHED POLICY

The change really began to take hold when he met the Rev, the man explained in a subdued voice. On that day, he was already clean and sober, was already determined to quit his life on the streets and in the homeless shelters, and had long ago given up the robberies and petty thefts that had financed his crack habit. So now what? He wasn't lacking in commitment or sense of purpose, but what he really needed now was a route from his past life into a job, a home, a family, a community. His past experience was not a reliable guide to finding the route out: his fatherless childhood and his life on the streets had not offered any clues either.

He had heard about the organization known as One Day at a Time (ODAAT), called "Oh-dat," and about the Reverend Henry Wells. He traveled to North Philadelphia and found the block where Rev. Wells and a group of ODAAT members were fixing up a vacant rowhouse to create a residence for incoming participants in the ODAAT recovery program. The porch, vestibule, and front hallway of the rehab-in-progress were cluttered with lumber, hardware, and equipment. The noise of hammering and power saws filled the air.

Someone gestured toward the stairway, and he walked up, finding himself standing in an empty hall, confronting a series of doorways. In one room he found a man busily engaged in carpentry, his trousers and shirt lightly coated with sawdust. The man stopped work-ing, and they began a friendly conversation. "Everybody's always look-ing for Rev. Wells. They're always asking 'Where's Rev. Wells?' 'Where's Rev. Wells?'" the sawdust-coated man said with amusement. "You know, that Rev. Wells must be a really important person." A moment later, the visitor figured it out: that worker in the unfinished room was the Rev. The experience was a little disarming. Henry Wells was different from the kind of pastor who would wear a tailored suit or drive to work in a Jaguar. The Rev was more like the person you pictured Jesus to be, someone who was close to—was one of—the people he served.

The Rev was no cult leader, no object of worship and devotion—but he was the master of a combination of skills that worked. He knew how to collaborate with participants in the ODAAT program, to guide them in their struggles to recover control of their lives, but he also knew how to lead. At a big meeting I had attended months earlier, he delivered a revival-style address that captured the attention and emotions of the crowd, a mix of ODAAT members and people who had never heard of the Rev or ODAAT before. He described with pas-sion the striving of the ODAAT members to regain their place in the world and told of their energy and seriousness, their commitment to a full-scale personal reconstruction of themselves. Shouts of "That's right!" "Yes sir!" and "Amen!" filled the air. At a climactic moment, the Rev called out to the ODAAT members in the audience, "Are you ever going to return to drugs again?" Thirty men leaped to their feet, fists in the air. "NO! NO! NO!" The room shook with the fierce release of their passion, anger, and pride.

A group of people were taking a walk-through of a recently com-pleted ODAAT residence. The house was quiet; most of the men were on the job in one of the organization's work crews, fixing up another vacant house or cleaning up the Fairmount Park lawn flanking Kelly Drive along the Schuylkill River. The message the plain, unfinished rooms conveyed was clear: this isn't home, and your journey isn't over yet. But as long as you stay here, we're together; you're us, and we're you.

They inspire feelings of discomfort, pity, and fear. They are called by collective names: the homeless, the chronically mentally ill,

ex–drug abusers. There are a lot more of them in the city than anywhere else. And, to some people, their visibility in cities is the
perfect picture of urban failure, a graphic illustration of an unman-
ageable, unsolvable problem.

Cities are the places where the metropolitan region's biggest
social problems can be found, and one of the hardest problems to
address in any region is the existence of these people: the individuals and families who will never be able to make their way in the
world unless they can find supportive housing (or "special-needs"
housing)—an affordable place to live, linked with health care or
human services delivered on-site or at a nearby, readily accessible
location. But cities are also the places where the best solutions to
these problems are located, and most cities have already produced
outstanding examples of supportive housing developed in an urban neighborhood setting, new neighborhood assets that provide
mutual benefit to the residents as well as the community at large.
In fact, so many great models of supportive housing have been
launched and sustained across the country during the past decade
that housing and neighborhood advocates are now in a position
to argue much more convincingly than ever before that problems
such as homelessness really are solvable.

Because available resources are limited, many of the successful
community-based models of supportive housing are small-scale and
low-profile. In terms of visibility and public recognition, even an
extraordinary supportive housing venture—a highly successful transitional housing program for formerly homeless women, for example—can't compare with a big downtown achievement such as
the topping-off of a monumental office tower or the opening of a
new stadium.

The biggest barrier standing in the way of larger-scale, higher-
profile special-needs housing production is the absence of a finished
special-needs policy consisting of two elements: ongoing commitments of readily usable federal and state support and effective program delivery at the local level. Although nearly every major city
has produced some highly successful supportive housing development or service programs for special-needs population groups in
recent years, no city has a complete, comprehensive special-needs
policy that efficiently organizes all available support resources and

program delivery systems to yield the greatest possible value. Just as the last decade was a time for constructing outstanding special-needs *models*, the coming years have to become the time for establishing outstanding special-needs *policy* to achieve bigger and better results.

This chapter has a very limited focus: it outlines some elements of a comprehensive supportive housing policy and describes how these policy elements relate to one special-needs group—homeless people. Special-needs policymaking deserves a more comprehensive treatment than this chapter provides or the limitations of this book allow. Because the special-needs population is so diverse, many different combinations of housing and services have to be considered in shaping special-needs policy: one housing/service blend for formerly homeless families, another for single men with AIDS, and so on. In addition, because each element of neighborhood reinvestment policy is affected by special-needs concerns, every one of the topics addressed in the preceding chapters has a particular special-needs relationship that needs to be defined and interpreted. For example, a neighborhood strategic plan (chapter 2) should identify special-needs population groups in the community and determine how available resources are going to be used to supply associated housing and services. In organizing housing finance strategies (chapter 3), particular consideration should be given to positioning the city to compete effectively for state and federal funding resources available for supportive housing and to using the flexibility of resources such as CDBG to produce more of the best supportive housing. Special needs–related adaptation and fine-tuning is necessary in order to make every element of reinvestment policy complete and fully effective.

The need for good special-needs policy has to be understood not just as an expression of humanitarian concern or moral obligation but as an economic survival issue that will decisively influence the future condition of cities and the regions to which they belong. Failure to establish a comprehensive, high-performance special-needs policy will have a severely damaging effect on efforts to promote and market the city, its attractions, and its quality of life. Untreated physically and mentally ill people will be constantly in evidence on the downtown streets, and poor-quality residential

facilities will be recognized as a chronic problem in many neighborhoods. These conditions convey several implicit but powerful
negative messages: that even the best-intentioned downtown improvement initiatives will never be fully successful; that a satisfactory integration of special-needs residency in city neighborhoods
can never be achieved, because people with special needs can't co-
exist with other residents of stable urban communities; and that
some serious urban problems can never really be solved.

The negative consequences of an unfinished special-needs
policy damage the downtown area and the neighborhoods in different ways. The downtown area is the city's primary center of private investment and employment, a key destination for tourists and
business travelers and, more recently, a growing housing market,
meeting an increased consumer demand for residency near "work
places . . . cultural amenities, and . . . a healthy urban environment."[1]
One key to success in the downtown arena is reliable management
of streets and public spaces. The desire for stronger management
is the principle underlying two kinds of downtown initiatives that
emerged and grew during the 1990s. One is the creation of business improvement districts, geographically specified areas within
which property owners pay a special tax to support an independent, quasi-public or nonprofit organization responsible for the delivery of services such as security and street cleaning (to achieve a
higher level of quality and responsiveness than is possible through
traditional government-agency management of these services) and
for improving the streetscape through the installation of new sidewalks, lighting, or landscaping. The other initiative is the enactment in many cities of local "anti-homeless," "anti-panhandling,"
or "sidewalk behavior" legislation intended to prohibit or restrict
a citizen's ability to sit or lie in a public place or to ask passersby
for money.

Efforts to implement downtown-management initiatives of
these kinds can have the effect of pitting two constituencies against
each other: the constituency of property owners, business owners,
economic development agencies, and government officials for
whom downtown improvement is a priority (a constituency referred
to below as "downtown advocates") and the people who develop,
operate, and provide various forms of assistance to supportive hous-

ing programs and development ventures (referred to below as "special-needs advocates"). From the perspective of the former, a homeless man lying on a downtown sidewalk or accosting pedestrians for money is a serious threat to economic development; if he stays there, his presence begins to undermine all the work devoted to making the downtown area a more attractive, appealing environment. From the perspective of the latter, that man is an example of the need for improved outreach—caseworkers on the street communicating with homeless people and, where possible, encouraging them to make use of affordable housing and service resources— as well as a need for more "safe havens," secure places where a homeless person can eat, sleep, or relax without feeling threatened.

A significant number of the homeless, substance-addicted, and/ or mentally ill people on the downtown streets are there because the "deinstitutionalization" policies that began in the 1960s—the policies that resulted in the closing of many public hospitals and government-funded mental institutions— were not accompanied by adequate funding for decent housing and appropriate managed care in the urban communities where the majority of these people would eventually seek shelter and services. The recent enactment of some of the more stringent sidewalk-behavior measures suggests that society is now apparently ready to acquiesce in at least one form of "reinstitutionalization" for some of these people: putting them in jail. One writer estimates that as many as 200,000 of the 1.8 million people behind bars in 1998 suffered from serious mental illness.[2]

There are only two alternatives to jail (if permanent life on the streets is ruled out as an option): emergency shelter or supportive housing. Although their overriding goal is simply getting people regarded as undesirable off the streets, downtown advocates are not calling for wholesale imprisonment of the downtown special-needs population, nor are they necessarily opposed to emergency shelter and services facilities being located in the downtown area. Most downtown advocates recognize the need for emergency shelter and services and understand that many of the sites where these are offered will have to be downtown, because downtowns are such a powerful magnet for people seeking lodging, money, or help. From the perspective of the downtown advocates, the existence of these resources is not necessarily incompatible with an attractive, marketable downtown, as long as the shelter and services are unobtrusively sited, are effective in drawing people off the streets, and are connected to a larger system that moves these people systematically into longer-term, neighborhood-based housing.

The desire to get people with combined housing and service needs off the downtown streets and into well-managed, neighborhood-based housing is a point of consensus for the downtown advocates and the special-needs advocates. For both groups, a key element of a comprehensive special-needs policy is that *the policy should pursue as a high priority those forms of intervention that are most effective in moving people from the downtown streets into supportive housing located in predominantly residential communities.*

One Philadelphia organization that has been highly effective in addressing this element of special-needs policy is the nonprofit Project H.O.M.E. (Housing Opportunities, Medical Care, and Education), founded in 1989 by Sister Mary Scullion and Joan Dawson McConnon.[3] Project H.O.M.E. has no formal link with downtown development interests—the organization's mission is "to work in partnership with chronically homeless persons in Philadelphia as they strive to attain their fullest potential as individuals and as members of the broader society"—but this group's approach to homelessness is highly responsive to the downtown-related problems and concerns described above. The people who live at Project H.O.M.E. residences are mostly nonwhites, are seriously mentally ill or suffering from substance-abuse disorders, and are formerly homeless and at high risk of becoming homeless again. Philadelphia's Center City is the target area for Project H.O.M.E. outreach activities, which take place every day and night of the year, with added teams during cold-weather months.

The short-term goal of the outreach is to create an informal relationship between the homeless person and the members of the outreach team. Initially, the team members try to engage the person they encounter in informal conversation, to introduce themselves, learn something about the person's background, and, if appropriate, to provide some basic information about day services available through Project H.O.M.E. and other providers. The primary purpose of this activity is not to transport people to shelters or to perform curbside diagnosis but to begin an informal communication that will gradually build a relationship of trust between homeless person and outreach worker.

Following the enactment of "sidewalk behavior" legislation in Philadelphia, Project H.O.M.E. devoted even more attention to reaching chronically homeless individuals. Some outreach teams respond to calls from the police and citizens regarding homeless individuals who are physically or mentally impaired and unable to walk to shelter. Other outreach teams maintain a "focus list" identifying individuals with whom team members regularly communicate on the street. Each team is responsible for insuring that services are made available to the neediest members of the street population and for following up with additional assistance as needed. Many of the people in greatest need are fearful of conditions in city shelters and are suspicious of professional caseworkers who demonstrate a clinical interest in them. The participation of formerly homeless peer outreach workers, who view the homeless people in terms of their emotional needs and desire for human companionship, has been particularly valuable in overcoming these feelings of fear and mistrust. One peer outreach worker told an interviewer, "A lot of case managers work with the mental health problem . . . but there is one thing that doesn't change and that's their emotions. Their feelings and their emotions. They hurt, they cry. And it kind of side steps the mental health. I can reach them because we are talking from an emotional standpoint."[4]

A homeless person who appears to have an interest in recovery may be invited to visit a Project H.O.M.E. worker at her office or to visit a Project H.O.M.E. residence for lunch and a tour. For homeless people who want to consider leaving the streets, three kinds of resources are available.

☐ *Safe havens* are fully staffed residences available to people who want to come in from the streets but may not be ready to enter a recovery program. Safe haven residents are not permitted to use drugs or alcohol on the premises and may not engage in violent or disruptive behavior. Medical services are available on-site, and referrals to mental and physical health resources are provided, along with opportunities for informal discussion about available program resources.

☐ *Highly supportive residences*, also staffed on a twenty-four-hour basis, are available to people who have stopped using drugs and alcohol for several months and are pursuing a specific recovery plan in coordination with a case worker. Meals and health care services are provided on-site. Residents clean their own rooms, do their own laundry at on-site facilities, and participate in counseling and group discussion sessions.

☐ *Minimally supportive residences* provide permanent housing for recovering individuals—apartments for people who are clean and sober, ready to live independently, and able to obtain any service support they need through nearby community-based agencies. Residents are responsible for cooking, laundry, cleaning, and daily chores, and most of them are expected to maintain their own budgets. Project H.O.M.E. provides counseling, educational programs, and training or job-readiness services.

A homeless person interested in living at a Project H.O.M.E. site may enter into any one of these types of residence, depending on his current condition and level of readiness to pursue recovery. Relapses in mental health and sobriety—which can result in a return to the streets—are anticipated and dealt with realistically, sometimes through placement in a hospital or more supportive environment. In all cases, Project H.O.M.E.'s goal is to work with homeless people to improve their physical and mental health and develop their job readiness, so that they can ultimately move to jobs and permanent housing.

When homeless people move off the streets, out of shelters and safe havens and into neighborhoods, the dialogue between homeless advocates and most downtown advocates ends, and a new dialogue—with new opportunities for misunderstanding, disagreement, and conflict—is joined between homeless advocates and members of residential communities. One of the reasons why special-needs policy is so important as an aspect of neighborhood reinvestment is because, when successful, special-needs ventures demonstrate that social diversity is a positive value, not a competitive disadvantage, and that a socially integrated urban neighborhood is a great place to live. Developers and promoters or middle-class and high-end suburban and new-town communities have effectively marketed the opposing worldview for decades: the view that escape and isolation from diversity and integration are fundamental to quality living. The products they offer are designed and marketed to display these qualities as virtues. As Andres Duany, a founder of the Congress for the New Urbanism, has stated convincingly in many presentations, the best suburban and exurban development offers a level of security, predictability, and reliability that cities can't match. Standing on gravel-covered dirt outside a model home in an emerging subdivision or new town, a developer can give a middle- or upper-income consumer a clear, credible presentation of the installation that is to take place on the bulldozed, graded acreage surrounding them: the new streets, the lot lines, the house sizes and types. When completed, the new houses will be identical to the model or will be precisely specified, based on clearly defined standards and controls published and promoted in advance. The consumer hearing this presentation doesn't know the people who will live in the other yet-to-be-built houses, but knows that the neighbors will be similar in the ways that matter: their income, education, professional affiliations, social standing, and career and life ambitions. The much-criticized homogenization of many suburban areas is a real advantage in terms of presentation and marketing. The fear of the unknown that can accompany social diversity never becomes a problem, because real diversity is absent from these places.

Both racial discrimination and discrimination against people with disabilities or supportive service needs can be found in many locations around the metropolitan region. But in the higher-end, newly built residential tracts outside the city, racial discrimination submerges, while bias against special-needs groups remains. White buyers of houses in the new subdivision will not be apprehensive about an African-American family moving into the tract, as long as the incoming family members possess the characteristics that matter, described above. In contrast, the history of suburban development and NIMBYism strongly suggests that the arrival of a formerly homeless family of any race—even a formerly homeless family with an employed head of household and well-behaved kids—would likely be viewed as a disaster for the new subdivision.

The urban counterpart to the suburban developer's marketing of the subdivision described above—a real estate salesperson showing a for-sale house in an existing urban neighborhood—is totally

different. Unless the neighborhood is a gated community, any assurance of security, predictability, and reliability ends at the lot line
defining the perimeter of the property. The salesperson standing
with a prospective buyer and viewing the streetscape from the front
yard can't speak with certainty about the future of the block—or
even the future of the house next door. The apartment building
on the corner could start accepting Section 8 certificate-holders who
may have recently emerged from city shelters. The big Victorian
house down the block could be converted into a residential treatment facility for drug abusers or a hospice for people with AIDS.
The church-and-parochial-school complex nearby could be closed
by the archdiocese and sold, possibly to a developer of housing for
homeless people. The consumer who rejects the opportunity to buy
a house in an urban neighborhood based on this uncertainty can
be called selfish, racist, exclusionary, or morally deficient—but it
doesn't matter. This uncertainty is a fact of life in many urban
neighborhoods and is not a significant issue in many neighborhoods outside the city. To address this uncertainty, special-needs
housing providers have to demonstrate that they can bring value
to a neighborhood rather than downgrade it.

Outstanding supportive housing ventures developed during the
late 1980s and 1990s have demonstrated that the best special-needs
housing development does not downgrade neighborhoods or reduce
property values and that, when planned, developed, and managed
appropriately, a special-needs venture can be a valued community
asset. Future reinvestment policy has to support the production of
more of the best kinds of special-needs ventures and to make possible the upgrading of supportive housing ventures that aren't providing sufficient benefit to both the people living there and to the
community at large. As important is another key element of a comprehensive special-needs policy: that *the policy should support a blend-
ing of special-needs activities with non–special needs neighborhood
reinvestment activities valued by the community at large.* In other words,
special-needs groups should give high priority to improving the
neighborhoods where they are active in order to create a better quality of life for everyone.

Experienced special-needs organizations have accomplished
this goal in many ways during recent years. One of the Philadel-

phia groups that has systematically linked its activities with the implementation of a broader neighborhood improvement plan is People's Emergency Center (PEC). PEC was founded in 1972 by a group of volunteers who opened an emergency shelter in a church basement near the University of Pennsylvania campus. After more than a decade of providing shelter and services for homeless women and children, PEC assembled financing to convert an abandoned warehouse into a headquarters facility and full-service residence. The latter, similar to sites managed by Project H.O.M.E., would incorporate three types of residency a dormitory-style shelter, transitional housing, and permanent, subsidized apartments for families ready for independent living. PEC's new headquarters was located about a dozen blocks from the organization's original shelter site, in a neighborhood that had no community development organization and had not been targeted for city-funded reinvestment programs in past years. PEC established a working relationship with three civic groups active in the area. The board president of one of these groups has served as PEC board vice president for many years.

PEC established its own community development corporation (PECCDC) in 1992 and began community planning intended to lead to the design of a broader neighborhood improvement program for the area surrounding PEC's headquarters. In 1994 the CDC completed its first venture: a gated playground, owned and maintained by the CDC, which was open to all neighborhood children. Following a period of planning with other community representatives, PECCDC acquired vacant properties scattered throughout the neighborhood and packaged them together as a twenty-four-unit rental development venture, Imani Homes. Although all of the apartments in Imani Homes were developed for formerly homeless people who were ready to move from PEC-supported transitional housing, neighborhood residents strongly backed this venture, for two reasons: they had confidence in PEC's capability to manage the apartments responsibly, and they were pleased that the development would "clean up" vacant houses dispersed on otherwise stable residential blocks throughout the community.

PECCDC organized a broader community planning initiative that included the completion of survey work, the convening of brainstorming sessions with neighborhood residents, and the publication of a neighborhood strategic plan in 1998. In addition to documenting existing conditions and summarizing the results of the community-wide discussions, the plan distinguished between improvement activities that PECCDC would complete as developer or producer (such as develop more housing and create a health center), activities that PECCDC would help others complete (such as the development of a tot lot and the publication of a community newsletter), and activities that PECCDC would support but not implement (such as revitalizing the Lancaster Avenue retail corridor, located in PECCDC's service area).[5]

PEC was not the only special-needs organization that succeeded in linking its activities with the interests of the community at large. One of Project H.O.M.E.'s priorities is to prevent homelessness and support neighborhood improvement through activities such as housing development (not limited to special-needs housing development), after-school programs, and landscaping vacant lots. In 1995, the Philadelphia Plan (the state tax credit funding program described in chapter 5) made possible the establishment of a ten-year funding commitment from Crown Cork & Seal, a local container manufacturer, to support Project H.O.M.E.–sponsored revitalization activities in two North Philadelphia neighborhoods where Project H.O.M.E. had already completed planning activities in close collaboration with local civic groups and block organizations. The primary focus of these activities was not special-needs housing and services but comprehensive neighborhood improvement. In one of these neighborhoods, the area around Saint Elizabeth's Church, Project H.O.M.E. maintains a former Catholic school as the location for a Head Start program and a Police Athletic League community recreation program. The former rectory of Saint Elizabeth's (closed a few years earlier, along with the church itself, as part of a downsizing and consolidation of Catholic church facilities in the city) is the location for Project H.O.M.E.–sponsored after-school programs and adult-education classes.

Linkage with neighborhoods is particularly important for preventing future homelessness. A recent study found that homeless people in the emergency shelter systems of New York and Philadelphia previously lived in neighborhoods experiencing housing vacancy and abandonment, overcrowding of occupied housing, higher-than-average unemployment rates, and higher-than-average rent-to-income ratios.[6] Other statistically noteworthy characteristics of these communities were high concentrations of poverty, African-American population, and female-headed households with young children. Providing more affordable housing and better services in neighborhoods with these characteristics is likely to be one of the most effective ways to prevent homelessness and reduce shelter admissions in the future.

When successful, the engagement of special-needs producers in neighborhood improvement creates a consensus shared by the sponsors of special-needs activities and members of the community. Establishing a consensus based on a history of collaborative planning that is responsive to community interests and concerns is one key to success in promoting social diversity in urban neighborhoods. But for the sponsors of one type of special-needs housing, achieving a consensus of this kind presents special difficulties. Group homes, providing a staff-supervised "congregate living" experience for populations as varied as people with chronic mental illness, recovering alcoholics, and adolescents just released from youth detention facilities, are a type of special-needs housing significantly different from the homeless housing programs described in this chapter. The vast majority of group-home sponsors don't have and can't develop the capability to form community development corporations or engage in a broad variety of neighborhood improvement activities. The activities of these organizations are governed by public-agency service contracts that do not support more than the cost of housing and supervising the residents of these sites. In addition, group-home sponsors looking for new locations gravitate toward certain types of urban neighborhoods—older communities containing larger detached or semidetached homes with lots of bedrooms—creating the possibility that an overconcentration of group residences will occur in some areas of the city.

To address this issue in one large section of West Philadelphia, a coalition of civic groups worked with the city's commissioners of human services and public health to create a policy specifically designed to address neighborhood concerns about existing and future group homes. All of the participants in the dialogue leading to the establishment of the new policy agreed on two principles:

that community-based living arrangements were one form of residency appropriate to the neighborhoods represented by the coalition; but that too many group homes produced disadvantages for both the community at large as well as the group-home residents themselves, because a disproportion of congregate housing in any particular neighborhood weakened the neighborhood's status as a diverse, mixed community—the very quality that supporters of congregate living arrangements value most.

This agreement was formalized through a "Residential Site Policy" applicable to "any residence of three or more unrelated persons which receives funding from the City . . . to deliver services to a population on-site via a provider agency."[7] The policy called for each city-funded provider agency to prepare an annual "Good Neighbor Plan" for review and approval prior to renewal of funding. The plan describes complaints received during the preceding year and explains how they were resolved; identifies any outstanding community-related issues and describes how they will be addressed; commits to participation in ongoing consultations with the community coalition; and outlines activities undertaken to maintain or improve the appearance and structure of the property. Community members have an opportunity to comment on the plan and recommend appropriate city action to address any outstanding neighborhood concerns. Under the policy, city agencies encourage providers interested in opening new facilities to consult with neighborhood organizations in advance and city agency staff reviews any proposals for new facilities through "an analysis of program design, clinical expertise, organizational experience, staffing patterns and qualifications, consumer preference as to location, consumer safety issues, public transportation availability, and the local zoning scheme."[8] Although this policy does not impose absolute limitations on the number and location of residential facilities or give community groups veto power over the placement of these facilities, the policy and the underlying city-neighborhood working relationship it documented provided an unprecedented opportunity for government and neighborhoods to anticipate and deal with the planning and management concerns associated with these sites.

Another key element of a finished supportive housing policy

is that *the policy should promote a strong working relationship between resident and service provider, aimed at enabling the resident to move to a condition of least possible dependence and greatest possible self-sufficiency.* A long-standing model of how to create, formalize, and manage this relationship is provided by a Philadelphia nonprofit group, Dignity Housing. The mission of Dignity Housing, founded in 1988 by a group of formerly homeless people and their supporters, is to "promote self-sufficiency and empowerment and to sustain independent living, thus decreasing dependency on federal, state and local government programs."[9] The organization manages 144 rental units—many of them single-family homes—located in various Philadelphia neighborhoods. All of Dignity Housing's dwelling units are supported by site-based Section 8 certificates, that form of rental assistance which is linked to a specific address rather than awarded to the tenant. The prospect of living in a Dignity Housing–managed home is an attractive one, because the Dignity Housing inventory consists of well-maintained, generous-sized properties located on good residential blocks in stable neighborhoods.

One important prerequisite for leasing a Dignity Housing unit is working with the organization's staff to prepare a Life Skills Development plan. This core element of the Dignity Housing approach is a requirement that "each tenant head of household develop and pursue life improvement goals . . . in the areas of education, employment/employment training, parenting, household management, budgeting, homeownership preparation, health and wellness, civic involvement and leadership development."[10] A review of the current status of the household's progress in achieving its Life Skills Development goals is conducted by the head of household and a Dignity Housing staff person on a quarterly basis, with an annual review prior to the renewal of the year-to-year lease, in order to "assess progress, identify and resolve problems, and determine the need for probationary measures or possible termination."[11]

Formerly homeless people referred from emergency shelters to Dignity Housing find the screening process leading to formalization of the Life Skills Development plan to be a challenging and demanding experience. A pivotal stage in this process is an interview between the applicant and a panel consisting of Dignity Housing staff, board, and resident representatives. One formerly homeless woman, now a Dignity Housing board member, described her interview as "very frightening," because "you realize these people are going to make or break you."[12] By the end of the orientation/ screening process, 10 to 15 percent of the applicants for Dignity Housing units withdraw because they aren't ready or willing to adhere to the requirements of the program; 10 percent are rejected because they fail drug tests; and another 5 percent are rejected by the review panel.[13] Those applicants that make their way through the process fully understand the connection between their fulfillment of the goals of the Life Skills Development plan and the fulfillment of the organizational mission of Dignity Housing.

Other capable providers of supportive housing establish similar performance-oriented relationships with residents. For example, each Project H.O.M.E. resident collaborates with a caseworker to prepare a service plan, called a "contract" by the residents, which specifies goals to be pursued during residency at the Project H.O.M.E. site. Service plan elements range from maintaining sobriety to completing course work required for a high-school degree.[14] This approach, like Dignity Housing's, emphasizes resident responsibility, in contrast to purely charitable endeavors—such as street feeding programs—that have no substantive value for homeless people or for the larger urban community of which they are a part. All other organizations interested in engaging in supportive housing activities should be required to adopt a similar approach.

There are three other key elements of a comprehensive supportive housing policy that require less explanation and illustration.

☐ The policy should support the creation and maintenance at the local level of a "continuum of care," a network of affordable-housing and service resources that helps people move systematically from emergency shelter into transitional housing and service programs designed to promote self-sufficiency and independent living. Capable supportive housing providers already are well aware of the value of a continuum of care, and 1990s HUD funding programs provided new support for this approach. In the coming years, the continuum of care should be expanded and stengthened, and its effectiveness maximized through better coordination between housing development agencies and human service agencies. However, HUD should reduce its funding for services in order to make available more dollars for housing development. Supportive services funding should come from the windfall of federal funding that "devolved" to state governments following the enactment of welfare reform. In Pennsylvania, as in other states, most of this money remains unspent.

☐ The policy should support pursuit of the only feasible route to substantially strengthening and expanding the continuum-of-care approach: enacting the changes to the public housing system described in chapter 6. Most, if not all, of the people threatened by homelessness are the people that the public housing system was designed to serve. Many people entering emergency shelters formerly lived in overcrowded, substandard public housing. Homeless and special-needs housing advocates should be in the front lines of the movement for public housing reform, because this system is the only major resource now available to address the needs of the constituencies they represent. A restructured, working public housing system is the only solution to the resource problem for the foreseeable future.

☐ The policy should establish a role for city government as the leading advocate for high-quality supportive housing production and as the mediator of conflicts that threaten to prevent capable special-needs developers from producing at capacity. The darkest period of the Rendell Administration was the one in which the city held up development funding for 1515 Fairmount Avenue, a Project H.O.M.E. permanent residence, in an attempt to accommodate political and neighborhood opponents of this venture. (The city finally relented after losing a court battle and being threatened with federal sanctions.) General expressions of support for special-needs housing and against NIMBYism are not sufficient. Local government has to defend its policy and push hard, when necessary, to achieve performance goals.

Does supportive housing really work? Although perfect results can never be achieved, supportive housing is the only workable approach for getting people off the downtown streets, providing safe places for them to live, and eventually helping them become residents of stable, attractive urban neighborhoods. Supportive housing ventures are not unlike the industrial or retail ventures implemented through public financing: the most successful of these ventures can bring great value to the city, but not all are as successful as one might wish—and even the best policy and the most generous public funding commitments won't guarantee success. As with other forms of urban development and improvement, success cannot be guaranteed or predicted. But one thing is certain: if our policy on supportive housing remains in its present unfinished state, urban social needs will spread and intensify, placing an ever greater economic burden on cities and metropolitan regions.

9

JUMP-START
AND PAYOFF

Back then, in 1978, you couldn't have asked for a better real-life test
of your public-speaking abilities. The sanctuary of Advent Lutheran
Church, located in the heart of West Kensington, another former industrial neighborhood in economic decline, was set up for a community meeting. About a hundred people were there already. As you
entered, you saw that the two back rows were occupied by a familiar
group: a cadre of professional community organizers and volunteer
neighborhood activists, trained to perform in the confrontational Saul
Alinsky style. The meeting was going to be disrupted within fifteen minutes. As an assistant project manager employed by the city, you were
there to explain a series of public programs, such as grants and low-
interest loans for home repair, and to start some coordinated planning for future improvements. They were there to achieve three goals:
expose the limitations of the city's programs, advocate for more city
funding, and establish a role for themselves as brokers of anticipated
community development resources—money for housing and services.

You were going to start explaining the programs, the target area,
the application process. They were going to start interrupting you with
questions, complaints, demands. You would lose control of the meeting quickly. They would keep the pressure on, convincing everyone of
their ability to achieve and maintain total disruption. Some of them

would storm out, shouting, "The city's program is an insult to our neighborhood!" or "The community will control its own destiny!" A lot of other members of the audience would follow, having given up hope of accomplishing anything.

Your challenge this evening: to deliver as much worthwhile information as you could before the shouting started. What key message were you going to try to get across within the limited time available? If you assumed that, at most, two statements of yours would be remembered by, at best, some of the people who had come to find out about the city's programs, what two statements would you choose?

Philadelphia has a time-honored protocol in which your political adversaries verbally sucker-punch you, defame you, slander you, and lie about you; then, after the dust settles, they shake your hand and tell you not to take it personally. I became acquainted with that protocol in the aftermath of those chaotic community meetings at Advent Lutheran Church. Some of the community activists and neighborhood organizers still remaining inside the church after the meeting engaged me in conversation about political goings-on downtown and in the neighborhood. Our dialogue was not unfriendly and not uninteresting, but— like the ruined meeting—it had little bearing on the larger reality. The rulers of government downtown, Mayor Frank L. Rizzo and City Council President George X. Schwartz, couldn't have cared less what these people or I were thinking or doing. The local ward leader and district city councilperson, Harry P. Jannotti, pouring drinks at his taproom a few blocks away, would make sure that any bright ideas we might have about how to change and reshape policy would be marginalized.

One opinion voiced by some of the advocates during these dialogues was that the city's neighborhood improvement programs were really nothing more than a smokescreen, concealing a secret plan to recycle the neighborhood for upper-income residency. Public money would be used to tear down older buildings and acquire property that would then be made available to well-heeled private developers. Luxury housing would be built and current residents—the ones to whom the loan and grant program was being presented—would be priced out of the area and forced to leave.

This view was a serious misunderstanding of the real, far worse, state of affairs: the city had absolutely no plan for the area; the people in the upper and middle ranks of local government had little or no understanding of the real needs of this distressed neighborhood; and no one in a position of real influence was doing anything to change these circumstances. A secret plan would have been relatively easy to expose, combat, and overturn. The lack of a plan, lack of an understanding, lack of a commitment, was an altogether different, possibly unresolvable problem.

The city's program chugged along. Homeowners began receiving repair grants. Our new vacant-house financing program was field-tested, was found successful, and was made permanent. New sidewalks were installed and street trees were planted. Our program activities helped some people get places to live or keep the homes they had, but no one could have mistaken these activities for a comprehensive approach that was going to change the neighborhood decisively. As the years went by, the neighborhood didn't get recycled for upper-income residency, but the city's program didn't noticeably slow the tide of disinvestment either. City funding got renewed every year, but a city-supported plan never emerged.

Neither did a neighborhood-supported plan. During the 1980s, the individuals who had led the advocacy of the late 1970s moved on to other jobs, in government or with nonprofit organizations. Some of their new jobs had a relationship to the neighborhood and its reinvestment needs; others did not. By 1990, the community-based groups that had played key roles in neighborhood organizing during the preceding decade were declining or had become inactive. Although community development corporations emerged in adjacent neighborhoods, no CDC got launched in West Kensington. Strategic plans were published and moved toward implementation in nearby areas during the 1990s, but not here.

Whose fault was it? The city's, for not making this neighborhood more of a priority? The activists', for undermining the government's well-intentioned program-delivery efforts? Everyone's, for not getting together and figuring out how best to create a unified reinvestment approach for the area? Or could it all be blamed on the hard-core economic disadvantages that continued to undermine the neighborhood and worsen its residents' quality of life during these years? No scientific device was available to measure relevant factors and extract precise answers to these questions.

Some years after my first encounters with the activists, the preschool program at Advent Lutheran lost its funding and closed down. After a time, the declining church congregation was dissolved, and the church closed too. The furnishings were carried out, and the building was locked and sealed. No one knew when the doors would open again.

Most government and private-sector leaders are reluctant to challenge the status quo and are unlikely to act on their own to improve policy or initiate reform. For this reason, people who care about urban communities often have to find the best ways to jump-start improvement and change, through neighborhood-level engagement in the city's political system and through other forms of advocacy— that activity which can be defined as the use of influence, persuasion, or coercion to promote a cause or pursue a goal.

Many people who are deeply committed to urban neighborhoods don't understand how valuable the city's existing political system can be as a vehicle for advocacy leading to positive change. As an illustration of this value, picture a special event held in a great hall, packed with people who have gathered there to celebrate a history-making occasion: politicians, civic leaders, government agency managers, community organizers, the media. Up front is a sight none of them have ever seen before: the mayor sharing the stage with the chairpersons and elected officers of the city's Democratic and Republican party organizations. The mayor welcomes everyone and introduces the political leaders flanking him. We're here because we all believe in our city's neighborhoods, he says, and because we want our neighborhoods to have a decisive role in choosing the elected leadership of our city and in influencing state and national elections. He explains the basic elements of the new policy, which is about to be ratified by both the local party organizations. The geographic context for this policy is a newly drafted map, projected onto a huge screen behind him, which divides the entire city into hundreds of compact geographic units, to be known in the future as *neighborhood empowerment districts*. Each district is of sufficient size to contain the residences of about five hundred registered voters. In neighborhoods with an average level of population density, one of these little districts would consist of five or six square city blocks. In all but the most spread-out neighborhoods, you could walk the entire district, passing down every street, in about an hour.

Here's how the new policy will work, the mayor continues. This year and every four years from now on, voters who participate in the spring primary election will choose representatives for the neighborhood empowerment districts where they live. If you're interested in running for this unpaid elective position in your neighborhood, all you have to do is get at least twenty district residents to sign a petition supporting your candidacy, then return the completed petition before the filing deadline for the primary election. When the votes are counted at the end of primary election day, the two highest vote getters within each district will become that district's *neighborhood empowerment coordinators* for the next four years. Each political party is going to elect two coordinators for every district in the city. Together, all the coordinators will constitute a volunteer army of activists, committed to representing the neighborhoods where they live.

Another map flashes onto the screen. The mayor uses a pointer to show how, under the new policy, clusters of twenty to twenty-five adjacent districts are going to be grouped together to form *area-wide opportunity zones.* All the elected coordinators whose districts are located within the same area-wide opportunity zone will meet together within a few weeks after the primary and elect a *zone leader* to represent them in the city's political system. In each zone, the mayor explains, the district coordinators and the zone leader are going to work together closely during their overlapping four-year terms. They will help community members get quicker and better responses to city-service requests, from towing away an abandoned car to repairing broken equipment in a local playground. They will mobilize neighborhood residents to become registered voters and to show up to vote on election days. They will endorse candidates in upcoming elections, for offices ranging from local judgeships to the U.S. presidency.

This whole network of representation and leadership, the mayor says, now creates the most direct link possible between urban communities, city hall, and the city's political system, to everyone's benefit. The mayor steps back, and the Democratic and Republican party leaders address the audience. They each express their unequivocal endorsement of the new policy, which is going to reenergize the city's political parties and increase citizen participation in the local electoral process. "Everyone's a winner," says one speaker, "and the biggest winners are the residents of our city's neighborhoods." The mayor and the party leaders raise their clasped hands in the air as cheers and applause swell up from the audience.

If held now, a special event of this kind would probably draw high praise from the news media and the city's private-sector leadership, and the crowd in the great hall would be likely to include many neighborhood activists ready to enthusiastically support the new policy. But an event of this kind will never take place—because it doesn't need to. A structure identical to the one described above has existed in most American cities for decades. What is surprising is that so many people who spend time advocating for the improvement of urban neighborhoods have not fully explored opportunities to use existing urban political structure as a tool for raising neighborhood interests to a higher level of political priority. Many neighborhood advocates are unable to name the geographic boundaries of the smallest political unit where they live or work, identify the people who serve as their local political representatives, or describe the process through which candidates for neighborhood-level elective positions are chosen.

The structure of the urban political system is a great framework for grass-roots community organizing, because it reduces the city to a network of small, manageable political units. In Philadelphia, these building blocks of the political system are called divisions, and the two party representatives elected from each division are called committeepersons. Divisions are grouped into clusters known as wards, and each party's elected committeepeople within each ward choose their own ward leader. The best ward leaders and the most active committeepeople play an important role—often the critical role—in getting neighborhood problems solved and in mobilizing voters to support endorsed candidates.

Committeepeople who are knowledgeable and responsible form long-term working relationships with staff members in the offices of local elected officials and learn how to use these relationships to get better delivery of city services to their neighborhoods. For their part, elected officials have a strong interest in nurturing and sustaining these relationships, because good committeepeople can have an important, sometimes decisive influence on voter turnout and election results. Just before election day, the best committee-people visit, phone, or circulate newsletters to every voting household in their divisions, encouraging residents to vote for endorsed candidates. All during the subsequent election day, the committee-person maintains a base of operations at curbside outside the polling place, handing out "sample ballots" and other information and dispensing advice. Because elections for some individual positions (such as Philadelphia's clerk of quarter sessions or register of wills) or some generic categories (such as Philadelphia's superior court judgeships) are seldom covered in the news media and never talked about on the street or in the workplace, many voters are inclined to follow the advice of a committeeperson they trust in deciding whom to vote for in these low-profile races. In the best-organized divisions, it doesn't matter how many field workers any given candidate, party organization, labor union, or other interest group assigns to congregate around the polling place; most of the voters walk directly to the committeeperson and pay attention only to the information they receive from this reliable source. In some parts of the city where poverty is high and literacy is below average, a voter arriving at the polls may receive from the committeeperson a handwritten list of numbers—no names or office titles, just the lever numbers of candidates endorsed by the committeeperson. Because the committeeperson is trusted and appreciated for past community service, the voter takes the list into the polling place, pulls the appropriate levers, then gives back the list so that the committeeperson can hand it on to the next person arriving to vote.

Candidates for elective office understand that this neighborhood-level vote-brokering role is critical to success at the polls. During the years when I served as a committeeperson in West Philadelphia, judicial candidates I opposed—even those candidates endorsed by the ward leader and the city's Democratic party organization—sometimes received fewer than half as many votes as the judicial candidates I supported. A dozen capable committeepeople committed to a particular candidate can make a significant difference in one area of a large city such as Philadelphia. A hundred committeepeople committed to a particular candidate can have a decisive influence on a citywide election.

Committeepeople who are at once ambitious and pragmatic and who set realistic goals as the basis for their participation in the local political system can deliver valuable results for the neighborhoods they represent. When the city closed down a fire station in my West Philadelphia neighborhood, the local community organization launched a plan to take over, develop, and reopen the building for some then-unspecified neighborhood-oriented use. The city's Department of Public Property opposed this plan, citing an established city policy that called for auctioning off "surplus" properties of this kind to the highest bidder. Neighborhood residents didn't like this approach, because of the risk that a speculator or someone else who had no interest in improving the community would be high bidder at the public auction. I asked for help from my ward leader, City Councilman Lucien Blackwell, and Councilman Blackwell subsequently contacted the Public Property commissioner and insisted that an exception to city policy be granted, in order to support the neighborhood organization's desire to control the conveyance of the fire station. A short time later, a City Council ordinance authorizing the transfer of the property to the neighborhood organization's development affiliate was drafted, advertised, scheduled for public hearing, and approved by City Council. The building was transferred out of city ownership and was later developed as the Firehouse Farmers Market, a fresh-food center with eight retailers, which quickly established itself as a key neighborhood attraction.

In some urban areas the neighborhood-level party structure is as fossilized and moribund as a dinosaur skeleton. Within these areas, neighborhood advocates have a great opportunity to flesh out the skeleton, bring the structure to life, and create a new level of political standing and respect for the community and its leaders. With this opportunity in mind, every neighborhood supporter needs to identify the local party representatives in the area where she lives or has an interest and figure out how to work closely with them—or, if an incumbent is ineffective or a position is vacant, how to get elected to one of these community-oriented party posts. One person's skill in rearranging and manipulating the neighborhood-level building blocks of the city's political system can produce big results. In 1998, Terry Gillen, a Southwest Center City community member with close ties to neighborhood groups, encouraged a number of local residents to run for committeeperson vacancies in several divisions within the Thirtieth Ward. A significant number of divisions gained new committeepeople as a result. This change, in turn, triggered an upset at the ward meeting following the spring primary, where a coalition of new committeepeople and some reelected ones chose Gillen as ward leader, ousting a veteran incumbent with long-standing ties to the city's Democratic party organization.

Because opportunities to hold office in the local political system are limited and not available to everyone, neighborhood supporters should also consider pursuing other kinds of advocacy opportunities. Assessing the value of each such opportunity is a matter of individual judgment. There are no universally accepted rules for determining whether a particular brand of advocacy is right or wrong, effective or ineffective. Advocacy can take many forms, from mailing a politely worded letter to the editor of a local newspaper to leading an aggressive disruption of a legislative hearing. Advocacy can be altruistic and high-minded or self-serving and exploitative. Advocacy can evoke sympathy, inspire fear and anger, or produce a feeling of deep frustration and helplessness. But every instance of advocacy—whether it comes in the form of a unique, one-time event or an extended multiyear campaign—can be characterized in terms of four elements, each of which should be examined and evaluated by advocates, their audiences, and their targets.

☐ *Issue/response.* What is the point of the advocacy? How have the advocates defined the issue? How are they saying they want the issue to be resolved?

☐ *Existing policy.* Is there a current policy that addresses this issue? Does it work? Whose characterization of current policy is more accurate, the advocates' or the policymakers'?

☐ *Participation opportunities.* Do concerned people have any real opportunities to work with policymakers to address the issue and pursue related goals? Or does existing policy rule out or discourage collaboration and initiative? Does the advocates' characterization of participation

opportunity differ from the policymakers'? If so, whose characterization is more accurate?

☐ *Big agenda.* What broader social, economic, and organizational concerns—whether articulated by the advocates or not—influence the issue and the advocacy? Are these concerns broad and generic matters
(such as poverty or race), or are they much more specific (such as
insufficient government resources to address the issue or a related
problem; or the advocates' use of the issue as the vehicle for publicity, membership building, or fund raising)?

In the 1978 West Kensington episode described at the beginning of this chapter, activists had clearly articulated the issue/re-
sponse element: the community needs and deserves a more
comprehensive neighborhood improvement program, and neighborhood advocates should play a central role in allocating publicly
controlled real estate and government money. The problem in West
Kensington, viewed in terms of the other three elements of advocacy, was that there was no existing policy of any substance, that
there were no good opportunities for interested people to collaborate with policymakers, and that big-agenda issues—the ruin of the
physical environment, the devastating loss of jobs and people, the
unresponsiveness of city government—dwarfed and overwhelmed
our small-time confrontations and dialogues.

The initiative of West Philadelphia residents that resulted in
the creation of the Residential Site Policy authorized by the commissioners of human services and public health (described in chapter 8) is a good example of a focused advocacy campaign that
produced positive results. West Philadelphia civic groups had previously tried to ignore all but the worst problems associated with
group homes in the area—problems such as poorly maintained
house exteriors and yards, excessive noise at night, and poor supervision of residents and visitors—or had tried to resolve these
problems through communications with group-home management
staff or middle managers at the public agencies that funded the residences. When these efforts proved inadequate and the problems
became too serious to ignore, the neighbors organized themselves
and insisted that the mayor and the departmental commissioners
get involved. The issue/response element: group-home development
in the area was uncontrolled, and existing group residences were

not being managed appropriately; for this reason, community members and city policymakers had to reach an understanding about how to prevent overconcentration of group homes in the area and how to deal with operational problems. Recognizing that the existing policy of referring community concerns to on-site staff and city agency managers was proving ineffective, the two commissioners created a new participation opportunity by agreeing to work directly with the neighborhood coalition to formulate a new policy. Two underlying big-agenda issues recognized by both parties helped cement the commitment to this process: the realization that overconcentration of group homes worsened the quality of life for group-home residents themselves, as well as for the neighborhood at large; and the understanding that, in this area of the city, the general community had a long tradition of tolerance and support for special-needs housing as part of a diverse community.

Seeking funding for a development venture is a common, elementary form of advocacy pursued year-round by neighborhood organizations, private developers, and their supporters in elected government and the private sector. Evaluation of this form of advocacy in terms of the four elements is relatively straightforward. The issue/response: a vacant property has to be developed, a needy population has to be housed, or a neighborhood has to be improved; therefore, a commitment of government funding is needed to support a particular development venture. Because advocacy of this kind is such a constant feature of public-sector life, the leaders of the city's neighborhood reinvestment programs have to establish and articulate a policy for the award of development subsidy funding and be clear and consistent about participation opportunities. These concerns are the subject of chapter 3, and the funding "gateway" described in that chapter is the city's definition of the participation opportunity, the way that developers can get access to available money through a process that is responsive and fair.

One December morning in 1993 a group of fifty people trooped into OHCD unannounced and began literally setting up camp in the reception area, unpacking blankets, clothing, food, and children's toys and arranging themselves on the carpeted floor. Television camera crews and newspaper reporters and photographers followed close behind. Most members of the group were young Latina and Caucasian women, some with small children, accompanied by college students and supervised by a small team of seasoned activists. They made three points clear: they were really angry; they wanted to meet with me personally; and they weren't going to leave.

We got acquainted quickly. The group's issue/response presentation, managed exclusively by one of the activists, was a unique blend of in-your-face confrontation and near-total misrepresentation.

We're a group of homeless people who are appealing to you because we have nowhere else to turn.

The women with children were poor, uneducated people who, it subsequently became apparent, lived in overcrowded, poor-quality housing, but none of them were part of the homeless street population. Neither the college students nor the group's organizers were homeless either.

We've tried to work within the system, but the system has failed us.

My assistant made a few quick phone calls and learned that, to the contrary, none of the members of the group were registered in city homeless shelters, and that only a handful had ever applied for Section 8 rental assistance.

We and our children need a place to sleep in safety tonight, and you are responsible for finding us decent housing.

The organizers of the group already knew that the city's emergency-shelter office, not OHCD, was responsible for providing overnight housing and services, and my staff had already found out that none of the members of the group had ever actually applied for emergency housing.

You own hundreds of vacant houses in Philadelphia that are sitting empty while homeless people are denied a decent place to live.

The truth was that the vast majority of vacant houses in Philadelphia were not owned or controlled by the city. Instead, the owners-of-record of most of these properties were people who had abandoned them and left the city; people who had remained in them, then died with-

out leaving a will; or businesses which had departed or dissolved. Those
vacant houses that the city did own were in terrible condition—roofless,
fire-damaged, structurally unsound—and were scheduled for demolition or for expensive, publicly subsidized rehabilitation. None were ready
for people to move into.

We want you to give us a hundred of these houses now. With sweat
equity contributed by our members and supporters, we'll fix them
up and turn them into homes for a hundred homeless families by
Christmas.

A lot more than sweat equity would be needed to rehabilitate the vacant houses actually owned by the city, and some of the members of
the group already knew this. In fact, one of the activists had received
a city grant months earlier to finance major-systems repair work at a
formerly vacant house held by the organization she represented. After the city-funded work had been completed, the organization members weren't able to finish other repair work on windows, doors, stairs,
and floors, and she had returned downtown several months later seeking more city funding. Because major-systems repair emergencies
were OHCD's top housing-preservation priority, no additional public
money was available for these repairs, and her request had been
denied.

During the preceding decade, Philadelphia had sponsored a series of unsuccessful homesteading programs, in which the city
would provide a free vacant house to a family that agreed to fix it
up and live in it. One important lesson learned through this experience was that a free house is not a quick-fix solution to the most
critical problems faced by an impoverished homeless or jobless family. Instead, the family members' emergency housing and service
needs have to be addressed immediately through government-
funded support programs. Then the family needs to move to transitional housing operated by an experienced provider—an organization
such as People's Emergency Center—and the head of household
needs to get a diploma or training certificate and find a job. Sad-
dling such a family with a vacant house rehabilitation project places
family members in jeopardy and makes it harder for them to confront and resolve problems that are even more critical than their
housing need.

The spokesperson pitched the group's issue/response forcefully and clearly: the system has failed us, so give us a hundred houses. As she made her presentation, the internal dynamic of the group became clear. Most of the women and children clustered in front of the television cameras didn't know anything about the city's programs, and the activists were far less interested in steering them to emergency shelter and transitional housing than they were in brokering a deal with the city. The organizers of the group didn't want to change policy; they wanted a payoff. Their under-the-surface big-agenda priorities were publicity and self-promotion. Why target OHCD? Because our CDBG funding was a lot more flexible than the funds managed by the city's emergency shelter office or the Philadelphia Housing Authority—flexible enough to pay for a negotiated settlement, in the form of a new house giveaway or a vacant house rehabilitation program tailor-made for the activists.

These contradictions, inconsistencies, and untruths didn't make the event at OHCD any less attractive a subject for media coverage. The camp-out at the OHCD reception area was a great photo opportunity—homeless families besiege housing office—and the activists' presentation was sound-bite perfect. The media crews weren't interested in considering the fine points of city policy or even in determining who was telling the truth. Other questions were more immediate and newsworthy: Can't you find houses for these families? Are you going to arrest these women and children? Where are they going to sleep tonight? Can't the city do something special for these people during this holiday season?

I refused to agree to the group's demands. The group refused to back off. Nobody went anywhere. That night, security guards cleared the reception area, and police officers arrested a few of the activists who refused to move. The group returned the next day, with a somewhat larger activist/college-student contingent, drawn by the media coverage. They staged demonstrations outside the building, then at the Convention Center and City Hall. I invited the group to meet with me and representatives of supportive-housing organizations such as PEC and Dignity Housing, and the demonstrators agreed to a get-together. Although our differences weren't resolved at this session, the meeting did provide an opportunity to give out some basic information about currently available housing and service resources. The meeting also provided confirmation, through closer observation, that the neediest members of the group were the least knowledgeable about available resources and that, homeless or not, they needed a lot of service support. For example, as a PEC representative later pointed out, the women's poor supervision of their kids during the meeting illustrated one serious problem: inadequate or nonexistent parenting skills.

We finally made a deal: no vacant houses or city funding would be committed to the group; instead, short-term rental assistance vouchers, accompanied by counseling made available through the nonprofit Tenants' Rental Assistance Corporation (TRAC), a service affiliate of the Tenants' Action Group, would be approved for each member of the group seeking housing. The TRAC program provides Section 8–like rental subsidy payments to help an individual or family move from dependency on government assistance to self-sufficiency. In coordination with a TRAC staff counselor, usually an individual who had once been homeless or in critical need of support services, a plan is created for improving the economic status of the individual or family during the months in which the rental subsidy is being dispensed. The overall goal of the program is to enable recipients of the rental assistance to complete education or training, find work, and begin to pay for their own housing (or to obtain longer-term Section 8 rental assistance, if necessary) by the time the temporary rental assistance payments end. All of the participants in the recent confrontations and dialogues supported this approach, some enthusiastically, others reluctantly. TRAC staff began taking applications and scheduling intake interviews, and the demonstrations ended.

Evaluating this resolution of the crisis months later, TRAC staff reported that a substantial number of the members of the group had failed to show up for appointments with TRAC counselors or work effectively with TRAC staff in fulfilling commitments to obtain services and pursue education or training. According to TRAC staff, women with children referred from the city shelter system to the TRAC rental assistance program had a substantially higher rate of follow-through. In other words, our deal was a victory for the activist leaders of the demonstrations but produced no added value for the special-needs constituency that all of us were supposed to be serving.

Even payoff advocacy, centered on getting some form of reward for the sponsors of the advocacy, can produce valuable insights into big-agenda concerns. At the time of the camp-out attempt described above, OHCD managed a number of programs to support the rehabilitation of vacant houses, but the agency had no vacant-house policy, no published approach that described the problem, identified the city's priorities, and established standards governing city intervention. City agencies were not doing enough to create more effective service-delivery systems for the Latino population, particularly for households headed by women. And the city was not doing enough to support homelessness-prevention strategies—in particular, counseling and financial assistance made available through neighborhood-based service agencies—to help address the housing needs of people living in overcrowded, substandard housing in the city's most distressed communities. The women with children who were the centerpiece of the group's advocacy wouldn't have joined the group and allowed themselves to be managed by the activist leaders if these problems hadn't been real.

My most significant and most unpleasant experience with payoff advocacy didn't start with an angry confrontation but with an ostensibly friendly phone call. Two lawyers associated with a public-interest group representing people with physical disabilities wanted to get together to talk informally about the city's policy. We met and reviewed the record. In general, OHCD had complied with federal regulations mandating that every rental housing venture we funded contain some apartments designed as accessible for people with disabilities, with features such as ramps, wider doorways, and first-floor bedrooms. In addition to this record of compliance, OHCD had made funding available to rental ventures sponsored by organizations that specialized in developing housing for people with disabilities, resulting in the production of more accessible units than the amount mandated by HUD. OHCD also funded a housing counseling agency that worked full-time to provide counseling services for people with disabilities. And OHCD had instituted a progressive policy requiring that, in every rental development supported with CDBG financing, at least 20 percent of the units had to be developed and maintained either for people with disabilities or for other residents with special needs.

At our meeting, we acknowledged that, although we shared a common understanding of the HUD rules governing the proportion of accessible units to be developed in rental housing, we differed in our interpretation of the regulations regarding sales housing ventures. The public-interest lawyers and their clients had always felt that the city should require accessible units in every OHCD-funded sales housing venture. OHCD staff disagreed: our position was that, in sales housing ventures, accessible units should only be produced in response to consumer demand. Why require a developer to outfit a house with ramps and first-floor bedrooms if the buyer isn't disabled or doesn't want these features? In addition, none of the participants in the meeting could cite a single instance in which a person with a disability had been unable to buy a house in an OHCD-supported venture because no accessible unit was available.

The wording of the HUD regulations was ambiguous as to whether a set-aside of accessible units was mandated in sales housing ventures, and HUD had never issued a clarification of these regulations. HUD staff who monitored Philadelphia's programs had never brought up the issue, leading OHCD staff to conclude that HUD supported the city's interpretation of the rules. In the broad scheme of things the issue seemed relatively small, because most OHCD-supported housing produced during the preceding decade was rental, not sales, and we all seemed to agree that the city's record in rental production for people with disabilities had met and, in some respects, exceeded federal requirements. The meeting ended, and I agreed to send the lawyers some additional information they had requested.

Not long afterward I received another phone call from the lawyers, with a new message: we're suing you. Citing undocumented, unsubstantiated allegations made by several disabled individuals—most of whom also happened to be members of advocacy groups—OHCD was being charged with violating federal law by denying affordable housing to people with physical disabilities. The lawyers explained that a lot of people with disabilities, including some of the complainants, recognized and respected OHCD's progressive role in advancing housing opportunities for the disabled. However, the lawsuit was necessary, they maintained, in order to resolve our differences over the interpretation of the HUD regulations on sales housing, as well as to produce "institutional change" at OHCD through a settlement agreement compelling the city to formalize new policy that would remain in effect after the current administration had left office. The litigation was just a way of achieving this goal, the lawyers explained, by making permanent some aspects of the progressive policy supported by the current administration and by adding new elements to strengthen and broaden this policy. If we could just reach agreement on a few basic issues, a settlement agreement could be drafted and the litigation settled almost immediately.

I found the legal action and its proffered justification annoying and frustrating. Why hadn't the lawyers and their clients tried to work with us to resolve our differences over the HUD regulations, possibly by forging a new policy that addressed all of our concerns and interests? Why hadn't the advocates named as plaintiffs in the suit taken the time to meet with me or my staff to explain their view of the issues and to give us a chance to address outstanding concerns? Some OHCD staff had long-standing, collaborative working relationships with some of the advocates named as plaintiffs, and no one could claim truthfully that OHCD had a history of unresponsiveness to the issues they cared about. To the contrary, the record showed, and the lawyers agreed, that OHCD policy was much more responsive than that of a lot of other local housing agencies around the country. So why was OHCD being targeted? Why not some other agency—the Philadelphia Housing Authority, for example, which at the time had a below-average record of performance in producing housing for people with disabilities? For the same reason that OHCD, and not PHA, was targeted by the advocates who wanted the hundred-house giveaway: OHCD, unlike the Housing Authority, had lots of relatively flexible funding that could be used to bankroll a special commitment of resources custom-tailored to address the advocates' interests.

The other shoe dropped shortly afterward, when the lawyers submitted to the court a series of demands that OHCD produce volumes of documentation regarding the city's provision of housing for people with disabilities during the preceding decade. The request for documentation was both a fishing expedition and an intimidation tactic, conveying an implicit threat: if you refuse to settle with us, we'll bury you in demands for paper. If the city chose to exercise its constitutional right to defend public policy in court, the lawyers' "requests for production of documents" would absorb thousands of hours of OHCD staff time in completing file searches and extracting requested documents. However, if we surrendered our right to defend the policy we believed in, the lawyers would withdraw their demands for documentation.

Accompanied by attorneys from the city's Law Department, I met with the plaintiffs' lawyers for the first time since the filing of the complaint. They opened the meeting by reemphasizing the plaintiffs' respect for OHCD's progressive record in providing housing for people with disabilities and their willingness to resolve outstanding issues quickly. By this time, the court had imposed specific deadlines for the "production of documents" demanded by the plaintiffs. In conciliatory fashion, the lawyers offered to approach the court to seek extensions of these deadlines, if OHCD would agree to enter into settlement negotiations immediately. What did the plaintiffs want? A set-aside of program funds, accompanied by a series of new programs and policy changes. My anger and frustration grew. The people who were about to bear the burden of the document-production orders were precisely those OHCD staff who had worked hardest to respond to the housing needs of people with disabilities and who had done more to support the plaintiffs' broad goals than anyone else in city government. Now, as the price of defending ourselves, they were about to become full-time file clerks. The days and weeks they would be spending on paper retrieval was time that they would ordinarily have devoted to working on accessible-housing issues and to helping disabled-housing organizations and their clients.

What made me really angry was the realization that the kind of negotiated settlement the lawyers wanted would amount to a court-sanctioned circumvention of the democratic process, that process through which housing policy and the city's housing budget are drafted by the city administration, presented for public review and response, then brought before the locally elected legislative body—in this case, Philadelphia's City Council—for another public review and response prior to implementation. The lawyers were

seeking a payoff that would preempt this process: an advance res-
ervation of funding and pledges of support for program activities
that would remain in place no matter what City Council and the
general public might want. The real message underlying this advocacy: we don't care about good policy; we care about getting paid.

And what about the danger of precedent setting? If I agreed to
a settlement, what would prevent the next public-interest advocacy
group from employing the same approach to carve out a set-aside
for the interest group they represented—persons with mental illness, for example, or the Latino population? A trend of challenges
to city policy could start, and, by the time the carve-outs ended,
there would be nothing left of mainstream public policy—that
policy authorized by elected government and supported by a majority of citizens interested in promoting the general good.

Following our dialogue with the public-interest lawyers, the
city's attorneys tried to calm me down. They patiently explained
the realities of the situation. The plaintiffs were well within their
rights to ask for the mountain of paper they had identified as part
of the discovery process. The advocates named as plaintiffs were
not under any obligation at this point to prove that OHCD had
denied them the opportunity to obtain affordable housing; in fact,
their personal experience wasn't really that relevant to the overall
case. The point of view the judge was likely to take also had to be
considered. The judge would probably regard our dispute as just
another disagreement between big government and representatives
of one of the needy constituencies that government was supposed
to be serving. Any issues of contention would probably be resolved
by the judge through a ruling that tilted in the direction of the
needy population, not the big government. More important, if the
case went to trial, the judge could conclude the litigation by issuing a court order far more demanding and wide-ranging than anything the plaintiffs were proposing as the basis for settlement. From
this perspective, the city's attorneys explained, the plaintiffs were
really doing OHCD a favor by offering to settle rather than to continue a litigation which would drain OHCD staff resources and
might produce a result far more at odds with my policymaking principles than anything the advocates were seeking.

Still feeling just as angry, I agreed to enter into settlement negotiations. A few months later, a settlement agreement was drafted, okayed by both parties, brought to the court, and authorized by the judge. The settlement agreement required us to make a number of commitments that we would have agreed to anyway if we had been given an opportunity to conduct, outside the context of a lawsuit, a dialogue with advocates for the disabled: to improve outreach and marketing for accessible units developed through OHCD's program; to increase funding for an existing program that financed the adaptation of owner-occupied houses for occupancy by people with disabilities; to schedule a special seminar on housing affordability issues affecting people with disabilities. The litigation also compelled OHCD to make a few commitments that we would not have agreed to in a dialogue with advocates and that seemed unlikely to make OHCD-supported housing any more available to prospective buyers who happened to be disabled. For example, the settlement agreement required OHCD to produce a certain number of new-construction sales housing units with bedrooms and full bathrooms on the first floor. The units were to be outfitted in this manner whether or not there were any buyers (with or without disabilities) who wanted houses with these features. The likely long-term effect of this provision: these specially designed houses for sale would be harder to market than other houses, and many of them would eventually be occupied by people who were not disabled and had no need for custom-designed accessibility features.

The encounters described above illustrate the need for city government to strongly and effectively advocate for its own policy. Local government leaders have to find the best ways to persuade interested people that the city has an appropriate and realistic neighborhood reinvestment policy—not just a collection of programs—and that this policy makes sense and deserves support. Local-government advocacy is strongest when city officials lead with the big agenda and set all implementation issues within that framework. Example: government funding to support neighborhood reinvestment is limited, and neighborhood needs significantly outweigh available resources; for this reason, in order to dispense available funding fairly and responsibly, all proposals for affordable-housing production must compete for development subsidy funding and must comply with published selection criteria. In contrast, grass-roots advocacy is most effective when advocates lead with their issue/response presentation. Example: our neighborhood needs more housing; give us funding to build houses on vacant lots. The city's policy has to anticipate and answer issue/response presentations to minimize the risk of a challenge which can only be resolved through ad hoc deal making and the appeasement of one special interest at the expense of the general public.

A skillfully articulated, widely promoted neighborhood reinvestment policy is the best way for local governments to defend themselves against payback advocacy launched from outside. Why is a particular neighborhood being designated as a target area for public investment? Why doesn't city government just give away vacant houses to homeless people? Why isn't the city using more of its housing budget for programs aimed at attracting and keeping middle-class residents? If jobs are more important than housing, why isn't more funding being dedicated to jobs programs? In Philadelphia, I had a great opportunity to address these questions and promote OHCD policy through publications on key issues—our Lower North Philadelphia housing production approach, described in chapter 2, for example—and through a series of annual conferences on big-agenda topics, from welfare reform to the future of CDCs. Other local-government leaders have to find similar opportunities in their own environments to publicly define key issues and show that the city is addressing them systematically. The traditional local-government approach, which defines reality in terms of existing public programs and complains about the need for more federal and state funding, will not succeed in elevating neighborhood reinvestment issues to a position of higher standing as priorities for the city and region.

Another particularly important reason why local government should strongly advocate for its policy is that good opportunities to change federal policy are rare and limited. OHCD's strongest defense against the payoff advocacy of the public-interest lawyers was the agency's generally strong past performance in producing accessible housing and in collaborating with advocates for people with disabilities. Without this strong record of performance, the legal challenge to OHCD and the associated terms of the settlement agreement demanded by the lawyers probably would have been far more severe. To resolve this issue at the national level, OHCD would have had to successfully challenge key provisions of fair housing law and the Americans with Disabilities Act—not a very realistic prospect. As decades of recent experience have shown, general-purpose advocacy—such as advocacy for better policy on neighborhood reinvestment—is far less effective at the national level than single-issue advocacy, as practiced by groups as varied as the Alzheimer's Association and the National Rifle Association. Although local neighborhood supporters should get involved in advocacy at the national level when the right opportunities emerge, their primary focus should be on creating the most defensible local policy possible in their particular environment.

For a number of reasons, national housing and community development groups, including professional associations like the National Association of Housing and Redevelopment Officials (NAHRO) and advocacy organizations like the National Low-Income Housing Coalition, have had limited success in conducting advocacy for better national policy on key neighborhood reinvestment issues. The broad national representation of the big professional associations and the dependence of their members on a continuation of existing federal programs administered by agencies such as HUD makes them unlikely vehicles for a focused, hard-charging advocacy for change. National advocacy organizations, on the other hand, are likely to have fewer resources and weaker political connections than supporters of the status quo policies affecting the interests of constituencies such as banks, insurance companies, or suburban real estate developers.

The only organization that has really succeeded in launching and sustaining a national advocacy centered on neighborhoods and investment issues is the Congress for the New Urbanism. Within a few years after its founding in 1993, CNU had drawn the attention of many professionals in planning and design fields, attracted national media coverage, produced a succession of well-attended annual meetings, influenced major federal funding programs, and enlisted the enthusiastic participation of several respected big-city mayors. As discussed in chapter 2, "traditional neighborhood design" as practiced by new urbanists is not the most effective strategic approach for urban neighborhoods struggling with disinvestment. As one travels from exurb and edge city toward inner-city communities, with every mile the new urbanism gets weaker and weaker as a guide to practice. But as a national advocate, CNU has called attention to many issues that are fundamentally important to supporters of urban neighborhoods: the value of planning and design approaches that promote diversity and a pedestrian-oriented street life; the need for more effective management of public spaces; and the desirability of marketing urban neighborhoods based on the competitive advantages they may possess over other residential communities in the region. In the coming years, the discussion of a national advocacy for neighborhood reinvestment should not focus on the limitations of the new urbanism but on a much more important question: What advocacy approach should supporters of urban neighborhoods pursue in order to be as effective as CNU in drawing the attention of professionals, attracting the media, producing well-attended annual events, influencing federal programs, and securing commitments of participation from big-city government leaders?

Whether skillfully organized or poorly managed, whether intended to benefit a broad constituency or a narrow organizational interest, all advocacy should be regarded as a learning experience that provides value in two ways: as a barometer that helps one measure the depth of public sentiment on a particular issue and as a test of the completeness and effectiveness of existing policy in addressing the issue. People who are interested in neighborhood reinvestment policy should look for this value in any form of advocacy that they find themselves compelled to initiate, react to, or resolve.

10

TO JUMP HIGHER,
TO RUN FARTHER

The framework for neighborhood recovery described in this book can be used to organize policy and pursue reinvestment opportunities in any city. However, because economic disinvestment affecting urban neighborhoods is a complex problem without precedent, no guaranteed prescription for neighborhood recovery exists—not in Philadelphia or anywhere else. Neighborhood supporters in every city can learn the elements of the framework, then decide how best to build out their own policy from this basic structure. Local leaders in government and neighborhoods can compare their city's current policy with the approach described in this book—their city's homeownership policy, for example, with that described in chapter 4—then make their own decisions about how to move ahead. Should current homeownership programs be expanded, reorganized, reoriented, downsized, eliminated? Should local homeownership program models be strengthened, or should programs that succeeded in other cities be studied, imported, and replicated? In each city, neighborhood supporters have to find that unique combination of activities that defines the city's reinvestment policy and works best in the local environment.

Get serious, stay focused, work harder are the imperatives that guided urban leaders in achieving the three best-publicized successes of the 1990s: lower crime, competent municipal government, and rejuvenated downtowns. The same imperatives have to be recognized by all the leaders of neighborhood reinvestment policy, from the city's mayor to the neighborhood block captain. *Get serious, stay focused, work harder.* Visioning, partnering, best practices, outcomes, cross-training, sustainability—none of these state-of-the-art buzzwords that permeate the high-priced needs assessments and planning studies of recent years have any analytical or prescriptive value unless local leadership is serious, focused, and determined to succeed in addressing the challenge of neighborhood reinvestment.

Neighborhood supporters can determine whether or not neighborhood reinvestment policy is working effectively in a particular city by assessing current activities in terms of four variables.

PEOPLE

Make a list of every government or government-controlled agency that has a role in the acquisition, financing, development, or management of real estate within the city, then rank each agency in terms of the staff's intelligence, competence, and responsiveness. Don't show me the results; I think I can predict them. In most cities, the highest scorer will be the agency that finances downtown development and other major private-sector development deals supported with public resources, such as revenue bonds, Section 108 loans, tax increment financing, and other financial incentives designed to attract and keep jobs and to generate tax ratables. The lowest scorer is likely to be the public housing authority or one of the CDBG-funded agencies responsible for managing community development activities. This disparity in professionalism shouldn't exist in any city; where it does exist, the city is broadcasting a message that neighborhood reinvestment is much lower in priority than downtown development and that lower-quality management and political interference are an accepted norm in the departments responsible for key neighborhood reinvestment activities.

What's it going to take to upgrade the low scorers to the level of professionalism demonstrated by the highest scorer? What are the mayor, the local legislature, and the board members and executives of these agencies doing to realize this change in the foreseeable future? Who needs to be fired, retired, laid off, transferred, or reassigned to make this happen? The mayor and the leaders of the local legislative body have to be the most vocal advocates for professionalism in the leadership and management of neighborhood reinvestment activities. If the city's elected leadership isn't dead serious about the issue of professionalism, the city's most distressed neighborhoods will continue to decline, without hope of recovery. In cities with a strong-mayor governmental structure, the mayor has to consistently support the people chosen to lead the city's neighborhood reinvestment approach. Government agency executives, in turn, have to make the tough but crucial decisions about managerial and operational changes that will improve performance. These tasks are difficult and often time-consuming, but they must be undertaken and carried through.

There is a bright side that emerges when this challenge is confronted. Housing and community development agencies in even the worst-run cities contain a significant number of idealistic, energetic younger women and men who care about neighborhoods and want to devote their professional lives to improving urban communities. Some of these people will be ready to make extraordinary commitments of their time and energy to leaders who appreciate what they can contribute and encourage their initiative. These people may or may not be future department heads, but their expanded participation in the implementation of neighborhood reinvestment policy is an important benefit that can be realized early in a campaign for organizational improvement and increased professionalism.

The leaders of organizations engaged in neighborhood reinvestment have to try to find ways to encourage ambitious people who want to move to higher positions or earn more performance-related compensation in the agency or organization where they work. This task is difficult in the current environment of limited funding resources and correspondingly limited financial rewards: due to ongoing funding constraints, staff costs have to be held down, staff turnover may not be frequent, and new job titles and promotion opportunities can't just be created at will. Despite these limitations, people with ambition are going to feel a greater sense of opportunity if all the appointive positions in agencies with neighborhood reinvestment responsibilities are being filled by competent people, while the ineffective or incompetent are being forced out or worked around. Within community development corporations, ambitious people can be encouraged by being given the opportunity to become players in performance-oriented development financing programs that are accessible year-round and that deliver more development subsidy funding, and associated developer fees, to organizations that produce more.

MONEY

Good policy is more valuable than money, but even the best policy won't produce good results for neighborhoods without a sustained flow of discretionary, flexible funding made available year after year. Urban neighborhoods can't recover without lots of capital invest-ment—the level and type of investment that federal and state governments have historically made to support highways, civic centers, and stadiums. "Reinventing government" initiatives designed to cut costs and increase productivity will produce some good results, but no amount of government reform, reorganization, and realignment is going to generate the capital needed for neighborhood recovery, because so much needs to be done, from cleaning up toxic industrial sites to funding supportive services and case management associated with new transitional housing. Because neighborhood reinvestment activities such as these don't generate user fees, prof-its, or rapid growth in tax ratables, they will always be dependent on public funding, most of which must come, as in the past, from the federal government.

So why can't the federal government do a better job of rein-venting itself with respect to neighborhood reinvestment policy? Although a more enlightened federal policy would be welcome, the experience of recent years—the years of the Clinton Administra-tion and the Contract-with-America Congress—strongly suggests that the prospects for fundamental change at the federal level are not good. Proposals for across-the-board budgetary increases for existing programs are likely to continue to go unanswered. Com-plaining about the insufficiency of funding or about related bureau-cratic and regulatory burdens is not likely to produce the policy changes that urban neighborhoods need. Worse yet, complaints of this kind may serve as the impetus for much-celebrated federal "reforms" that actually reduce the net resources available to cities. The HOPE VI program and the Section 202 public housing downsizing mandate, discussed in chapter 6, are two examples of federally imposed "solutions" that have resulted in disadvantages and resource loss for urban neighborhoods.

The approach that will be most effective in future efforts to secure funding for neighborhood reinvestment is a two-part strategy: lobbying for increased funding of existing programs that are nationally recognized as productive and cost-effective (programs such as CDBG, HOME, and the Low Income Housing Tax Credit); and advocating for a public housing reform policy that maintains current funding levels but provides more flexibility and local discretion to cities with strong performance records.

Rust-belt cities with older housing possessing characteristics such as masonry construction, historical significance, lead paint and asbestos, "party-wall" attachment to adjacent houses, and location on otherwise good residential blocks with a high level of occupancy, have to address a particularly difficult money-related issue: the high cost of housing rehabilitation. As discussed in chapter 1, a "clean slate" approach to development, through urban-renewal-style acquisition, relocation, demolition, and large-scale new construction isn't possible or desirable in many older urban neighborhoods today. On relatively good blocks, the cost of hand-demolishing a vacant house located between two attached, occupied houses and "infilling" the gap with a new house can be substantial. In older cities, a top-priority landmark venture involving vacant-house rehabilitation may require significant investment in lead and asbestos abatement, structural stabilization, and restoration of historic features, producing a much higher than average rehabilitation cost.

Where these conditions exist, local government should pursue vacancy prevention and lower-cost rehabilitation strategies, as described in chapter 2. The city's housing finance agency, the equivalent of Philadelphia's RDA, has to enforce tough underwriting standards to hold down the cost of rehabilitation. At the same time, however, the city's policymakers have to be prepared to support top-dollar commitments of development subsidy funding for top-quality rehabilitation of strategically important properties. In the Cecil B. Moore area of North Philadelphia, per-unit development subsidy for the rehabilitation of a badly deteriorated, historically certified, generous-sized rowhouse consistently exceeded seventy-five thousand dollars—more than the median sales price of a single-family home in the Philadelphia market. However, because the Cecil B. Moore neighborhood was part of the strategically important Lower North Philadelphia area—the city's top-priority target area for housing production—high-cost rehabilitation was supported as part of the cost of reclaiming this older neighborhood as a viable new residential community. Everyone should be concerned about high development subsidies; but if cost becomes the primary consideration guiding neighborhood reinvestment policy, then areas such as the Cecil B. Moore district will be abandoned despite their strategic value, and fundamental questions about the future of these areas will be defaulted to future generations of policymakers.

Arguing that good policy takes precedence over cost reduction is particularly difficult because neighborhood development ventures are subjected to greater scrutiny and exposed to more criticism than downtown projects. In most cities, no one critiques the cost of the marble floors in the new hotel, the window treatments in the new civic center, the cost of the exterior design proposed for the new retail complex, or other design features of downtown development to which the city is providing subsidies and financial incentives. But many people will feel justified in criticizing all high-cost housing production as a waste of government money. More often than not, these critics happen to be people who enjoy the benefit of the mortgage interest deduction, a government subsidy that provides higher-income households with much more taxpayer-financed value than the development subsidy associated with affordable-housing production activities. Good neighborhood reinvestment is as important to the city as good downtown development, and leaders of neighborhood reinvestment have to wage a convincing public-relations campaign against the current double standard by which high-cost neighborhood ventures are automatically assumed to be wasteful, while high-cost downtown projects are routinely exempted from cost-related scrutiny.

How are the leaders of the city's neighborhood reinvestment policy defining and managing these money issues? Who is leading the initiative for public housing reform? Are underwriting standards for publicly subsidized development ventures published and consistently applied to proposals for development funding? Does the city's elected leadership consistently support the city housing finance agency's role as enforcer of these standards? How does the city establish an upper limit for per-unit rehabilitation cost? What is going to be done with vacant houses that can't be rehabilitated within this established cost limit? The answers to these and related questions will show how well the city is handling the money variable.

INTEGRATION

How can we get whites and blacks to live together comfortably in urban neighborhoods, or encourage other racial and ethnic mixes in the city's communities? What's the best way to encourage income mixing and bring more middle-income people back into the city's lower-income communities? The answer to both questions is the same: improve the public schools, make the neighborhoods safer, and make the local tax structure more competitive with that of nearby suburban areas. The best possible package of housing incentives designed to encourage racial and ethnic integration or attract middle-income residency won't bring decisive change if the issues of schools, safety, and taxes aren't addressed decisively.

Although housing programs are secondary in importance to these overriding priorities, housing incentives can still play an important role in promoting racial/ethnic integration and middle-income/lower-income integration. The best housing strategies for encouraging both kinds of integration are not real estate development projects but consumer-oriented programs linked to the purchase of a house in the city's for-sale market, programs such as the Philadelphia housing counseling and settlement assistance activities described in chapter 4. As indicated in this chapter, an analysis of program results suggests that Philadelphia's consumer-oriented approach accelerated the expansion of the Latino population outward from concentrated areas of residency and enabled a significant

number of African-American buyers to move into more racially integrated neighborhoods.

The most effective housing incentive for mixed-income residency attempted in Philadelphia during recent years is a program
launched by the University of Pennsylvania in 1998. The Penn program, structured as a consumer-oriented approach, offered any university employee who purchased a home in West Philadelphia a
choice of either a fifteen-thousand-dollar cash payment at settlement or annual payments of three thousand dollars for seven years
following settlement. Within months after the opening of this program, dozens of university employees, from buildings-and-grounds
workers to tenured faculty, had already made use of it to buy homes
in West Philadelphia. The West Philadelphia real estate market grew
measurably stronger, and the many for-sale signs long evident in
the area began to vanish.

Both the city-sponsored housing counseling and settlement assistance program (funded entirely with public money) and the University of Pennsylvania program (funded entirely with university
money) demonstrate that consumer-oriented, market-linked incentives will stimulate home sales and can substantially improve the
private real estate market. Dollar for dollar, these kinds of incentives are far more effective than government-subsidized real estate
development, in terms of generating more real estate sales, raising
property values, and promoting integration. In each city, the extent to which local government and major employers are supporting consumer choice is an important test of the effectiveness of
overall neighborhood reinvestment policy.

While working to promote mixed-income residency, cities
should determine how to recover the resources lost during the past
decade in one critical area: affordable housing for the lowest-
income citizens. What are the leaders of the city's neighborhood
reinvestment policy doing to support more production of high-
quality transitional and permanent housing for citizens with special needs? What is being done to address the housing and service
needs of those people who, displaced from downsized or closed-
down public housing sites, have been issued Section 8 certificates
instead? In the biggest cities, the HOPE VI and Section 202 transformations of troubled conventional public housing sites are gen-

erating an unprecedented level of displacement and an associated resettlement and integration problem that cities need to understand, confront, and solve.

PRESENTATION

During the 1990s an interesting trend began to emerge in Philadelphia's downtown area. Companies that had moved out years earlier to relocate elsewhere in the region, primarily to suburban office campuses, began leasing Center City office space and moving some of their workforce back into Philadelphia.[1] This trend was limited in scale and impact—the companies weren't abandoning the suburbs altogether, and these "return" decisions, by themselves, weren't transforming the Center City office market—but each decision to come back meant the recovery of jobs for Philadelphia.

Why did these businesses decide to move workers back to Philadelphia? The city offered attractive financing to some of them, but other factors also influenced the "return" decisions. The downtown area had become much safer and more attractive than it had been during the preceding two decades, thanks in large measure to the accomplishments of the Center City District, the private business improvement district organization devoted to downtown management. City government had improved substantially under the Rendell Administration, and Mayor Rendell's success in overcoming a colossal budget deficit and producing a series of annual budget surpluses was recognized as solid evidence of improved local governance. Finally, the corporate decision makers recognized that the downtown area possessed an intangible value that suburban office campuses couldn't match: the value realized when people work in close proximity to their associates, customers, and clients and can meet them or encounter them unexpectedly in an office building, on the street, or at a restaurant or coffee shop. The best electronically networked suburban office can't offer comparable opportunities for people to meet face to face, transact business in person, and enjoy one another's company.

Some serious downtown problems were still very much in evidence at the time when companies began making these "return" decisions. Homeless people could still be seen on the sidewalks,

crime had not vanished (although crime rates had dropped substantially), and no one could guarantee continued improvement
in future local-government administrations. Despite these limitations, the corporate decisions to move back showed that supporters of Philadelphia's downtown were succeeding in presenting its
competitive advantages, in highlighting recent improvements, and
in conveying a message that the city was getting better and better.

Urban neighborhoods need to be able to deliver a similar kind
of presentation during the coming years, a presentation that emphasizes the values of urban living and calls attention to improvements recently completed or currently under way. The 1990s were
the first decade in which the disadvantages of suburban living—
the isolation, the overcrowded infrastructure, the emerging social
problems—began to be widely publicized in the news media and
in popular literature.[2] Supporters of urban neighborhoods have to
find highly effective ways to present what should be recognized as
the most logical alternative to the suburbs: finding a great place to
live in the city, in the kind of new-hometown setting where people
are able to get acquainted with their neighbors, where the physical plan of the community is pedestrian-friendly and interesting,
and where other urban attractions—stores, museums, universities,
the parks, the waterfront—are readily accessible.

Most of the people who demand a perfect, full-service living
environment—with round-the-clock security and highly supervised
management of streets and public spaces—will never consider living in the city under any circumstances. But most people don't demand perfection in a neighborhood environment, just as the
business leaders who made "return" decisions weren't expecting
perfection in the downtown environment. A lot of people will move
to and live in an urban community that contains some vacant
houses and that includes some people who are jobless, formerly
homeless, or in need of specialized assistance such as community-
based mental health services. If the neighborhood's primary assets—
houses and people—are generally attractive, if the real estate market
appears to be relatively stable, and if existing neighborhood problems appear to be solvable, many people will buy into an urban
neighborhood and stay there for years.

A successful presentation of urban neighborhoods has to be linked to an effective improvement strategy—sometimes documented in a neighborhood strategic plan—that shows how neighborhood problems are being addressed through a sequence of improvements that produces visible progress each year. This documented series of actions, in turn, has to be supported by a great neighborhood reinvestment policy, established and promoted by local-government leaders and managers as the basis for setting priorities, creating performance standards, and committing resources. A great neighborhood reinvestment policy for the coming years is neither a government-guaranteed total-improvement approach, like the urban renewal policy that produced Society Hill and Yorktown during the sixties, nor an approach that cedes control either to neighborhood-based organizations or to the developers of today's highly managed state-of-the-art, high-end new towns or gated communities. Instead, the best neighborhood reinvestment policy for the future is the one which recognizes that current limitations and hardships require government and neighborhood interests to be disciplined and systematic in their use of available resources.

The task of carrying out a neighborhood strategy in an uncertain environment, while simultaneously addressing the broader urban issues of schools, safety, and taxes, is a formidable one, and some cities will find it difficult to organize and implement a strategic approach for presenting currently distressed neighborhoods successfully to consumers and the general public during the coming years. Municipal government has to continue to improve. The best people have to be found to lead government policy and advance neighborhood initiative. Available resources have to be managed creatively and responsibly. Major new threats to stability, of which the greatest now is the nation's poorly conceived, badly coordinated welfare reform policy, have to be confronted and dealt with.

The urban environment is constantly changing; certainty and predictability are nowhere to be found. As we plan and implement, the earth moves beneath our feet. We can neither look back nor defer taking responsibility for problems that the current generation of leaders needs to confront and resolve now. In each city, the question is,

Are we ready? Are we ready to make a serious commitment to urban neighborhoods, to support a goal of total recovery for these places of high risk and big opportunity?

In late December 1998, at the end of the next-to-last year of the Rendell Administration, I thought about my goals, plans, and dreams for the coming months. One high-ranking dream: to make the OHCD budget hearing, likely to be scheduled in May, into a celebration of the success of Philadelphia neighborhood reinvestment policy.

In the scenario I imagined, a throng of excited people poured into City Council chambers, filling up the rows of seats facing in from three sides, pressing up against the marble walls in the rear, crowding up along the front rail behind the councilpersons' desks, looking down from the mezzanine. Council's Finance Committee stopped the budget hearing to allow time for hundreds of people, most of whom had traveled in groups bused from their neighborhoods to City Hall, to enter and find places to sit or stand. A homemade banner hung over the mezzanine rail facing front. The inscription could be seen easily from across the room: THANK YOU, blocked out in foot-high capitals.

The turnout for this housing budget hearing was the biggest in more than a decade—the biggest since the dismal free-for-all period during the 1980s, when the mayor, council leadership, and the housing director were hopelessly disconnected from one another. Back then, the hearings sometimes went on for days, with testimony and debate continuing past midnight. By the time the housing budget had passed through this gauntlet and had been voted out of Finance Committee, no one was really pleased—not the council members, not the mayor's staff and the exhausted housing agency staff, and certainly not the neighborhood constituencies who tried to influence the direction of the city's programs, some through a play-by-the-rules approach, others through challenges and confrontations.

Today was a welcome contrast from those bleak days and nights. This time, citizens had come to acclaim the city's policy. Some people crowding into the big room remembered that dark earlier period. A few of them had been among the most vocal critics of the city's approach during those years. Other people in council chambers that day had only recently become engaged in neighborhood work, and the city's recent years of success were their only frame of reference, their first and only impression of what a neighborhood reinvestment policy should be. The experience would be inspiring and unforgettable for everyone present—at least, that's what I hoped.

As I thought about the budget hearing and other events in the upcoming final year, questions that had confronted me long before came drifting back: What do you want to happen? And what are you going to do? There was really no way to predict how the coming year's budget hearing would actually turn out, and it would be impossible for me or anyone else to orchestrate an event like the one I was imagining. Every position in City Council would be up for election that year, just like the mayor's seat. By the time of the budget hearing, the end of Mayor Rendell's administration would be six or seven months away. Some of the incumbent City Council members might be preparing to leave office. The early-May mayoral primary would be over, and the best-organized neighborhood constituencies would already be scoping out opportunities to collaborate politically with the Democratic and Republican victors. Under these circumstances, the scene at the budget hearing might be entirely different from what I hoped: it might turn into a public airing of grievances about the failures and shortcomings of current city policy and a launchpad for new challenges that would need to be confronted during the late months of this administration and the first months of the next. The hearing could turn ugly and revive the spirit of those bad old days, portending the start of a now free-for-all.

But even if it could happen, what message would be conveyed through the outpouring of public support in the budget hearing scenario that I imagined? What would the people who saw this spectacular display of enthusiasm and good will say or think about it? Would it come off as a big accolade for me? In earlier years, as an outsider, I had hated the paternalism of some previous OHCD administrations, the implicit message conveyed to favored constituencies: "I'm an important person, and I'll take care of you, provided you show the proper respect at the appropriate time." A testimonial to me would convey the message that payback for services rendered was a foundation of city policy. Besides, my leadership and my policy were not universally acclaimed—far from it. For every enthusiastic supporter, there were plenty of other people who thought of me as too narrowly focused, as inflexible, as not sufficiently receptive to new opportunities for innovation and collaboration, as overly supportive of a less-than-perfect staff infrastructure.

To other people, the event would convey a message about Mayor Rendell's leadership and about how the next mayor should deal with neighborhood issues. Some people would always think that Rendell didn't care about neighborhoods or that he hadn't really backed up my leadership of OHCD during the past years. They were wrong. Rendell had been outspoken in his criticism of the welfare-reform policy approved by his friend Bill Clinton, and in dozens of public appearances he had repeatedly warned audiences against concluding that the 1990s successes of big-city downtowns meant that economic recovery for urban neighborhoods would inevitably follow. The mayor and I never worked together closely on a day-to-day basis, but he listened to me, absorbed my memos on program-development issues, memorized and recited data from the policy papers I wrote, and publicly endorsed my stance on every major issue. On several occasions, I would send over a summary description of a new program involving a major new funding commitment; he reviewed the material, discussed it with Council President Street, saw to it that any related questions were dealt with, and approved the program and the money within a week or two. During each of the difficult middle years of the administration, the mayor and his chief of staff, David L. Cohen, agreed to my request for an annual end-of-year meeting away from City Hall to talk over big-agenda issues and consider our policy direction for the coming months. We met in a conference room at Rendell's former law firm. I reported on OHCD's achievements, identified problems, and described upcoming opportunities. The two of them scribbled pages of notes, like a couple of college students at the last class before midterms. The experience was a powerful, unforgettable expression of loyalty and respect.

Would my hoped-for version of the budget hearing prove to anyone that the city's neighborhood reinvestment policy was really succeeding? There was some clear evidence of success: those ten thousand first-time homebuyers; the once-homeless people now living and working independently; the formerly jobless men and women now employed in good construction, precision-industry, and computer-related jobs. That group of people, those direct beneficiaries, could fill a stadium. But neither I nor anyone else who really knew

Philadelphia's neighborhoods well would contend that my ability to identify a great many direct beneficiaries of our policy proved that the city's
residential communities were bound for recovery. Despite the successes of past years, the view from the city's worst neighborhoods—
or from the worst sections of some of the better-off neighborhoods—was
still too bleak. No one could argue convincingly that, thanks to city
policy, the tide of disinvestment had turned and neighborhoods were
getting better and better.

Philadelphia neighborhoods were not progressing steadily toward
some ideal condition of well-being. What had really been accomplished,
in this imperfect time, this less-than-ideal place, was a setting of the
stage: the creation of an environment where the implementers of
neighborhood reinvestment policy could deliver their best performances
and where people witnessing the results of our policy could feel that
positive change was beginning to happen, that neighborhoods were
once again becoming places of interest and opportunity. Our success
was the inspiration and ambition of all the people gathered on that
day. Our success was every voice resounding in that big room.

Notes

INTRODUCTION

1. Michael E. Porter, "The Competitive Advantage of the Inner City," *Harvard Business Review*, May–June 1995, 55–71. See also responses published in *Harvard Business Review*, July–August 1995,144–154.

1   A STRATEGIC PROBLEM

1. Donna Ladd, "No Home for the Holidays," *Springs Magazine*, December 1996, 35–38.
2. New Jersey Casino Control Commission, Licence Division, *Casino Employment by Zip Code* (Atlantic City: New Jersey Casino Control Commission, November 17, 1997).
3. U.S. Bureau of the Census, 1990.
4. Robert J. Butera, "Urban Convert: How 'Mr. Suburbia' Learned to Love Center City," *Philadelphia Forum*, July 11, 1996, 1, 4.
5. The Yorktown background information which follows is summarized from Office of Housing and Community Development (OHCD), *Learning from Yorktown* (Philadelphia: City of Philadelphia, 1996), 1–3.
6. This important feature was pointed out to me by Joanne Barnes Jackson.
7. Quoted in OHCD, 2.
8. Quoted in OHCD, 3.
9. Quoted in OHCD, 6.
10. OHCD, 2.

2   ADVANCING THE PLAN

1. Witold Rybczynski has written of this consumer perspective in "What Kind of Cities Do We Need?" *Wharton Real Estate Review* 1, no. 1 (1997): 64–69.
2. Anthony Downs, "The Challenge of Our Declining Big Cities," *Housing Policy Debate* 8, no. 2 (1997): 359–408.
3. Office of Housing and Community Development (OHCD), *Vacant Property Prescriptions: A Reinvestment Strategy* (Philadelphia: City of Philadelphia, 1995).

4. Todd W. Bressi, "Planning the American Dream," in Peter Katz, ed., *The New Urbanism: Toward an Architecture of Community* (New York: McGraw-Hill, 1994), xxv.

5. See, for example, Elizabeth Plater-Zyberk's comments in David Mohney, ed., "Seaside and the Real World: A Debate on American Urbanism," *ANY* 1 (July-August 1993): 6–39.

3   TROPHIES AND LANDMARKS

1. Russell F. Weigley, ed., *Philadelphia: A 300–Year History* (New York: W. W. Norton & Company, 1982), 652.

2. See, for example, Nicholas Lemann, *The Promised Land: The Great Black Migration and How It Changed America* (New York: Vintage Books, 1991), 249–252.

4   THE NEW HOMEOWNERSHIP

1. Fannie Mae Foundation, *African American and Hispanic Attitudes on Homeownership* (Washington, D.C.: Fannie Mae Foundation, 1998),14, 15.

2. The statistics that follow are published in Office of Housing and Community Development, *Philadelphia Neighborhood Homebuyers: Summary Data; Housing Counseling and Settlement Assistance Program* (Philadelphia: City of Philadelphia, 1998).

3. Harriet Newburger, "Search Activity and Mobility Patterns of Lower-Income Homebuyers in Philadelphia: Preliminary Findings" (Bryn Mawr College, Department of Economics, 1996).

5   CDCS ON THE EDGE

1. Information about the Mercado is taken from Monica Rhor, "A Taste of Home," *Philadelphia Inquirer*, June 2, 1998, F1, F3.

2. Neal R. Peirce and Curtis W. Johnson, "Reinventing the Region: The Peirce Report," *Philadelphia Inquirer*, March 26, 1995, H2.

3. David Osborne and Ted Gaebler, *Reinventing Government: How the Entrepreneurial Spirit Is Transforming the Public Sector* (Reading, Mass.: Addison-Wesley Publishing Company, 1992), 49–75.

4. Commonwealth of Pennsylvania, Department of Community Affairs, Bureau of Human Resources, "Instructions for Submitting an Application for Fiscal Year 1995–96 Neighborhood Assistance Program/Comprehensive Service Program" (Harrisburg, 1995), 3.

6   SECOND-GENERATION SEGREGATION

1. Actually, this profile is a composite of several tenant council leaders with whom I became acquainted between 1993 and 1999, one of the periods in which OHCD pursued an active interest in public housing issues.

2. Public housing–related line items in the fiscal 1999 HUD budget appropriation include $10.327 billion for housing certificates, $3 billion for the public housing capital fund, $2.818 billion for the operating fund, $625 million for the HOPE VI program, and $310 million for drug elimination programs.

3. U.S. Congress, Joint Committee on Taxation, *Estimates of Federal Tax Expenditures for Fiscal Years 1996–2000* (Washington, D.C., 1995) cited in Stephen G. Cecchetti and Peter Rupert, "Mortgage Interest Deductibility and Housing Process," *Economic Commentary*, February 1, 1998, 1–7.

4. Former Pennsylvania House Majority Leader Robert O'Donnell has used this phrase to characterize the state legislative process.

5. Peter Nicholas, "A Push to Cluster Section 8 Tenants Is Likely," *Philadelphia Inquirer*, October 2, 1997, B1, B6.

6. U.S. Department of Housing and Urban Development, *Assessment of the Reasonable Revitalization Potential of Certain Public Housing Required by Law* (24 CFR 971).

7. Peter Nicholas, "PHA Is Urged to Downsize Housing," *Philadelphia Inquirer*, March 29, 1998, B1, B7.
8. Nicholas, "PHA Is Urged to Downsize Housing."

7   WORKING THE ECONOMY

1. YouthBuild Philadelphia, *YouthBuild Philadelphia Charter School Class of 1998 Yearbook* (Philadelphia: Youthbuild, 1998).
2. Thomas Ferrick, Jr., "Obsolete? Try Vital; Don't Look Now—No, Do. Downtown Philadelphia Appears to Be in the Midst of a Building Boom," *Philadelphia Inquirer*, November 23, 1997, F1.
3. Philadelphia Business Journal, *Book of Business Lists, 1999* (Philadelphia: Philadelphia Business Journal, 1999), 94.
4. Greater Philadelphia First, *An Economic Development Strategy for the Greater Philadelphia Region* (Philadelphia: Greater Philadelphia First, 1995).
5. Philadelphia Business Journal, 9, 11.
6. The CBC program summary that follows is based on information published in Barbara A. Coscarello, "Public/Private Job-Training amidst Chaos in a Changing Marketplace" (paper presented at the Fifty-ninth National Conference of the American Society for Public Administration, Seattle, Washington, May 9–13, 1998).
7. Campus Boulevard Corporation, "CBC Medical Administration Job Training Program: Student Evaluation Comments—Cycle Two" (Philadelphia: Campus Boulevard Corporation, undated).
8. Greater Philadelphia First, *An Economic Development* Strategy, 9.
9. Greater Philadelphia First, *Greater Philadelphia First's Employer-Driven Workforce Development Demonstration Projects* (Philadelphia: Greater Philadelphia First, undated).
10. Greater Philadelphia First, "Sectoral Research" (undated report), 46.
11. Greater Philadelphia First, *Greater Philadelphia First's Employer-Driven Workforce Demonstration Projects.*
12. Greater Philadelphia First, *Greater Philadelphia First's Employer-Driven Workforce Demonstration Projects.*
13. Communities in Schools of Philadelphia, "Resume" (fact sheet) (Philadelphia: Communities in Schools of Philadelphia, undated).
14. Joseph A. Slobodzian, "Judge Rejects Set-Aside Law for Third Time," *Philadelphia Inquirer*, January 12, 1995, B1.
15. U.S. Congress, *Housing and Urban Development Act of 1968.*
16. City of Philadelphia, *Executive Order 95–2: Neighborhood Benefit Strategy* (Philadelphia, 1995).

8   THE UNFINISHED POLICY

1. Brookings Institution, Center on Urban and Metropolitan Policy, and Fannie Mae Foundation, *Rouse Forum Survey: A Rise in Downtown Living* (New York: Brookings Institution, 1998), 1.
2. Eric Schlosser, "The Prison-Industrial Complex," *Atlantic Monthly* 282, no. 6 (1998): 51–77.
3. Philadelphia Health Management Corporation, *None of Us Are Home until All of Us Are Home; Supporting the Homeless: The Project H.O.M.E. Approach* (Philadelphia: Philadelphia Health Management Corporation, 1997). This publication was made possible through a grant awarded to PHMC by the Substance Abuse and Mental Health Services Administration (SAMHSA).
4. Philadelphia Health Management Corporation, 38.
5. People's Emergency Center, *Neighborhood Strategic Plan for Saunders Park/West Powelton* (Philadelphia: People's Emergency Center, 1998), 1, 2.
6. Dennis P. Culhane, Chang-Moo Lee, and Susan M. Wachter, "Where the Homeless Come from: A Study of the Prior Address Distribution of Families Admitted to Public Shelters in New York City and Philadelphia," *Housing Policy Debate* 7, no. 2 (1996): 327–365.

7. City of Philadelphia, Department of Public Health and Department of Human Services, "DPH/DHS University City Pilot Residential Site Policy."

8. City of Philadelphia, "Residential Site Policy."

9. Dignity Housing, *Dignity Housing: Building Community, Creating Leaders, Making Change* (brochure) (Philadelphia: Dignity Housing, undated).

10. Dignity Housing, *Dignity Housing Year 21 Proposal and Budget Submission to the Office of Housing and Community Development* (Philadelphia: Dignity Housing, 1995), 1.

11. Dignity Housing, *Year 21 Proposal*, 1.

12. Bruce Millar, "Rebuilding Homes—and Lives," *Chronicle of Philanthropy* 5, no. 24 (1993):1, 8.

13. Millar, 8.

14. Philadelphia Health Management Corporation, 49, 50.

10 TO JUMP HIGHER, TO RUN FARTHER

1. Andrea Knox, "Center City Gets to Take a Bow: Day & Zimmerman's Returning," *Philadelphia Inquirer*, December 19, 1995, D1, D2.

2. See, for example, James Howard Kunstler, *The Geography of Nowhere: The Rise and Decline of America's Man-Made Landscape* (New York: Simon & Schuster, 1993); Jerry Adler, "Bye-Bye, Suburban Dream," *Newsweek*, May 15, 1995, 40–60.

Index

Advent Lutheran Church, 205, 206, 208

advocacy/advocates, 64; at Advent Lutheran Church, 205–208, 214; Congress for the New Urbanism and, 227, 228; defined, 208; in demonstrations at OHCD, 215–220; downtown and special-needs, compared, 190–192, 194, 203; elements of, 213, 214; forms of and opportunities to pursue, 213; general-purpose vs. single-issue, 227; as learning experience, 228; in litigation over disabled housing, 220–227; national, for neighborhood reinvestment, 228; national organizations and, 227; payoff, 220, 226; political system and, 208–213; and reinvestment funding, 25, 26, 85; and Residential Site Policy, 214, 215; and Section 8 issues, 145, 146; seeking development funding as a form of, 215

affirmative action, 36

affordable housing, 25, 39, 65, 68; CDCs and nonprofit group production of, 114, 119; for lowest-income citizens, 236; for people with physical disabilities, 221, 224; to prevent homelessness, 199; public housing as, 138

"affordability gap," 157

African Americans: in Campus Boulevard Corporation service area, 170; and home purchases in integrated neighborhoods, 236; and homelessness, 199; and ownership of assets, 88–92; and racial/ethnic concentration, 98; reparations to, 91; and subsidized housing programs, 90; set-asides for businesses owned by, 179; and transformation of race, 163; and UCH strategy, 99; in Yorktown, 20–22

age: as characteristic of blighted neighborhoods, 9, 11; of residents, 10; of housing, 63

Allegheny West Foundation, 128

About the Author

John Kromer was appointed Director of the City of Philadelphia's Office of Housing and Community Development in January 1992. He lives with his family in Philadelphia.